Biography

Dolores Delgado Campbell teaches at American River College in Sacramento, CA. She has taught there since 1972. Her areas of teaching specialization are Women in American History and Mexican American History.

In 1991, Dolores rewrote the curriculum for History 16W (Women in American History) to include the history of Latina, Native American, Asian American and African American women. The course meets the multicultural requirement for graduation from American River College and transfer requirements to the University of California and California State University.

Dolores holds a B.S. from the University of Texas, El Paso and MA and MS from California State University, Sacramento. She is a Chicana and part Tigua Indian from El Paso, Texas. Dolores received the Patron's Chair Award for in excellence in teaching from American River College in 1997.

Preface

The reader was an idea that came to me while struggling to find a multicultural U. S. women's history text. There are many new materials being published that deal with women's history, however the new materials continue to have too little coverage about women of color. My biggest frustration has been not only finding multicultural women's history texts, but a truly inclusive text that dealt with Latina, Native American, African American and Asian American women. The reader includes material about European American women, including some documents and articles that I consider very necessary to the study of women in U. S. history.

I am personally indebted to my student assistant and friend, Patsy Olmstead for her help in selecting and compiling materials for this reader. Patsy shared my enthusiasm while doing the multitude of tasks needed to produce this reader. I am also grateful to my husband, Duane, who advised me on many aspects of the reader and was there to give me a hug when I needed one.

Table of Contents

African American Women

Mexican American Women

Asian American Women

Documents

1972

"Equal Rights Amendment"

Sec. 1. Equality of rights under the law shall not be denied or abridged by the United States or by any State on account of sex.
Sec. 2. The Congress shall have the power to enforce, by appropriate legislation, the provisions of this article.
Sec. 3. This amendment shall take effect two years after the date of ratification.

1970

Gloria Steinem, Testimony Before Subcommittee on Constitutional Amendments on Proposed E.R.A. Amendment

The Equal Rights Amendment, which used the wording first proposed by Susan B. Anthony in the nineteenth century, was approved by Congress in 1972 and sent to the states for ratification. Because the amendment failed to gain approval in three-quarters of the state legislatures, it was not enacted. The following testimony before the Senate Committee on the Judiciary was presented by Gloria Steinem, editor of Ms. Magazine, in 1970.

My name is Gloria Steinem. I am a writer and editor. I have worked in several political campaigns, and am currently a member of the Policy Council of the Democratic National Committee

During twelve years of working for a living, I've experienced much of the legal and social discrimination reserved for women in this country. I have been refused service in public restaurants, ordered out of public gathering places, and turned away from apartment rentals; all for the clearly-stated sole reason that I am a woman. And all without the legal remedies available to blacks and other minorities. I have been excluded from professional groups, writing assignments on so-called "unfeminine" subjects such as politics, full participation in the Democratic Party, jury duty, and even from such small male privileges as discounts on airline fares. Most important to me, I have been denied a society in which women are encouraged, or even allowed, to think of themselves as first-class citizens and responsible human beings.

However, after two years of researching the status of American women, I have discovered that I am very, very lucky. Most women, both wage-earners and housewives, routinely suffer from humiliation and injustice than I do.

As a freelance writer, I don't work in the male-dominated hierarchy of an office...I am not one of the millions of women who must support a family. Therefore, I haven't had to go on welfare because there are no day care centers for my children while I work, and I haven't had to submit to the humiliating welfare inquiries about my private and sexual life, inquiries from which men are exempt. I haven't had to brave the sex bias of labor unions and employers, only to see my family subsist on a median salary 40% less than the male median salary.

I hope this committee will hear the personal, daily injustices suffered by many women--

professionals and day laborers, women housebound by welfare as well as suburbia. We have all been silent for too long. We won't be silent anymore.

The truth is that all our problems stem from the same sex-based myths. We may appear before you as white radicals or the middle-aged middleclass or black soul sisters, but we are *all* sisters in fighting against these outdated myths. Like radical myths, they have been reflected in our laws. Let me list a few:

That Women Are Biologically Inferior to Men

In fact, an equally good case can be made for the reverse. Women live longer than men, even when the men are not subject to business pressures...

However, I don't want to prove the superiority of one sex to another. That would only be repeating a male mistake. English scientists once definitively proved, after all, that the English were descended from the angels, while the Irish were descended from the apes; it was the rationale for England's domination of Ireland for more than a century. The point is that science is used to support current myth and economics almost as much as the church was.

What we do know is that the difference *between* two races or two sexes is much smaller than the differences to be found *within* each group. Therefore, in spite of the slide show on female inferiorities that I understand was shown to you yesterday, the law makes more sense when it treats individuals, not groups bundled together by some condition of birth...

That Women Are Already Treated Equally In This Society

I'm sure there has been ample testimony to prove that equal pay for equal work, equal chance for advancement, and equal training or encouragement is obscenely scarce in every field, even those like food and fashion industries, that are supposedly "feminine."

A deeper result of social and legal injustice, however, is what sociologists refer to as "Internalized Aggression." Victims of aggression absorb the myth of their own inferiority, and come to believe that their group is in fact second class.

Women suffer this secondclass treatment from the moment they are born. They are expected to be rather than achieve, to function biologically rather than learn. A brother, whatever his intellect, is more likely to get the family's encouragement and education money, while girls are often pressured to conceal ambition and intelligence, to "Uncle Tom."

I interviewed a New York public school teacher who told me about a black teenager's desire to be a doctor. With all the barriers in mind, she suggested he be a veterinarian instead.

The same day, a high school teacher mentioned a girl who wanted to be a doctor. The teacher said, "How about a nurse."

Teachers, parents, and the Supreme Court may exude a protective, well-meaning rationale, but limiting the individual's ambition is doing no one a favor. Certainly not this country. It needs all the talent it can get.

That American Women Hold Great Economic Power

51% of all shareholders in this country are women. That's a favorite male-chauvinist statistic. However, the number of shares they hold is so small that the total is only 18% of all shares. Even those holdings are often controlled by men.

Similarly, only 5% of all the people in the country who receive $10,000 a year or more, earned or otherwise, are women. And that includes all the famous rich widows.

The constantly-repeated myth of our economic power seems less testimony to our real power than to the resentment of what little power we do have.

That Children Must Have Full-Time Mothers

American mothers spend more time with their homes and children than those of any other society we know about. In the past, joint families, servants, a prevalent system in which grandparents raised the children, or family field work in the agrarian systems--all these factors contributed more to child care than the labor-saving devices of which we are so proud.

The truth is that most American children seem to be suffering from too much Mother, and too little Father. Part of the program of Women's Liberation is a return of fathers to their children. If laws permit women equal work and pay opportunities, men will then be relieved of their role as sole breadwinner. Fewer ulcers, fewer hours of meaningless work, equal responsibility for his own children: these are a few of the reasons that Women's Liberation is Men's Liberation, too.

As for the psychic health of the children, studies show that the quality of time spent by parents is more important than the quantity. The most damaged children were not those whose mothers worked, but those whose mothers preferred to work but stayed home out of role-playing desire to be a "good mother."

QUESTIONS

1. Read the proposed Equal Rights Amendment. Why do you think it created such a storm of debate in the early 1970's? If it were proposed today, do you think it would have a better chance of being passed?
2. What are the "sex-based myths" that Steinem identifies in her 1970 testimony? Do you think these "myths" are still believed today?

National Organization for Women (NOW), Statement of Purpose

In 1966 the National Organization for Women was established. It quickly became the nation's largest and most influential feminist organization.
The following document is the organization's "Statement of Purpose."

We, men and women who hereby constitute ourselves as the National Organization for Women, believe that the time has come for a new movement toward true equality for all women in America, and toward a fully equal partnership of the sexes, as part of the world-wide revolution of human rights now taking place within and beyond our national borders.

The purpose of NOW is to take action to bring women into full participation in the mainstream of American society now, exercising all the privileges and responsibilities thereof in truly equal partnership with men.

We believe the time has come to move beyond the abstract argument, discussion and symposia over the status and special nature of women which has raged in America in recent years; the time has come to confront, with concrete action, the conditions that now prevent women from enjoying the equality of opportunity and freedom of choice which is their right as individual Americans, and as human beings.

NOW is dedicated to the proposition that women first and foremost are human beings, who, like all other people in our society, must have the chance to develop their fullest human potential. We believe that women can achieve such equality only by accepting to the full the challenges and responsibilities they share with all other people in our society, as part of the decision-making mainstream of American political, economic and social life. We organize to initiate or support action, nationally or in any part of this nation, by individuals or organizations, to break through the silken curtain of prejudice and discrimination against women in government, industry, the professions, the churches, the political parties, the judiciary, the labor unions, in education, science, medicine, law, religion and every other field of importance in American society....

There is no civil rights movement to speak for women, as there has been for Negroes and other victims of discrimination. The National Organization for Women must therefore begin to speak.

WE BELIEVE that the power of American law, and the protection guaranteed by the U.S. Constitution to the civil rights of all individuals, must be effectively applied and enforced to isolate and remove patterns of sex discrimination, to ensure equality of opportunity in employment and education, and equality of civil and political rights and responsibilities on behalf of women, as well as for Negroes and other deprived groups.

We realize that women's problems are linked to many broader questions of social justice; their solution will require concerted action by many groups. Therefore, convinced that human rights for all are indivisible, we expect to give active support to the common cause of equal rights for all those who suffer discrimination and deprivation, and we call upon other organizations committed to such goals to support our efforts toward equality for women.

WE DO NOT ACCEPT the token appointment of a few women to high-level positions in government and industry as a substitute for a serious continuing effort to recruit and advance women according to their individual abilities. To this end, we urge American government and industry to mobilize the same resources of ingenuity and command with which they have solved problems of far greater difficulty than those now impeding the progress of women.

WE BELIEVE that this nation has a capacity at least as great as other nations, to innovate new social institutions which will enable women to enjoy true equality of opportunity and responsibility in society, without conflict with their responsibilities as mothers and homemakers. In such innovations, America does not lead the Western world, but lags by decades behind many European countries. We do not accept the traditional assumption that a woman has to choose between marriage and motherhood, on the one hand, and serious participation in industry or the professions on the other. We question the present expectation that all normal women will retire from job or profession for ten or fifteen years, to devote their full time to raising children, only to reenter the job market at a relatively minor level. This in itself is a deterrent to the aspirations of women, to their acceptance into management or professional training courses, and to the very possibility of equality of opportunity or real choice, for all but a few women. Above all, we reject the assumption that these problems are the unique responsibility of each individual woman, rather than a basic social dilemma which society must solve. True equality of opportunity and freedom of choice for women requires such practical and possible innovations as a nationwide network of child-care centers, which will make it unnecessary for women to retire completely from society until their children are grown, and national programs to provide retraining for women who have chosen to care for their own children full time.

WE BELIEVE that it is as essential for every girl to be educated to her full potential of human ability as it is for every boy--with the knowledge that such education is the key to effective participation in today's economy and that, for a girl as for a boy, education can only be serious where there is expectation that it will be used in society. We believe that American educators are capable of devising means of imparting such expectations to girl students. Moreover, we consider the decline in the proportion of women receiving higher and professional education to be evidence of discrimination. This discrimination may take the form of quotas against the admission of women to colleges and professional schools; lack of encouragement by parents, counselors and educators; denial of loans or fellowships; or the traditional or arbitrary procedures in graduate and professional training geared in terms of men, which inadvertently discriminate against women. We believe that the same serious attention must be given to high school dropouts who are girls as to boys.

WE REJECT the current assumptions that a man must carry the sole burden of supporting himself, his wife, and family, and that a woman is automatically entitled to lifelong support by a man upon her marriage, or that marriage, home and family are primarily woman's world and responsibility--hers, to dominate, his to support. We believe that a true partnership between the sexes demands a different concept of marriage, an equitable sharing of the responsibilities of home and children and of the economic burdens of their support. We believe that proper recognition should be given to the economic and social value of homemaking and child care. To these ends, we will seek to open a reexamination of laws and mores governing marriage and divorce, for we believe that the current state of "half-equality" between the sexes discriminates against both men and women, and is the cause of much unnecessary hostility between the sexes.

WE BELIEVE that women must now exercise their political rights and responsibilities as American citizens. They must refuse to be segregated on the basis of sex into separate-and-not-equal ladies' auxiliaries in the political parties, and they must demand representation according to their numbers in the regularly constituted party committees--at local, state, and national levels-and in the informal power structure, participating fully in the selection of candidates and political decision-making, and running for office themselves.

IN THE INTERESTS OF THE HUMAN DIGNITY OF WOMEN, we will protest and endeavor to change the false image of women now prevalent in the mass media, and in the texts, ceremonies, laws, and practices of our major social institutions. Such images perpetuate contempt for women by society and by women for themselves. We are similarly opposed to all policies and practices--in church, state, college, factory, or office--which, in the guise of protectiveness, not only deny opportunities but also foster in women self-denigration, dependence, and evasion of responsibility, undermine their confidence in their own abilities and foster contempt for women.

NOW WILL HOLD ITSELF INDEPENDENT OF ANY POLITICAL PARTY in order to mobilize the political power of all women and men intent on our goals. We will strive to ensure that no party, candidate, President, senator, governor, congressman, or any public official who betrays or ignores the principle of full equality between the sexes is elected or appointed to office. If it is necessary to mobilize the votes of men and women who believe in our cause, in order to win for women the final right to be fully free and equal human beings, we so commit ourselves.

WE BELIEVE THAT women will do most to create a new image of women by *acting* now, and by speaking out in behalf of their own equality, freedom, and human dignity--not in pleas for special privilege, nor in enmity toward men, who are also victims of the current half-equality between the sexes--but in an active, self-respecting partnership with men. By so doing, women will develop confidence in their own ability to determine actively, in partnership with men, the conditions of their life, their choices, their future and their society.

QUESTIONS

1. How do you think your parents would have reacted to the contents of this statement in 1966? Would they have found it radical? Moderate? Would they have agreed with its position that women needed their own civil rights movement to speak for them?
2. How do you think the situation of women has changed since this statement was written? If it were to be rewritten today, what parts would you eliminate, strengthen, weaken, add?

Abortion as a Legal and Feminist Issue

Roe v. Wade

By 1968, women's right to legal abortions had become a central tenet, and one of the most controversial demands, of the developing women's movement. In 1970, New York State became the first to reform its abortion laws, an act followed by fifteen other states and the District of Columbia by 1972. Still, it was estimated that 2,500 illegal abortions were taking place every day, many performed at great risk to women's health.

In 1973, the United States Supreme Court ruled by a 7-2 margin in the cases of *Roe* v. *Wade* and *Doe* v. *Bolton* that the constitutional right of privacy "is broad enough to encompass a woman's decision whether or not to terminate her pregnancy." The "right of privacy" was a legal doctrine developed from the Ninth and Fourteenth Amendments to shield certain areas of private action from state intervention. In this excerpt from Justice Blackmun's majority opinion, the court discusses the historical and legal background of abortion, paying special attention to the interest of the state in protecting the health and welfare of individuals. The court does not agree that women have an absolute right to terminate pregnancies, but rules that in the first trimester (three months of pregnancy) women can legally choose to seek an abortion. After the first trimester, however, it is appropriate for the states to intervene to regulate access and conditions. Note the total absence of feminist rhetoric such as women's right to control their own bodies in the reasoning: the decision turns on the right of privacy, and especially the confidentiality of the doctor-patient relationship. Like birth control, abortion is treated as a medical, not a feminist issue.

Roe v *Wade* remains one of the most controversial Supreme Court decisions ever handed down. It provoked a Right to Life movement that seeks to overturn the liberalization of abortion laws either in the states or by constitutional amendment. The issue has become so hotly polarized, both among the public at large and in legal and medical circles, that the future of abortion in the United States remains in doubt.

MR. JUSTICE BLACKMUN delivered the opinion of the Court.

This Texas federal appeal and its Georgia companion, *Doe* v. *Bolton, post,* p.179, present constitutional challenges to state criminal abortion legislation. The Texas statutes under attack here are typical of those that have been in effect in many States for approximately a century. The Georgia statutes, in contrast, have a modern cast and are a legislative product that, to an extent at least, obviously reflects the influences of recent attitudinal change, of advancing medical knowledge and techniques, and of new thinking about an old issue.

We forthwith acknowledge our awareness of the sensitive and emotional nature of the abortion controversy, of the vigorous opposing views, even among physicians, and of the deep and seemingly absolute convictions that the subject inspires. One's philosophy, one's experiences, one's exposure to the raw edges of human existence, one's religious training, one's attitudes toward life and family and their values, and the moral standards one establishes and seeks to observe, are all likely to influence and to color one's thinking and conclusions about abortion.

In addition, population growth, pollution, poverty, and racial overtones tend to complicate and not to simplify the problem.

Our task, of course, is to resolve the issue by constitutional measurement, free of emotion and of predilection. We seek earnestly to do this, and, because we do, we have inquired into, and in this opinion place some emphasis upon, medical and medical-legal history and what that history reveals about man's attitudes toward the abortion procedure over the centuries. We bear in mind, too, Mr. Justice Holmes' admonition in his now-vindicated dissent in *Lochner* v. *New York*, 198 U.S. 45, 76 (1905):

> "[The Constitution] is made for people of fundamentally differing views, and the accident of our finding certain opinions natural and familiar or novel and even shocking ought not to conclude our judgment upon the question whether statues embodying them conflict with the Constitution of the United States."...

Three reasons have been advanced to explain historically the enactment of criminal abortion laws in the 19th century and to justify their continued existence.

It has been argued occasionally that these laws were the product of a Victorian social concern to discourage illicit sexual conduct. Texas, however, does not advance this justification in the present case, and it appears that no court or commentator has taken the argument seriously. The appellants and *amici* contend, moreover, that this is not a proper state purpose at all and suggest that, if it were, the Texas statutes are overbroad in protecting it since the law fails to distinguish between married and unwed mothers.

A second reason is concerned with abortion as a medical procedure. When most criminal abortion laws were first enacted, the procedure was a hazardous one for the woman. This was particularly true prior to the development of antisepsis. Antiseptic techniques, of course, were based on discoveries by Lister, Pasteur, and others first announced in 1867, but were not generally accepted and employed until about the turn of the century. Abortion mortality was high. Even after 1900, and perhaps until as late as the development of antibiotics in the 1940's, standard modern techniques such as dilation and curettage were not nearly so safe as they are today. Thus, it has been argued that a State's real concern in enacting a criminal abortion law was to protect the pregnant woman, that is, to restrain her from submitting to a procedure that placed her life in serious jeopardy.

Modern medical techniques have altered this situation. Appellants and various *amici* refer to medical data indicating that abortion in early pregnancy, that is, prior to the end of the first trimester, although not without its risk, is now relatively safe. Mortality rates for women undergoing early abortions, where the procedure is legal, appear to be as low as or lower than the rates for normal childbirth. Consequently, any interest of the State in protecting the woman from an inherently hazardous procedure, except when it would be equally dangerous for her to forgo it, has largely disappeared. Of course, important state interests in the area of health and medical standards do remain. The State has a legitimate interest in seeing to it that abortion, like any other medical procedure, is performed under circumstances that insure maximum safety for the patient. This interest obviously extends at least to the performing physician and his staff, to the facilities involved, to the availability of aftercare, and to adequate provision for any complication or emergency that might arise. The prevalence of high mortality rates at illegal "abortion mills" strengthens, rather than weakens, the State's interest in regulating the conditions under which abortions are performed. Moreover, the risk to the woman increases as her pregnancy continues.

Thus, the State retains a definite interest in protecting the woman's own health and safety when an abortion is proposed at a late stage of pregnancy.

The third reason is the State's interest--some phrase it in terms of duty--in protecting prenatal life. Some of the argument for this justification rests on the theory that a new human life is present from the moment of conception. The State's interest and general obligation to protect life then extends, it is argued, to prenatal life. Only when the life of the pregnant mother herself is at stake, balanced against the life she carries within her, should the interest of the embryo or fetus not prevail. Logically, of course, a legitimate state interest in this area need not stand or fall on acceptance of the belief that life begins at conception or at some other point prior to live birth. In assessing the State's interest, recognition may be given to the less rigid claim that as long as at least *potential* life is involved, the State may assert interests beyond the protection of the pregnant woman alone.

Parties challenging state abortion laws have sharply disputed in some courts the contention that a purpose of these laws, when enacted, was to protect prenatal life. Pointing to the absence of legislative history to support the contention, they claim that most state laws were designed solely to protect the woman. Because medical advances have lessened this concern, at least with respect to abortion in early pregnancy, they argue that with respect to such abortions the laws can no longer be justified by any state interest. There is some scholarly support for this view of original purpose. The few state courts called upon to interpret their laws in the late 19th and early 20th centuries did focus on the State's interest in protecting the woman's health rather than in preserving the embryo and fetus. Proponents of this view point out that in many States, including Texas, by statute or judicial interpretation, the pregnant woman herself could not be prosecuted for self-abortion or for cooperating in an abortion performed upon her by another. They claim that adoption of the "quickening" distinction through received common law and state statutes tacitly recognizes the greater health hazards inherent in late abortion and impliedly repudiates the theory that life begins at conception.

It is with these interests, and the weight to be attached to them, that this case is concerned...

In view of all this, we do not agree that, by adopting one theory of life, Texas may override the rights of the pregnant woman that are at stake. We repeat, however that the State does have an important and legitimate interest in preserving and protecting the health of the pregnant woman, whether she be a resident of the State or a nonresident who seeks medical consultation and treatment there, and that it has still *another* important and legitimate interest in protecting the potentiality of human life. These interests are separate and distinct. Each grows in substantiality as the woman approaches term and, at a point during pregnancy, each becomes "compelling."

With respect to the State's important and legitimate interest in the health of the mother, the "compelling" point, in the light of present medical knowledge, is at approximately the end of the first trimester. This is so because of the now-established medical fact, referred to above at 149, that until the end of the first trimester mortality in abortion may be less than mortality in normal childbirth. It follows that, from and after this point, a State may regulate the abortion procedure to the extent that the regulation reasonably relates to the preservation and protection of maternal health. Examples of permissible state regulation in this area are requirements as to the qualifications of the person who is to perform the abortion; as to the licensure of that person; as to the facility in which the procedure is to be performed, that is, whether it must be a hospital or may be a clinic or some other place of less-than-hospital status; as to the licensing of the facility; and the like.

This means, on the other hand, that, for the period of pregnancy prior to this "compelling" point, the attending physician, in consultation with his patient, is free to determine, without regulation by the State, that, in his medical judgment, the patient's pregnancy should be terminated. If that decision is reached, the judgment may be effectuated by an abortion free of interference by the State.

With respect to the State's important and legitimate interest in potential life, the "compelling" point is at viability. This is so because the fetus then presumably has the capability of meaningful life outside the mother's womb. State regulation protective of fetal life after viability thus has both logical and biological justifications. If the State is interested in protecting fetal life after viability, it may go so far as to proscribe abortion during that period, except when it is necessary to preserve the life or health of the mother.

Measured against these standards, Art. 1196 of the Texas Penal Code, in restricting legal abortions to those "procured or attempted by medical advice for the purpose of saving the life of the mother," sweeps too broadly. That statute makes no distinction between abortions performed early in pregnancy and those performed later and it limits to a single reason, "saving" the mother's life, the legal justification for the procedure. The statute, therefore, cannot survive the constitutional attack made upon it here...

To summarize and to repeat:

1. A state criminal abortion statute of the current Texas type, that excepts from criminality only a *life-saving* procedure on behalf of the mother, without regard to pregnancy stage and without recognition of the other interests involved, is violative of the Due Process Clause of the Fourteenth Amendment.

(a) For the stage prior to approximately the end of the first trimester, the abortion decision and its effectuation must be left to the medical judgment of the pregnant woman's attending physician.

(b) For the stage subsequent to approximately the end of the first trimester, the State, in promoting its interest in the health of the mother, may, if it chooses, regulate the abortion procedure in ways that are reasonably related to normal health.

(c) For the stage subsequent to viability, the State in promoting its interest in the potentiality of human life may, if it chooses, regulate, and even proscribe, abortion except where it is necessary, in appropriate medical judgment, for the preservation of the life or health of the mother.

2. The State may define the term "physician," as it has been employed in the preceding numbered paragraphs of this Part XI of this opinion, to mean only a physician currently licensed by the State, and may proscribe any abortion by a person who is not a physician as so defined...

This holding, we feel, is consistent with the relative weights of the respective interests involved, with the lessons and examples of medical and legal history, with the lenity of the common law, and with the demands of the profound problems of the present day. The decision leaves the State free to place increasing restrictions on abortion as the period of pregnancy lengthens, so long as those restrictions are tailored to the recognized state interests. The decision vindicates the fight of the physician to administer medical treatment according to his professional judgment up to the points where important state interests provide compelling justifications for intervention. Up to those points, the abortion decision in all its aspects is inherently, and primarily, a medical decision and basic responsibility for it must rest with the physician. If an individual practitioner abuses the privilege of exercising proper medical judgment, the usual remedies, judicial and intraprofessional, are available.

Source: *Roe et al. v. Wade, District Attorney of Dallas County*, 410 U.S. 113 (1973), pp. 116-117, 147-152, 162-166. Notes have been omitted.

Elizabeth Cady Stanton, *Declaration of Sentiments* (1848)

Elizabeth Cady Stanton (1848-1902) played a major role in drafting the Declaration that was presented at the convention at Seneca Falls, New York, in 1848. The Declaration is possibly the most significant document in the history of U.S. women. It summarized the way in which feminists believed men usurped power and tyrannized women. The document paralleled the Declaration of Independence--the abusive power of men was substituted for that of England. The inclusion of the demand for women's suffrage proved to be the most controversial aspect of the argument for woman's rights. What is meant by the Declaration's allegation that men have assigned to women "a sphere of action?" Did the Declaration deny or uphold the view of women's moral superiority? In what ways did the Declaration speak for all women? In what ways did it reflect the particular experience of white middle-class women?*

When, in the course of human events, it becomes necessary for one portion of the family of man to assume among the people of the earth a position different from that which they have hitherto occupied, but one to which the laws of nature and of nature's God entitle them, a decent respect to the opinions of mankind requires that they should declare the causes that impel them to such a course.

We hold these truths to be self-evident: that all men and women are created equal; that they are endowed by their Creator with certain inalienable rights; that among these are life, liberty and the pursuit of happiness; that to secure these rights governments are instituted, deriving their just powers from the consent of the governed. Whenever any form of government becomes destructive of these ends, it is the right of those who suffer from it to refuse allegiance to it, and to insist upon the institution of a new government, laying its foundation on such principles, and organizing its powers in such form, as to them shall seem most likely to effect their safety and happiness. Prudence, indeed, will dictate that governments long established should not be changed for light and transient causes; and accordingly all experience has shown that mankind are more disposed to suffer, while evils are sufferable, than to right themselves by abolishing the forms to which they are accustomed. But when a long train of abuses and usurpations, pursuing invariably the same object, evinces a design to reduce them under absolute despotism, it is their duty to throw off such government, and to provide new guards for their future security. Such has been the patient sufferance of the women under this government, and such is now the necessity which constrains them to demand the equal station to which they are entitled.

*From "Declaration of Sentiments," ed. Elizabeth Cady Stanton, Susan B. Anthony, and Matilda J. Gage, in *History of Woman Suffrage* (Rochester: Charles Mann, 1881), I: 67-94.

The history of mankind is a history of repeated injuries and usurpations on the part of man toward woman, having in direct object the establishment of an absolute tyranny over her. To prove this, let facts be submitted to a candid word.

He has never permitted her to exercise her inalienable right to the elective franchise.

He has compelled her to submit to laws, in the formation of which she had no voice.

He has withheld from her rights which are given to the most ignorant and degraded men--both natives and foreigners.

Having deprived her of this first right of citizen, the elective franchise, thereby leaving her without representation in the halls of legislation, he has oppressed her on all sides.

He has made her, if married, in the eye of the law, civilly dead.

He has taken from her all right in property, even to the wages she earns.

He has made her, morally, an irresponsible being, as she can commit many crimes with impunity, provided they be done in the presence of her husband. In the covenant of marriage, she is compelled to promise obedience to her husband, he becoming, to all intents and purposes, her master, the law giving him power to deprive her of her liberty, and to administer chastisement.

He has so framed the laws of divorce, as to what shall be the proper causes, and in case of separation, to whom the guardianship of the children shall be given, as to be wholly regardless of the happiness of women--the law, in all cases, going upon a false supposition of the supremacy of man, and giving all power into his hands.

After depriving her of all rights as a married woman, if single, and the owner of property, he has taxed her to support a government which recognizes her only when her property can be made profitable to it.

He has monopolized nearly all the profitable employments, and from those she is permitted to follow, she receives but a scanty remuneration. He closes against her all the avenues to wealth and distinction which he considers most honorable to himself. As a teacher of theology, medicine, or law, she is not known.

He has denied her the facilities for obtaining a thorough education, all colleges being closed against her.

He allows her in Church, as well as in State, but a subordinate position, claiming Apostolic authority for her exclusion from the ministry, and, with some exceptions, from any public participation in the affairs of the Church.

He has created a false public sentiment by giving to the world a different code of morals for men and women, by which the moral delinquencies which exclude women from society are not only tolerated, but deemed of little account in man.

He has usurped the prerogative of Jehovah himself, claiming it as his right to assign for her a sphere of action, when that belongs to her conscience and to her God.

He has endeavored, in every way he could, to destroy her confidence in her own powers, to lessen her self-respect, and to make her willing to lead a dependent and abject life.

Now, in the view of this entire disfranchisement of one-half of the people of this country, their social and religious degradation, in view of the unjust laws above mentioned, and because women do feel themselves aggrieved, oppressed, and fraudulently deprived of their most sacred rights, we insist that they have immediate admission to all the rights and privileges which belong to them as citizens of the United States.

In entering upon the great work before us, we anticipate no small amount of misconception, misrepresentation, and ridicule; but we shall use every instrumentality within our power to effect our object. We shall employ agents, circulate tracts, petition the State and National legislatures, and endeavor to enlist the pulpit and the press on our behalf. We hope this Convention will be followed by a series of Conventions embracing every part of the country.

Native American Women

In this section I have chosen articles that reflect the diverse experience within the Native American Nations. The "Iroquois Women" is an excerpt from a Jusuit priest's journal with his observations of the role of Iroquois women's involvement in tribal government. "Captivity with the Seneca and Delawares" tells a different story about a female captured by Indians. The story of the removal of the Cherokee from the southern United States to Indian Territory in 1838 is told in "Cherokee Women and the Trail of Tears." In 1879, Indian activist Susette LaFlesche wrote about "The Plight of the Ponca Indians" from her own personal experience. The last article is an extensive description about "American Indian Women at the Center of Indigenous Resistance in Contemporary North America."

Iroquois Women in Government

Pierre de Charlevoix, 1721
Pierre de Charlevoix, Journal of a Voyage to North America, *2 vols. (London: 1761 [Chicago: The Caxton Club, 1923]), 2:19-20, 23-27.*

When Europeans compared Indian and white societies, they noted that women sometimes inherited leadership roles in their tribes and that, in the unique case of the Iroquois, some women played a prominent role in government. In practice, the formal authority that Iroquois tribes granted to women was subordinate to that of male chiefs and the village council of elders. Still, the Iroquois matrons had a legitimate voice in public affairs, which neither European women--nor most other Indian women--could claim.

Pierre de Charlevoix (1682-1761) a Jesuit priest who traveled from Quebec to the Gulf of Mexico, described the civic roles of Iroquoian-speaking Huron women in a letter to an unidentified woman correspondent in 1721. Among these Indians, Charlevoix points out, the role of chief was inherited through the female line. Older women also played a special part in government. According to his account, they could select and unseat male chiefs, serve as assistants to chiefs, and oversee the public treasury. Debating issues separately, the women also had their own representative, or orator, to express their views to the all male council of elders.

It must be agreed, Madam, that the nearer we view our Indians, the more good qualities we discover in them: most of the principles which serve to regulate their conduct, the general maxims by which they govern themselves, and the essential part of their character discover nothing of the barbarian...

In the northern parts, and wherever the Algonquin tongue prevails, the dignity of chief is elective; and the whole ceremony of election and installation consists in some feasts, accompanied with dances and songs: the chief elect likewise never fails to make the panegyrick of his predecessor, and to invoke his genius. Amongst the Hurons, where this dignity is hereditary, the succession is continued through the women, so that at the death of a chief, it is not his own, but his sister's son who succeeds him; or, in default of which, his nearest relation in the female line. When the whole branch happens to be extinct, the noblest matron of the tribe or in the nation chooses the person she approves of most, and declares him chief...

Nay more, each family has a right to choose a counselor of its own, and an assistant to the chief, who is to watch for their interest, and without whose consent the chief can undertake nothing. These counselors are, above all things, to have an eye to the public treasury; and it is properly they who determine the uses it is to be put to. They are invested with this character in a general council, but they do not acquaint their allies with it, as they do at the elections and installations of their chief. Amongst the Huron nations, the women name the counselors, and often choose persons of their own sex.

This body of counsellors or assistants is the highest of all; the next is that of the elders, consisting of all those who have come to the years of maturity. I have not been able to find exactly what this age is. The last of all is that of the warriors; this comprehends all who are able to bear arms. This body has often at its head, the chief of the nation or town; but he must first have distinguished himself by some signal action of bravery; if not, he is obliged to serve as a subaltern, that is, as a single centinel; there being no degrees in the militia of the Indians.

In fact, a large body may have several chiefs, this title being given to all who ever commanded; but they are not therefore the less subject to him who leads the party; a kind of general, without character or real authority, who has power neither to reward nor punish, whom his soldiers are at liberty to abandon at pleasure and with impunity, and whose orders notwithstanding are scarce ever disputed: so true it is, that amongst a people who are guided by reason and inspired with sentiments of honour and love for their country, independence is not destructive of subordination; and, that a free and voluntary obedience is that on which we can always rely with the greatest certainty. Moreover, the qualities requisite are, that he be fortunate, of undoubted courage, and perfectly disinterested. It is no miracle, that a person possessed of such eminent qualities should be obeyed.

The women have the chief authority amongst all the nations of the Huron language; if we except the Iroquois canton of Onneyouth, in which it is in both sexes alternately. But if this be their lawful constitution, their practice is seldom agreeable to it. In fact, the men never tell the women anything they would have to be kept secret; and rarely any affair of consequence is communicated to them, though all is done in their name, and the chiefs are no more than their lieutenants. What I have told your Grace of the grandmother of the hereditary chief of the Hurons of the Narrows, who could never obtain a missionary for her own town, is a convincing proof that the real authority of the women is very small: I have been however assured, that they always deliberate first on whatever is proposed in council; and that they afterwards give the result of their deliberation to the chiefs, who make the report of it to the general council, composed of the elders; but in all probability this is done only for form's sake, and with the restrictions I have already mentioned. The warriors likewise consult together, on what relates to their particular province, but can conclude nothing of importance which concerns the nation or town; all being subject to the examination and control of the council of elders, who judge in the last resource.

It must be acknowledged, that proceedings are carried on in these assemblies with a wisdom and a coolness, and a knowledge of affairs, and I may add generally with a probity, which would have done honour. to the areopagus of Athens, or to the senate of Rome, in the most glorious days of those republics: the reason of this is, that nothing is resolved upon with precipitation; and that those violent passions, which have so much disgraced the politics even of Christians, have never prevailed amongst the Indians over public good...

Each tribe has an orator in every town, which orators are the only persons who have a liberty to speak in the public councils and general assemblies: they always speak well and to the purpose. Besides this natural eloquence, and which none who are acquainted with them will dispute, they have a perfect knowledge of the interests of their employers, and an address in placing the best side of their own cause in the most advantageous light, which nothing can exceed. On some occasions, the women have an orator, who speaks in their name, or rather acts as their interpreter.

Mary Jemison's "Captivity" with the Senecas and Delawares

The Seven Years' War (or the French and Indian War, as Americans preferred to call it) was indeed a vast "struggle for the Continent." Indeed, it was in many ways a world war. But its effects--of all wars--often came into the lives of ordinary people in drastic and shocking ways.

During the frontier struggles of the early 1750's that set the stage for the war, a fifteen-year-old girl named Mary Jemison became first the captive, then the adopted sister, then the wife of Native Americans--Shawnee, Seneca, and Delaware. Many years later, as an old woman, she dictated an account of her experience

The night was spent in gloomy forebodings. What the result of our captivity would be, it was out of our power to determine, or even imagine. At times, we could almost realize the approach of our masters to butcher and scalp us; again, we could nearly see the pile of wood kindled on which we were to be roasted; and then we would imagine ourselves at liberty, alone and defenseless in the forest, surrounded by wild beasts that were ready to devour us. The anxiety of our minds drove sleep from our eyelids; and it was with a dreadful hope and painful impatience that we waited for the morning to determine our fate.

The morning at length arrived, and our masters came early and let us out of the house, and gave the young man and boy to the French, who immediately took them away. Their fate I never learned, as I have not seen nor heard of them since.

I was now left alone in the fort, deprived of my former companions, and of every thing that was near or dear to me but life. But it was not long before I was in some measure relieved by the appearance of two pleasant-looking squaws, of the Seneca tribe, who came and examined me attentively for a short time, and then went out. After a few minutes' absence, they returned in company with my former masters, who gave me to the squaws to dispose of as they pleased.

The Indians by whom I was taken were a party of Shawnees, if I remember right, that lived, when at home, a long distance down the Ohio.

My former Indian masters and the two squaws were soon ready to leave the fort, and accordingly embarked--the Indians in a large canoe, and the two squaws and myself in a small one--and went down to Ohio. When we set off, an Indian in the forward canoe took the scalps of my former friends, strung them on a pole that he placed upon his shoulder, and in that manner carried them, standing in the stern of the canoe directly before us, as we sailed down the river, to the town where the two squaws resided.

On the way we passed a Shawnee town, where I saw a number of heads, arms, legs, and other fragments of the bodies of some white people who had just been burned. The parts that remained were hanging on a pole, which was supported at each end by a crotch stuck in the ground, and were roasted or burnt black as a coal. The fire was yet burning; and the whole appearance afforded a spectacle so shocking that even to this day the blood almost curdles in my veins when I think of them.

At night we arrived at a small Seneca Indian town, at the mouth of a small river that was called by the Indians, in the Seneca language, She-nan-jee, about eighty miles by water from the fort, where the two squaws to whom I belonged resided. There we landed, and the Indians went on; which was the last I ever saw of them.

Having made fast to the shore, the squaws left me in the canoe while they went to their wigwam or house in the town, and returned with a suit of Indian clothing, all new, and very clean and nice. My clothes, though whole and good when I was taken, were now torn in pieces, so that I was almost naked. They first undressed me, and threw my rags into the river; then washed me clean and dressed me in the new suit they had just brought, in complete Indian style; and then led me home and seated me in the center of their wigwam.

I had been in that situation but a few minutes before all the squaws in the town came in to see me. I was soon surrounded by them, and they immediately set up a most dismal howling, crying bitterly, and wringing their hands in all the agonies of grief for a deceased relative.

Their tears flowed freely, and they exhibited all the signs of real mourning. At the commencement of this scene, one of their number began, in a voice somewhat between speaking and singing, to recite some words to the following purport, and continued the recitation till the ceremony was ended; the company at the same time varying the appearance of their countenances, gestures, and tone of voice, so as to correspond with the sentiments expressed by their leader.

"Oh, our brother! alas! he is dead--he has gone; he will never return! Friendless he died on the field of the slain, where his bones are yet lying unburied! Oh! who will not mourn his sad fate?...His spirit has seen our distress, and sent us a helper whom with pleasure we greet. Deh-he-wa-mis has come: then let us receive her with joy !--she is handsome and pleasant! Oh! she is our sister, and gladly we welcome her here. In the place of our brother she stands in our tribe. With care we will guard her from trouble; and may she be happy till her spirit shall leave us."

In the course of that ceremony, from mourning they became serene-joy sparkled in their countenances, and they seemed to rejoice over me as over a long-lost child. I was made welcome among them as a sister to the two squaws before mentioned, and was called Deb-he-wa-mis; which, being interpreted, signifies a pretty girl, a handsome girl, or a pleasant, good thing. That is the name by which I have ever since been called by the Indians.

I afterward learned that the ceremony I at that time passed through was that of adoption. The two squaws had lost a brother in Washington's war, sometime in the year before, and in consequence of his death went up to Fort Du Quesne on the day on which I arrived there, in order to receive a prisoner, or an enemy's scalp, to supply their loss. It is a custom of the Indians, when one of their number is slain or taken prisoner in battle, to give to the nearest relative of the dead or absent a prisoner, if they have chanced to take one; and if not, to give him the scalp of an enemy.

My sisters were very diligent in teaching me their language; and to their great satisfaction, I soon learned so that I could understand it readily, and speak it fluently. I was very fortunate in falling into their hands; for they were kind, good-natured women; peaceable and mild in their dispositions; temperate and decent in their habits and very tender and gentle toward me. I have great reason to respect them, though they have been dead a great number of years.

In the second summer of my living at Wiishto, I had a child, at the time that the kernels of corn first appeared on the cob. When I was taken sick, Sheninjee [her husband] was absent, and I was sent to a small shed on the bank of the river, which was made of boughs, where I was obliged to stay till my husband returned. My two sisters, who were my only companions, attended me; and on the second day of my confinement my child was born; but it lived only two days. It was a girl; and notwithstanding the shortness of the time that I possessed it, it was a great grief to me to lose it.

After the birth of my child I was very sick, but I was not allowed to go into the house for two weeks; when, to my great joy, Sheninjee returned, and I was taken in, and as comfortably provided for as our situation would admit. My disease continued to increase for a number of days;

and I became so far reduced that my recovery was despaired of by my friends, and I concluded that my troubles would soon be finished. At length, however, my complaint took a favorable turn, and by the time the corn was ripe I was able to get about. I continued to gain my health, and in the fall was able to go to our winter quarters, on the Saratoga, with the Indians.

From that time nothing remarkable occurred to me till the fourth winter of my captivity, when I had a son born, while I was at Sciota. I had a quick recovery, and my child was healthy. To commemorate the name of my much-lamented father, I called my son Thomas Jemison.

QUESTIONS

1. Why do you think Jemison was so surprised at the fact that she was "adopted" rather than killed outright?
2. Why do you think Jemison does not speak of trying to escape?

Cherokee Women and the Trail of Tears

Theda Perdue

One hundred and fifty years ago, in 1839, the United States forced the Cherokee Nation west of the Mississippi River to what later would become the state of Oklahoma. The Cherokees primarily occupied territory in the Southeast that included north Georgia, northeastern Alabama, southeastern Tennessee, and southwestern North Carolina. In the three decades preceding removal, they experienced a cultural transformation. Relinquishing ancient beliefs and customs, the leaders of the nation sought to make their people culturally indistinguishable from their white neighbors, in the hope that through assimilation they could attain their ancestral homeland. White land hunger and racism proved too powerful, however, and the states in which the Cherokees lived, particularly Georgia, demanded that the federal government extinguish the Indians' title and eject them from the chartered boundaries of the states. The election of Andrew Jackson in 1828 strengthened the states' cause.

While President Jackson promoted the policy of removing eastern Indians to the west, he did not originate the idea. Thomas Jefferson first suggested that removal beyond the evils of "civilization" would benefit the Indians and provide a justification for his purchase of Louisiana. In 1808 to 1810 and again in 1817 to 1819, members of the Cherokee Nation migrated to the west as the Cherokee land base shrank. But the major impetus for total removal came in 1830 when Congress, at the urging of President Jackson, passed the Indian Removal Act which authorized the President to negotiate cessions of Indian land in the east and transportation of native peoples west of the Mississippi. Although other Indian Nations, such as the Choctaws, signed removal treaties right away, the Cherokees refused. The Nations' leaders retained legal counsel and took its case against repressive state legislation to the United States Supreme Court (*Cherokee Nation v. Georgia*, 5 Peters 1). The Cherokee Nation won, however, on the grounds that the Cherokees constituted a "domestic dependent" nation--not a foreign state under the U.S. Constitution. The state's failure to respond to the decision and the federal government's refusal to enforce it prompted an unauthorized Cherokee faction to negotiate removal. In December 1835, these disaffected men signed the Treaty of New Echota by which they exchanged the Cherokee Nation's territory in the southeast for land in the west. The United States Senate ratified the treaty, and in the summer of 1838, soldiers began to round up Cherokees for deportation. Ultimately, the Cherokees were permitted to delay until fall and to manage their own removal, but this leniency did little to ameliorate the experience the Cherokees called the "trail of tears." The weather was unusually harsh that winter; cold, disease, hunger, and exhaustion claimed the lives of at least four thousand of the fifteen thousand people who travelled the thousand miles to the west.

The details of Cherokee removal have been recounted many times by scholars and popular writers. The focus of these accounts has tended to be political: they have dealt primarily with the United States' removal policy, the negotiation of removal treaties, and the political factionalism which the removal issue created within Cherokee society. In other words, the role of men in this event has dominated historical analysis. Yet women also were involved, and it seems appropriate to reexamine the "trail of tears" using gender as a category of analysis. In particular, what role did women play in removal? How did hey regard the policy? Did their views differ from those of men? How did the removal affect women? What were their experiences along the "trail of tears"? How did they go about reestablishing their lives in their new homes in the West? How does this kind of analysis amplify or alter our understanding of the event?

The Treaty of New Echota by which the Cherokee Nation relinquished its territory in the Southeast was signed by men. Women were present at the rump council that negotiated the treaty, but they did not participate in the proceedings. They may have met in their own council-- precedents for women's councils exist—but if they did not, no record remains. Instead, they probably cooked meats and cared for the children while their husbands discussed treaty terms with the United States commissioner. The failure of women to join in the negotiation and signing of the Treaty of New Echota does not necessarily mean that women were not interested in the disposition of tribal land, but it does indicate that the role of women had changed dramatically in the preceding century.

Traditionally, women had a voice in Cherokee government. They spoke freely in council, and the War Woman (or Beioved Woman) decided the fate of captives. As late as 1787, a Cherokee woman wrote Benjamin Franklin that she had delivered an address to her people urging them to maintain peace with the new American nation. She had filled the peace pipe for the warriors, and she enclosed some of the same tobacco for the United States Congress in order to unite symbolically her people and his in peace. She continued:

> I am in hopes that if you Rightly consider that woman is the mother of All--and the Woman does not pull Children out of Trees or Stumps nor out of old Logs, but out of their Bodies, so that they ought to mind what a woman says.

The political influence of women, therefore, rested at least in part on their maternal biological role in procreation and their maternal role in Cherokee society, which assumed particular importance in the Cherokee's matrilineal kinship system. In this way of reckoning kin, children belonged to the clan of their mother, and their only relatives were those who could be traced through her.

The Cherokees were not only matrilineal, they also were matrilocal. That is, a man lived with his wife in a house which belonged to her. Or perhaps more accurately, to her family. According to the naturalist William Bartram, "Marriage gives no right to the husband over the property of his wife; and when they part she keeps the children and property belonging to them. The "property" that women kept included agricultural produce--corn, squash, beans, sunflowers, and pumpkins-- stored in the household's crib. Produce belonged to women because they were the principal farmers. This economic role was ritualized at the Green Corn Ceremony every summer, when an old woman presented the new corn crop. Furthermore, eighteenth-century travelers and traders normally purchased corn from women instead of men, and in the 1750's the garrison at Fort Loudoun, in present-day eastern Tennessee, actually employed a female purchasing agent to procure corn. Similarly, the fields belonged to the women who tended them, or rather to the women's lineages. Bartram observed that "their fields are divided by proper marks and their harvest is gathered separately." While the Cherokees technically held land in common and anyone could use unoccupied land, improved fields belonged to specific matrilineal households.

Perhaps this explains why women signed early deeds conveying land titles to the Proprietors of Carolina. Agents who made these transactions offered little explanation for the signatures of women on these documents. In the early twentieth century, a historian speculated that they represented a "renunciation of dower," but it may have been that the women were simply parting with what was recognized as theirs, or they may have been representing their lineages in the negotiations.

As late as 1785, women still played some role in the negotiation of land transactions. Nancy Ward, the Beloved Woman of Chota, spoke to the treaty conference held at Hopewell, South Carolina to clarify and extend land cessions stemming from Cherokee support of the British in the American Revolution. She addressed the assembly as the "mother of warriors" and promoted a peaceful resolution to land disputes between the Cherokees and the United States. Under the terms of the Treaty of Hopewell, the Cherokees ceded large tracts of land south of the Cumberland River in Tennessee and Kentucky and west of the Blue Ridge Mountains in North Carolina. Nancy Ward and the other Cherokee delegates to the conference agreed to the cession not because they believed it to be just but because the United Stares dictated the terms of the treaty.

The conference at Hopewell was the last treaty negotiation in which women played an official role, and Nancy Ward's participation in that conference was somewhat anachronistic. In the eighteenth century, the English as well as other Europeans had dealt politically and commercially with men, since men were the hunters and warriors in Cherokee society and Europeans were interested primarily in military alliances and deerskins. As relations with the English grew increasingly important to tribal welfare, women became less significant in the Cherokee economy and government. Conditions in the Cherokee Nation following the American Revolution accelerated the trend. In their defeat, the Cherokees had to cope with he destruction of villages, fields, corn cribs, and orchards which had occurred during the war, and the cession of hunting grounds which accompanied the peace. In desperation, they turned to the United States government, which proposed to convert the Cherokees into replicas of white pioneer farmers in the anticipation that they would then cede additional territory (presumably hunting grounds they no longer needed). While the government's so-called "civilization" program brought some economic relief, it also helped produce a transformation of gender roles and social organization. The society envisioned for the Cherokees, one which government agents and Protestant missionaries zealously tried to implement, was one in which a man farmed and headed a household composed only of his wife and children. The men who gained power in eighteenth-century Cherokee society--hunters, warriors, and descendants of traders--took immediate advantage of this program in order to maintain their status in the face of a declining deerskin trade and pacification, and then diverted their energy, ambition, and aggression into economic channels. As agriculture became more commercially viable, these men began to farm or to acquire African slaves to cultivate their fields for them. They also began to dominate Cherokee society, and by example and legislation, they altered fundamental relationships.

In 1808, a Council of headmen (there is no evidence of women participating) from Cherokee towns established a national police force to safeguard a person's holdings during life and "to give protection to children as heirs to their father's property, and to the widow's share," thereby changing inheritance patterns and officially recognizing the patriarchal family as the norm. Two years later a council representing al seven matrilineal clans, but once again apparently including no women, abolished the practice of blood vengeance. This action ended one of the major functions of clans and shifted the responsibility for punishing wrongdoers to the national police force and tribal courts. Matrilineal kinship clearly did not have a place in the new Cherokee order.

We have no record of women objecting to such legislation. In fact, we know very little about most Cherokee women because written documents reflect the attitudes and concerns of a male Indian elite or of government agents and missionaries. The only women about whom we know very much are those who conformed to expectations. Nancy Ward, the Beloved Woman who favored peace with the United States, appears in the historical records, while other less cooperative Beloved Women are merely unnamed, shadowy figures. Women such as Catherine Brown, a model of Christian virtue, gained the admiration of missionaries, and we have a memoir of Brown's life; other women who removed their children from mission schools incurred the missionaries' wrath, and they merit only brief mention in mission diaries. The comments of government agents usually focused on those native women who demonstrated considerable industry by raising cotton and producing cloth (in this case, Indian men suffered by comparison), not those who grew corn in the matrilineage's fields. In addition to being biased and reflecting only one segment of the female population, the information from these sources is secondhand; rarely did Indian women, particularly traditionalists, speak for themselves.

The one subject on which women did speak on two occasions was land. In 1817 the United States sought a large cession of Cherokee territory and removal of those who lived on the land in question. A group of Indian women met in their own council, and thirteen of them signed a message which was delivered to the National Council. They advised the council:

> The Cherokee ladys now being present at the meeting of the Chiefs and warriors in council have thought it their duties as mothers to address their beloved Chiefs and warriors now assembled.
> Our beloved children and head men of the Cherokee nation we address you warriors in council[. W]e have raised all of you on the land which we now have, which God gave us to inhabit and raise provisions[. W]e know that our country has once been extensive but by repeated sales has become circumscribed to a small tract and never have thought it our duty to interfere in the disposition of it till now, if a father or mother was to sell all their lands which they had to depend on[,] which their children had to raise their living on[,] which would be bad indeed and to be removed to another county[. W]e do not wish to go to an unknown country which we have understood some of our children wish to go over the Mississippi but this act of our children would be like destroying your mothers. Your mother and sisters ask and beg of you not to part with any more of our lands.

The next year, the National Council met again to discuss the possibility of allotting Cherokee land to individuals, an action the United States government encouraged as a preliminary step to removal. Once again, Cherokee women reacted:

> We have heard with painful feelings that the bounds of the land we now possess are to be drawn into very narrow limits. The land was given to us by the Great Spirit above as our common right, to raise our children upon, & to make support for our rising generations. We therefore humbly petition our beloved children, the head men and warriors, to hold out to the last in support of our common rights, as the Cherokee nation have been the first settlers of this land; we therefore claim the right of the soil...We therefore unanimously join in our meeting to hold our country in common as hitherto.

Common ownership of land meant in theory that the United States government had to obtain cessions from recognized, elected Cherokee officials who represented the wishes of the people. Many whites favored allotment because private citizens then could obtain individually owned tracts of land through purchase, fraud, or seizure. Most Cherokees recognized this danger and objected to allotment for that reason. The women, however, had an additional incentive for opposing allotment. Under the laws of the states in which the Cherokees lived and of which they would become citizens if land were allotted, married women had few property rights. A married woman's property, even property she held prior to her marriage, belonged legally to her husband. Cherokee women and matrilineal households would have ceased to be property owners.

The implications for women became apparent in the 1830's, when Georgia claimed its law was in effect in the Cherokee country. Conflicts over property arose because of uncertainty over which legal system prevailed. For example, a white man, James Vaught, married the Cherokee, Catherine Gunter. She inherited several slaves from her father, and Vaught sold two of them to General Isaac Wellborn. His wife had not consented to the sale and so she reclaimed her property and took them with her when the family moved west. General Wellborn tried to seize the slaves just as they were about to embark, but a soldier, apparently recognizing her claim under Cherokee law, prevented him from doing so. After removal, the General appealed to Principal Chief John Ross for aid in recovering the slaves, but Ross refused. He informed Wellborn: "By the laws of the Cherokee Nation, the property of husband and wife remain separate and apart and neither of these can sell or dispose of the property of the other." Had the Cherokees accepted allotment and come under Georgia law, Wellborn would have won.

The effects of the women's protests in 1817 and 1818 are difficult to determine. In 1817 the Cherokees ceded tracts of land in Georgia, Alabama, and Tennessee, and in 1819 they made an even larger cession. Nevertheless, they rejected individual allotments and strengthened restrictions on alienation of improvements. Furthermore, the Cherokee Nation gave notice that they would negotiate no additional cessions--a resolution so strongly supported that the United States ultimately had to turn to a small unauthorized faction in order to obtain the minority treaty of 1835.

The political organization which existed in the Cherokee Nation in 1817 to 1818 had made it possible for women to voice their opinion. Traditionally, Cherokee towns were politically independent of one another, and each town governed itself through a council in which all adults could speak. In the eighteenth century, however, the Cherokees began centralizing their government in order to restrain bellicose warriors whose raids jeopardized the entire nation, and to negotiate as a single unit with whites. Nevertheless, town councils remained important, and representatives of traditional towns formed the early National Council. This National Council resembled the town councils in that anyone could address the body. Although legislation passed in 1817 created an Executive Committee, power still rested with the council, which reviewed all committee acts.

The protests of the women to the National Council in 1817 and 1818 were, however, the last time women presented a collective position to the Cherokee governing body. Structural changes in Cherokee government more narrowly defined participation in the National Council. In 1820 the council provided that representatives be chosen from eight districts rather than from traditional towns, and in 1823 the committee acquired a right of review over acts of the council. The more formalized political organization made it less likely that a group could make its views known to the national government.

As the Cherokee government became more centralized, political and economic power rested increasingly in the hands of a few elite men who adopted the planter lifestyle of the white, antebellum South. A significant part of the ideological basis for this lifestyle was the cult of domesticity, in which the ideal woman confined herself to home and hearth while men contended with the corrupt world of government and business. The elite adopted the tenets of the cult of domesticity, particularly after 1817, when the number of Protestant missionaries, major proponents of this feminine ideal, increased significantly, and their influence on Cherokee society broadened.

The extent to which a man's wife and daughters conformed to the idea quickly came to be one measure of his status. In 1818 Charles Hicks, who later served as Principal Chief, described the most prominent men in he Nation as "those who have for the last 10 or 20 years been pursuing agriculture & kept their women & children at home & in comfortable circumstances." Eight years later, John Ridge, one of the first generation of Cherokees to have been educated from childhood in mission schools, discussed a Cherokee law which protected the property rights of a married woman and observed that "in many respects she has exclusive & distinct control over her own, particularly among the less civilized." The more "civilized" presumably left such maters to men. Then Ridge described suitable activities for women: "They sew, they weave, they spin, they cook our meals and act well the duties assigned them by Nature as mothers." Proper women did not enter business or politics.

Despite the attitudes of men such as Hicks and Ridge, women did in fact continue as heads of households and as businesswomen. In 1828 the *Cherokee Phoenix* published the obituary of Oo-dah-less who had accumulated a sizeable estate through agriculture and commerce. She was "the support of a large family," and she bequeathed her property "to an only daughter and three grandchildren." Oo-dah-less was not unique. At least one-third of the heads of household listed on the removal roll of 1835 were women. Most of these were not as prosperous as Oo-dah-less, but some were even more successful economically. Nineteen owned slaves (190 men were slaveholders), and two held over twenty slaves and operated substantial farms.

Nevertheless, these women had ceased to have a direct voice in Cherokee government. In 1826 the council called a constitutional convention to draw up a governing document for the nation. According to legislation which provided for election of delegates to the convention, "No person but a free male citizen who is full grown shall be entitled to vote." The convention met and drafted a constitution patterned after that of the United States. Not surprisingly, the constitution which male Cherokees ratified in 1827 restricted the franchise to "free male citizens" and stipulated that "no person shall be eligible to a seat in the General Council, but a free Cherokee male, who shall have attained the age of twenty-five. Unlike the United States Constitution, the Cherokee document clearly excluded women, perhaps as a precaution against women who might assert their traditional right to participate in politics instead of remaining in the domestic sphere.

The exclusion of women from politics certainly did not produce the removal crisis but it did mean that a group traditionally opposed to land cession could no longer be heard on the issue. How women would have voted is also unclear. Certainly by 1835, many Cherokee women, particularly those educated in mission schools, believed that men were better suited to deal with political issues than women, and a number of women voluntarily enrolled their households to go west before the forcible removal of 1838 to 1839. Even if women had united in active opposition to removal, it is unlikely that the United States and aggressive state governments would have paid any more attention to them than they did to the elected officials of the nation who opposed removal or the fifteen thousand Cherokees, including women (and perhaps children), who petitioned the United States Senate to reject the Treaty of New Echota. While Cherokee legislation may have made women powerless, federal authority rendered the whole Nation impotent.

In 1828 Georgia had extended state law over the Cherokee Nation, and white intruders who invaded its territory. Georgia law prohibited Indians, both men and women, from testifying in court against white assailants, and so they simply had to endure attacks on person and property. Delegates from the Nation complained to Secretary of War John H. Eaton about the lawless behavior of white intruders:

> Too many there are who think it an act of trifling consequence to oust an Indian family from the quiet enjoyment of all the comforts of their own firesides, and to drive off before their faces the stock that gave nourishment to the children and support to the aged, and appropriate it to the satisfaction of avarice.

Elias Boudinot, editor of the bilingual *Cherokee Phoenix,* even accused the government of encouraging the intruders in order to force the Indians off their lands, and he published the following account:

> A few days since two of these white men came to a Cherokee house, for the purpose, they pretended, of buying provisions. There was no person about the house but one old woman of whom they inquired for some corn, beans etc. The woman told them she had nothing to sell. They then went off in the direction of the field belonging to this Cherokee family. They had not gone but a few minutes when the woman of the house saw a heavy smoke rising from that direction. She immediately hastened to the field and found the villains had set the woods on fire but a few rods from the fences, which she found already in a full blaze. There being a very heavy wind that day, the fire spread so fast, that her efforts to extinguish it proved utterly useless. The entire fence was therefore consumed in a short time. It s said that during her efforts to save the fence the men who had done the mischief were within sight, and were laughing heartily at her.

The Georgia Guard, established by the state to enforce its law in the Cherokee country, offered no protection and, in fact, contributed to the lawlessness. The *Phoenix* printed the following notice under the title "Cherokee Women, Beware.":

> It is said that the Georgia Guard have received orders, from the Governor we suppose, to inflict corporeal punishment on such females as shall hereafter be guilty of insulting them. We presume they are to be the judges of what constitutes *insult*.

Despite harassment from intruders and the Guard, most Cherokees had no intention of going west, and in he spring of 1838 they began to plant their crops as usual. Then United States soldiers arrived, began to round up the Cherokees, and imprisoned them in stockades in preparation for deportation. In 1932 Rebecca Neugin, who was nearly one hundred years old, shared her childhood memory and family tradition about removal with historian Grant Foreman:

When the soldier came to our house my father wanted to fight, but my mother told him that the soldiers would kill him if he did and we surrendered without a fight. They drove us out of our house to join other prisoners in a stockade. After they took us away, my mother begged them to let her go back and get some bedding. So they let her go back and she brought what bedding and a few cooking utensils she could carry and had to leave behind all of our other household possessions.

Rebecca Neugin's family was relatively fortunate. In the process of capture, families were sometimes separated and sufficient food and clothing were often left behind. Over fifty years after removal, John G. Burnett, a soldier who served as an interpreter, reminisced:

Men working in the fields were arrested and driven to stockades. Women were dragged from their homes by soldiers whose language they could not understand. Children were often separated from their parents and driven into the stockades with the sky for a blanket and the earth for a pillow.

Burnett recalled how one family was forced to leave the body of a child who bad just died and how a distraught mother collapsed of heart failure as soldiers evicted her and her three children from their homes. After their capture, many Cherokees had to march miles over rugged mountain terrain to the stockades. Captain L. B. Webster wrote his wife about moving eight hundred Cherokees from North Carolina to the central depot in Tennessee: "We were eight days in making the journey (80 miles), and it was pitiful to behold the women & children, who suffered exceedingly--as they were all obliged to walk, with the exception of the sick."

Originally the government planned to deport all the Cherokees in the summer of 1838, but the mortality rate of the three parties that departed that summer led the commanding officer, General Winfield Scott, to agree to delay the major removal until fall. In the interval, the Cherokees remained in the stockades, where conditions were abysmal. Women in particular often became individual victims of their captors. The missionary Daniel Butrick recorded the following episode in his journal:

The poor Cherokees are not only exposed to temporal evils, but also to every species of moral desolation. The other day a gentleman informed me that he saw six soldiers about two Cherokee women. The women stood by a tree, and the soldiers with a bottle of liquor were endeavoring to entice them to drink, though the women, as yet were resisting them. He made this known to the commanding officer but we presume no notice was taken of it, as it was reported that those soldiers had those women with them the whole night afterwards. A young married woman, a member of the Methodist society was at the camp with her friends, though her husband was not there at the time. The soldiers, it is said, caught her, dragged her about, and at length, either through fear, or otherwise, induced her to drink; and then seduced her away, so that she is now an outcast even among her own relatives. How many of the poor captive women are thus debauched, through terror and seduction, that eye which never sleeps, alone can determine.

When removal finally got underway in October, the Cherokees were in a debilitated and demoralized state. A white minister who saw them as they prepared to embark noted: "The women did not appear to as good advantage as did the men. All, young and old, wore blankets which almost hid them from view" The Cherokees had received permission to manage their own removal, and they divided the people into thirteen detachments of approximately one thousand each. While some had wagons, most walked. Neugin rode in a wagon with other children and some elderly women, but her older brother, mother, and father "walked all the way." One observer reported that "even aged females, apparently nearly ready to drop in the grave, were traveling with heavy burdens attached to the back." Proper conveyance did not spare well-to-do

Cherokees the agony of removal, the same observer noted:

> One lady passed on in her hack in company with her husband, apparently with as much refinement and equipage as any of the mothers of New England; and she was a mother too and her youngest child, about three years old, was sick in her arms, and all she could do was to make it comfortable as circumstances would permit…She could only carry her dying child in her arms a few miles farther, and then she must stop in a stranger-land and consign her much loved babe to the cold ground, and that without pomp and ceremony, and pass on with the multitude

This woman was not alone. Journals of the removal are largely a litany of the burial of children, some born "untimely."

Many women gave birth alongside the trail: at least sixty-nine newborns arrived in the West. The Cherokees' military escort was often less than sympathetic. Daniel Butrick wrote in his journal that troops frequently forced women in labor to continue until they collapsed and delivered "in the midst of the company of soldiers." One man even stabbed an expectant mother with a bayonet. Obviously, many pregnant women did not survive such treatment. The oral tradition of a family from southern Illinois, through which the Cherokees passed, for example, includes an account of an adopted Cherokee infant whose mother died in childbirth near the family's pioneer cabin. While this story may be apocryphal, the circumstances of Cherokee removal make such traditions believable.

The stress and tension produced by the removal crisis probably accounts for a post-removal increase in domestic violence, of which women usually were the victims. Missionaries reported that men, helpless to prevent seizure of their property and assaults on themselves and their families, vented their frustrations by beating wives and children. Some women were treated so badly by their husbands that they left them, and this dislocation contributed to the chaos in the Cherokee Nation in the late 1830's.

Removal divided the Cherokee Nation in a fundamental way, and the Civil War magnified that division. Because most signers of the removal treaty were highly acculturated, many traditionalists resisted more strongly the white man's way of life and distrusted more openly those Cherokees who imitated whites. This split between "conservatives," those who sought to preserve the old ways, and "progressives," those committed to change, extended to women. We know far more, of course, about "progressive" Cherokee women who left letters and diaries which in some ways are quite similar to those of upper-class women in the antebellum South. In letters, they recounted local news such as "they had Elick Cockrel up for steeling horses" and "they have Charles Reese in chains about burning Harnages house" and discussed economic concerns: "I find I cannot get any corn in this neighborhood, and so of course I shall be greatly pressed in providing provision for my family." Nevertheless, family life was the focus of most letters: "Major is well and tryes hard to stand alone he will walk soon. I would write more but the baby is crying."

Occasionally we even catch a glimpse of conservative women who seem to have retained at least some of their original authority over domestic matters. Red Bird Smith, who led a revitalization movement at the end of the nineteenth century, had considerable difficulty with his first mother-in-law. She "influenced" her adopted daughter to marry Smith through witchcraft and, as head of the household, meddled rather seriously in the couple's lives. Interestingly, however, the Kee-Too-Wah society which Red Bird Smith headed had little room for women.

Although the society had political objectives, women enjoyed no greater participation in this "conservative" organization than they did in the "progressive" republican government of the Cherokee Nation.

Following removal, the emphasis of legislation involving women was on protection rather than participation. In some ways, this legislation did offer women greater opportunities than the law codes of the states. In 1845 the editor of the *Cherokee Advocate* expressed pride that "in this respect the Cherokees have been considerably in advance of many of their white brethren, the rights of their women having been amply secured almost ever since they had written laws." The Nation also established the Cherokee Female Seminary to provide higher education for women, but like the education women received before removal, students studied only those subjects considered to be appropriate for their sex.

Removal, therefore, changed little in terms of the status of Cherokee women. They had lost political power before the crisis of the 1830's, and events which followed relocation merely confirmed new roles and divisions. Cherokee women originally had been subsistence-level farmers and mothers, and the importance of these roles in traditional society had made it possible for them to exercise political power. Women, however, lacked the economic resources and military might on which political power in the Anglo-American system rested. When the Cherokees adopted the Anglo-American concept of power in the eighteenth and nineteenth centuries, men became dominant. But in the 1830's the chickens came home to roost. Men, who had welcomed the Anglo-American basis for power, now found themselves without power. Nevertheless, they did not question the changes they had fostered. Therefore, the tragedy of the trail of tears lies not only in the suffering and death which the Cherokees experienced but also in the failure of many Cherokees to look critically at the political system which they had adopted--a political system dominated by wealthy, highly acculturated men, and supported by an ideology that made women (as well as others defined as "weak" or "inferior") subordinate. In the removal crisis of the 1830's, men learned an important lesson about power; it was a lesson women had learned well before the "trail of tears."

Reprinted with permission from the *Journal of Women's History*, Vol. 1, No. 1 (Spring 1989).

Questions

1. Why were the Cherokee removed to Oklahoma from Southeastern U.S.?
    What was the outcome of the removal?

2. How did the cession of lands by the Cherokee contribute to their "REMOVAL" to Oklahoma?

3. Describe how the education of Cherokee Indian women in Mission Schools influenced their adoption of the domestic role model.

Susette LaFlesche, *The Plight of the Ponca Indians* (1879)

An Omaha Indian, Susette LaFlesche (1854-1903) spent her childhood on a reservation. She devoted her life to documenting Native American suffering. Both in terms of cultural back-ground and the extent of their victimization, Native American Women's life experiences were vastly different from those of European American Women. What particular "wrongs" does LaFlesche address? In what way is her account similar to that of Zitkala-Sa?

I have lived all my life, with the exception of two years, which I spent at school in New Jersey, among my own tribe, the Omahas, and I have had an opportunity, such as is accorded to but few, of hearing both sides of the "Indian question." I have at times felt bitterly toward the white race, yet were it not for some who have shown all kindness, generosity and sympathy toward one who had no claims on them but that of common humanity, I shudder to think what I would now have been. As it is, my faith in justice and God has sometimes almost failed me, but, I thank God, only almost. It crushed our hearts when we saw a little handful of poor, ignorant, helpless, but peaceful people, such as the Poncas were, oppressed by a mighty nation, a nation so powerful that it could well have afforded to show justice and humanity if it only would. It was so hard to feel how powerless we were to help those we loved so dearly, when we saw our relatives forced from their homes and compelled to go to a strange country at the point of the bayonet. The whole Ponca tribe were rapidly advancing in civilization; cultivated their farms, and their schoolhouses and churches were well filled, when suddenly they were informed that the government required their removal to Indian Territory. My uncle said it came so suddenly upon them that they could not realize it at first, and they felt stunned and helpless. He also said if they had had any idea of what was coming, they might have successfully resisted; but as it was, it was carried rigidly beyond their control. Every objection they made was met by the word "soldier" and "bayonet." The Poncas had always been a peaceful tribe, and were not armed, and even if they had been they would rather not have fought. It was such a cowardly thing for the government to do! They sold the land which belonged to the Poncas to the Sioux, without the knowledge of the owners, and, as the Poncas were perfectly helpless and the Sioux well armed, the government was not afraid to move the friendly tribe.

The tribe has been robbed of thousands of dollars' worth of property, and the government shows no disposition to return what belongs to them. That property was lawfully theirs; they had worked for it; the annuities which were to be paid to them belong to them. It was money promised by the government for land they had sold to the government. I desire to say that all annuities paid to Indian tribes by the government are in payment for land sold by them to the government, and are not charity. The government never gave any alms to the Indians, and we all know that through the "kindness" of the "Indian ring" they do not get the half of what the government actually owes them. Its seems to us sometimes that the government treats us with less consideration than it does even the dogs.

*From Susette LaFlesche, *"The Plight of the Ponca Indians,"* in *Daily Advertiser* (Boston) November 26, 1879, 4.

American Indian Women
At the Center of Indigenous Resistance
in
Contemporary North America

M. Annette Jaimes with Theresa Halsey

A people is not defeated until the hearts of its woman are on the ground.
Traditional Cheyenne Saying

The United States has not shown me the terms of my surrender.
Marie Lego
Pit River Nation, 1970

The two brief quotations forming the epigraph of this chapter were selected to represent a constant pattern of reality within Native North American life from the earliest times. This is that women have always formed the backbone of indigenous nations on this continent. Contrary to those images of meekness, docility and subordination to males with which we women typically have been portrayed by the dominant culture's books and movies, anthropology, and political ideologues of both rightist and leftist persuasions, it is women who have formed the very core of indigenous resistance to genocide and colonization since the first moment of conflict between Indians and invaders. In contemporary terms, this heritage has informed and guided generations of native women such as the elder Marie Lego, who provided crucial leadership to the Pit River Nation's land claims struggle in northern California during the 1970's.

In Washington state, women such as Janet McCloud (Tulalip) and Ramona Bennett (Puyallup) had already assumed leading roles in the fishing rights struggles of the 60's, efforts which, probably more than any other phenomena, set in motion the "hard-line" Indian liberation movements of the modern day. These were not political organizing campaigns of the ballot and petition sort. Rather, they were, and continue to be, conflicts involving the disappearance of entire peoples. As Bennett has explained the nature of the fishing rights confrontations:

> At this time, our people were fighting to preserve their last treaty right--the right to fish. We lost our land base. There was no game in the area…We're dependent not just economically but culturally on the right to fish. Fishing is part of our art forms and religion and diet, and the entire culture is based around it. And so when we talk about [Euroamerica's] ripping off the right to fish, we're talking about cultural genocide.

The fish-ins, discussed in Chapter Seven, were initially pursued within a framework of "civil disobedience" and "principled nonviolence," which went nowhere other than to incur massive official and quasi official violence in response. "They [the police] came right on the reservation with a force of three hundred people," Bennett recounts. "They gassed us, they clubbed people around, they laid $125,000 bail on us. At that time I was a member of the Puyallup Tribal Council and I was spokesman for the camp [of local fishing rights activists]. And I told them what our policy was: that we were there to protect our Indian fishermen. And because I used a voice-gun, I'm being charged with inciting a riot. I'm faced with an eight year sentence." It was an elder Nisqually woman who pushed the fishing rights movement in western Washington to adopt the policy of armed self-defense which ultimately proved successful (the struggle in eastern Washington took a somewhat different course to the same position and results):

Finally, one of the boys went down to the river to fish, and his mother went up on the bank. And she said: "This boy is nineteen years old and we've been fighting on this river for as many years as he's been alive. And no one is going to pound my son around, no one is going to arrest him. No one is going to touch my son or I'm going to shoot them." And she had a rifle...Then we had an armed camp in the city of Tacoma.

The same sort of dynamic was involved in South Dakota during the early 1970's, when elder Oglala Lakota women such as Ellen Moves Camp and Gladys Bissonette assumed the leadership in establishing what was called the Oglala Sioux Civil Rights Organization (OSCRO) on the Pine Ridge Reservation. According to Bissonette, "Every time us women gathered to protest or demonstrate, they [federal authorities] always aimed machine guns at us women and children." In response, she became a major advocate of armed self-defense at the reservation hamlet of Wounded Knee in 1973, remained within the defensive perimeter for the entire 71 days the U.S. government besieged the Indians inside, and became a primary negotiator for what was called the "Independent Oglala Nation." Both women remained quite visible in the Oglala resistance to U.S. domination despite a visual counterinsurgency war waged by the government on Pine Ridge during the three years following Wounded Knee.

At Big Mountain, in the former "Navajo-Hopi Joint Use Area" in Arizona, where the federal government is even now attempting to forcibly relocate more than 10,000 traditional Dine (Navajos) in order to open the way for corporate exploitation of the rich coal reserves underlying their land, it is again elder women who have stood at the forefront of resistance, refusing to leave the homes of their ancestors. One of them, Pauline Whitesinger, was the first to physically confront government personnel attempting to fence off her land. Another, Katherine Smith, was the first to do so with a rifle. Such women have constituted a literal physical barrier blocking consummation of the government's relocation/mining effort for more than a decade. Many similar stories, all off them accruing from the past quarter-century, might be told in order to demonstrate the extent to which women have galvanized and centered contemporary native resistance.

The costs of such uncompromising (and uncompromised) activism have often been high. To quote Ada Deer, who, along with Lucille Chapman, became an essential spokesperson for the Menominee restoration movement in Wisconsin during the late 1960's and early '70's: "I wanted to get involved. People said I was too young, too naïve--you can't fight the system. I dropped out of law school. That was the price I had to pay to be involved." Gladys Bissonette lost a son, Pedro, and a daughter, Jeanette, murdered by federal surrogates on Pine Ridge in the aftermath of Wounded Knee. Other native women, such as American Indian Movement (AIM) members Tina Trudell and Anna Mae Pictou Aquash, have paid with their own and sometimes their children's lives for their prominent defiance of their colonizers. Yet, it stands as a testament to the strength of American Indian women that such grim sacrifices have served, not to deter them from standing up for the rights of native people, but as an inspiration to do so. Mohawk activist and scholar Shirley Hill Witt recalls the burial of Aquash after her execution-style murder on Pine Ridge:

Some women had driven from Pine Ridge the night before--a very dangerous act--"to do what needed to be done." Young women dug the grave. A ceremonial tipi was set up...A woman seven months pregnant gathered sage and cedar to be burned in the tipi. Young AIM members were pallbearers: they laid her on pine boughs while spiritual leaders spoke the sacred words and performed the ancient duties. People brought presents for Anna Mae to take with her to the spirit world. They also brought presents for her two sisters to carry back to Nova Scotia with them to give to her orphaned daughters...The executioners of Anna Mae did not snuff out a meddlesome woman. They exalted a Brave Hearted Woman for all time.

The motivations of indigenous women in undertaking such risks are unequivocal. As Maria Sanchez, a leading member of the Northern Cheyenne resistance to corporate "development" of their reservation puts it: "I am the mother of nine children. My concern is for their future, for their children, and for future generations. As a woman, I drew strength from the traditional spiritual people...from my nation. The oil and gas companies are building a huge gas chamber for the Northern Cheyennes." Pauline Whitesinger has stated, "I think there is no way we can survive if we get moved to some other land away from ours. We are just going to waste away. People tell me to move, but I've got no place to go. I am not moving anywhere, that is certain." Roberta

Blackgoat, another leader of the Big Mountain resistance, concurs: "If this land dies, the people die with it. We are a nation. We will fight anyone who tries to push us off our land." All across North America, the message from native women is the same. The explicitly nationalist content of indigenous women's activism has been addressed by Lorelei DeCora Means, a Minne-conjou Lakota AIM member and one of the founders of Women of All Red Nations (WARN):

> We are American *Indian women,* in that order. We are oppressed, first and foremost, as American Indians, as peoples colonized by the United States of America, *not* as women. As Indians, we can never forget that. Our survival, the survival of every one of us—man, woman and child--as *Indians* depends on it. Decolonization is the agenda, the whole agenda, and until it is accomplished, it is the only agenda that counts for American Indians. It will take every one of us--every single one of us--to get the job done. We haven't got the time, energy or resources for anything else while our lands are being destroyed and our children are dying of avoidable diseases and malnutrition. So we tend to view those who come to us wanting to form alliances on the basis of "new" and "different" or "broader" and "more important" issues to be a little less than friends, especially since most of them come from the Euroamerican population which benefits most directly from our ongoing colonization.

As Janet McCloud sees it:

> Most of these 'progressive' non-Indian ideas like "class struggle" would at the present time divert us into participating as "equals" in our own colonization. Or, like "women's liberation," would divide us among ourselves in such a way as to leave us colonized in the name of "gender equity." Some of us can't help but think maybe a lot of these "better ideas" offered by non-Indians claiming to be our "allies" are intended to accomplish these sorts of diversions and disunity within our movement. So, let me toss out a different sot of "progression" to all you marxists and socialists and feminists out there. *You* join *us* in liberating *our* land and lives. Lose the privilege *you* acquire at *our* expense by occupying *our* land. Make *that* your first priority for as long as it takes to make it happen. *Then* we'll join you in fixing up whatever's left of the class and gender problems in your society, and our own, if need be. *But,* if you're not willing to do that, then don't presume to tell *us* how we should go about our liberation, what priorities and values we should have. Since you're standing on our land, we've got to view you as just another oppressor trying to hang on to what's ours. And that doesn't leave us a whole lot to talk about, now does it?

Myths of Male Dominance

A significant factor militating against fruitful alliances--or even dialogue--between Indians and non-Indians is the vast and complex set of myths imposed and stubbornly defended by the dominant culture as a means of "understanding" Native America both historically and topically. Aspects of the mythology are discussed throughout this volume, especially Chapters One, Twelve, Fourteen, and Fifteen. As concerns indigenous women in particular, this fantastical lexicon includes what anthropologist Eleanor Burke Leacock has termed the "myths of male dominance." Adherence to its main tenets of the stereotypes involved seems to be entirely trans-ideological within the "mainstream" of American life, a matter readily witnessed by recent offerings in the mass media by Paul Valentine, a remarkably reactionary critic for the *Washington Post*, and Barbara Ehrenreich, an ostensibly socialist-feminist columnist for *Time Magazine* and several more progressive publications.

In a hostile review of the film *Dances with Wolves* published in April 1991, Valentine denounces producer-director Kevin Costner for having "romanticized" American Indians. He then sets forth a series of outlandish contentions designed to show how nasty things really were in North America before Europeans came along to set things right. An example of the sheer absurdity with which his polemic is laced is a passage in which he has "the Arapaho of eastern Colorado...igniting uncontrolled grass fires on the prairies" which remained barren of grass "for many years afterward," causing mass starvation among the buffalo (as any high school botany student might have pointed out, a fall burn-off actually *stimulates* spring growth of most grasses, prairie grasses included). He then proceeds to explain the lot of native women in precontact times as being the haulers of "the clumsy two stick travois used to transport a family's belongings on the nomadic seasonal treks" (there were virtually no precontact "nomads" in North America, and dogs were used to drag travois prior to the advent of horses).

Ehrenreich, for her part, had earlier adopted a similar posture in a *Time* Magazine column arguing against the rampant militarism engulfing the United States during the fall of 1990. In her first paragraph, while taking a couple of gratuitous and utterly uninformed shots at the culture of the southeast African Masai and indigenous Solomon Islanders, she implies America's jingoist policies in the Persian Gulf had "descended" to the level of such "primitive"--and male dominated--"warrior cultures" as "the Plains Indian societies," where "the passage to manhood allowing young males to marry required the blooding of the spear, the taking of a scalp or head." Ehrenreich's thoroughly arrogant use of indigenous cultures as a springboard upon which to launch into the imagined superiority of her own culture and views is no more factually supportable than Valentine's, and is every bit as degrading to native people of *both* genders. Worse, she extends her "analysis" as a self-proclaimed "friend of the oppressed" rather than as an unabashed apologist for the status quo.

The truth of things was, of course, rather different. Contra Ehrereich's thesis, the Salish/Kootenai scholar D'Arcy McNickle long ago published the results of lengthy and painstaking research which showed that 70 percent or more of all precontact societies in North America practiced no form of warfare at all (for a description of the sort of "war" practiced by the remainder, see Chapter Twelve.) This may have been due in part to the fact that, as Laguna researcher Paula Gunn Allen has compellingly demonstrated in her recent book, *The Sacred Hoop*, traditional native societies were never "male dominated" and there were likely no "warrior cultures" worthy of the name before the European invasion. There is no record of *any* American Indian society, even after the invasion, requiring a man to kill in war before he could marry. To the contrary, military activity--including being a literal warrior--was never an exclusively male sphere of endeavor.

Although it is true that women were typically accorded a greater social value in indigenous tradition--both because of their biological ability to bear children, and for reasons which will be discussed below--and therefore tended to be noncombatant to a much greater degree than men, female fighters were never uncommon once the necessity of real warfare was imposed by Euroamericans. These included military commanders like Cousaponakeesa--Mary Matthews Musgrove Bosomworth, the "Creek Mary" of Dee Brown's 1981 novel--who led her people in a successful campaign against the British at Savannah during the 1750's. Lakota women traditionally maintained at least four warrior societies of their own, entities which are presently being resurrected. Among the Cherokees, there was Da'nawa-gasta, or "Sharp War," an especially tough warrior and head of a women's military society. The Piegans maintained what has been mistranslated as "Manly-Hearted Women," more accurately understood as being "Stong-Hearted Women," a permanent warrior society. The Cheyennes in particular fielded a number of strong women fighters, such as Buffalo Calf Road (who distinguished herself at both the Battle of the Rosebud in 1876 and during the 1878 "Cheyenne Breakout"), amidst the worst period of the wars of annihilation waged against them by the United States. Many other native cultures produced comparable figures, a tradition into which the women of the preceding section fit well, and which serves to debunk the tidy (if grossly misleading and divisive) male/female, warlike/ peaceful dichotomies deployed by such Euroamerican feminist thinkers as Ehrenreich and Robin Morgan.

More important than their direct participation in military activities was native women's role in making key decisions, not only about matters of peace and war, but in all other aspects of socioeconomic existence. Although Gunn Allen's conclusion that traditional indigenous societies added up to "gynocracies" is undoubtedly overstated and misleading, this is not to say that Native American women were not politically powerful. Creek Mary was not a general *per se*, but essentially head of state within the Creek Confederacy. Her status was that of "Beloved Woman," a position better recorded with regard to the system of governance developed among the Cherokees slightly to the north of Creek domain:

Cherokee women had the right to decide the fates of captives. Decisions that were made by vote of the Women's Council and relayed to the district at large by the War Woman or Pretty Woman. The decisions had to be made by female clan heads because a captive who was to live would be adopted into one of the families whose affairs were directed by the clan-mothers. The clan-mothers also had the right to wage war, and as Henry Timberlake wrote, the stories about Amazon women warriors were not so farfetched considering how many Indian women were famous warriors and powerful voices in the councils...The war women carried the titled Beloved Women, and their power was great...The Women's Council, as distinguished from the District, village, or Confederacy councils, was powerful in a number of political and socio-spiritual ways, and may have had the deciding voice on which males would serve on the Councils...Certainly the Women's Council was influential in tribal decisions, and its spokeswomen served as War Women and Peace Women, presum-ably holding offices in the towns designated as red towns and white towns, respectively. Their other powers included the right to speak in the men's Council [although men lacked a reciprocal right, under most circumstances], the right to choose whom and whether to marry, the right to bear arms, and the right to choose the extramarital occupations.

While Creek and Cherokee women "may" have had the right to select which males assumed positions of political responsibility, this was unquestionably the case within the Haudenosaunee {Six Nations Iroquois Confederacy) of New York state. Among the "Sixers," each of the fifty extended families (clans) was headed by a clan mother. These women formed a council within the confederacy which selected the males which would hold positions on a second council, composed of men, representing the confederacy's interests, both in formulation of internal policies and in conduct of external relations. If at any time, particular male council members adopted positions or undertook policies perceived by the women's council as being contrary to the people's interests, their respective clan mothers retained the right to replace them. Although much diminished after two centuries of U.S. colonial domination, this "Longhouse" form of government is ongoing today.

The Haudenosannee were hardly alone among northeastern peoples in according women such a measure of power. At the time of the European arrival in North America, the Narragansett of what is now Rhode Island were headed by a "sunksquaw," or female chief. The last of these, a woman named Magnus, was executed along with ninety other members of the Narraganset government after their defeat by English Major James Talcot in 1675. During the same period, the Esopus Confederacy was led, at least in part, by a woman named Mamanuchqua (also known as Mamareoktwe, Mamaroch, and Mamaprocht). The Delawares *generically* referred to themselves as "women," considering the term to be supremely complimentary. Among other Algonquin peoples of the Atlantic Coast region--e.g., the Wampanoag and Massachusetts Confederacies, and the Niaticks, Scaticooks, Niantics, Pictaways, Powhatans, and Caconnets-- much the same pattern prevailed:

From before 1020 until her death in 1677, a squaw-sachem known as the "Massachusetts Queen" by the Virginia colonizers governed the Massachusetts confederacy. It was her fortune to preside over the confederacy's destruction as the people were decimated by disease, war, and colonial manipulations...Others include the Pocasett sunksquaw Weetamoo, who was King Philip's ally and "served as a war chief commanding over 300 warriors" during his war with the British...Awashonks, another [woman head of state] of the Mid-Atlantic region, was squaw-sachem of the Sakonnet, a [nation] allied with the Wampanoag Confederacy. She [held her office] in the latter part of the seventeenth century. After fighting for a time against the British during King Philip's War, she was forced to surrender. Because she then convinced her warriors to fight with the British, she was able to save them from enslavement in the West Indies.

Women's power within traditional Indian societies was also grounded in other ways. While patrilineal/patrilocal cultures did exist, most precontact North American civilizations functioned on the basis of matrilineage and matrilocality. Insofar as family structures centered upon the identities of wives rather than husbands--men joined women's families, not the other way around--and because men were usually expected to relocate to join the women they married, the context of native social life was radically different from that which prevailed (and prevails) in European and Euro-derived cultures.

> Many of the largest and most important Indian peoples were matrilineal...Among these were: in the East, the Iroquois, the Siouan [nations] of the Piedmont and Atlantic coastal plain, the Mohegan, the Delaware, various other [nations] of southern New England, and the divisions of the Powhatan Confederacy in Virginia; in the South, the Creek, the Choctaw, the Chickasaw, the Seminole, and the [nations] of the Caddoan linguistic family; in the Great Plains, the Pawnee, the Hidatsa, the Mandan, the Oto, the Missouri, and the Crow and other Siouan [nations]; in the Southwest, the Navajo, and the numerous so-called Pueblo [nations], including the well known Hopi, Laguna, Acoma, and Zuni.

In many indigenous societies, the position of women was further strengthened economically, by virtue of their owning all or most property. Haudenosannee women, for example, owned the fields which produced about two-thirds of their people's diet. Among the Lakota, men owned nothing but their clothing, a horse for hunting, weapons and spiritual items; homes, furnishings, and the like were the property of their wives. All a Lakota woman needed to do in order to divorce her husband was to set his meager personal possessions outside the door of their lodge, an action against which he had no appeal under traditional law. Much the same system prevailed among the Anishinabe and numerous other native cultures. As Mary Oshana, an Anishinabe activist, has explained it:

> Matrilineal [nations] provided the greatest opportunities for women: women in these [nations] owned houses, furnishings, fields, gardens, agricultural tools, art objects, livestock and horses. Furthermore, these items were passed down through female lines. Regardless of their marital status, women had the right to own and control property. The woman had control of the children and if marital problems developed the man would leave the home.

Additional reinforcement of motive women's status accrues from the spiritual traditions of most of North America's indigenous cultures. First, contrary to the Euroamerican myth that American Indian spiritual leaders are invariably something called "medicine men," women have always held important positions in this regard. Prime examples include Coocoochee of the Mohawks, Sanapia of the Comanches, and Pretty Shield of the Crows. Among the Zuni and other Puebloan cultures, women were members of the Rain Priesthood, the most important of that society's religious entities. Women are also known to have played crucial leadership roles within Anishinabe, Blackfeet, Chalula, and Dine spiritual practices, as well as those other native societies.

More important in some ways, virtually all indigenous religions on this continent exhibit an abundant presence of feminine elements within their cosmologies. When contrasted to the hegemonic masculinity of the deities embraced by such "world religions" as Judaism, Christianity, and Islam--the corresponding male supremacism marking those societies which adhere to them-- the real significance of concepts like Mother Earth (universal), Spider Woman (Hopi and Dine), White Buffalo Calf Woman (Lakota), Grandmother Turtle (Iroquois), Sky Woman (Iroquois), Hard Beings Woman and Sand Altar Woman (Hopi), First Woman (Abanaki), Thought Woman (Laguna), Corn Woman (Cherokee), and Changing Woman (Dine) becomes rather obvious. So too does the real rather than the mythical status of woman in traditional Native American life. Indeed, as Dine artist Mary Morez has put it, "in [our] society, the woman is the dominant figure who becomes the wise one with old age. It's a [matrilineal/matrilocal] society, you know. But the Navajo woman never demands her status. She achieves, earns, accomplishes it through maturity. That maturing process is psychological. It has to do with one's feelings for the land and being part of the whole cycle of nature. It's difficult to describe to a non-Indian.

Bea Medicine, a Hunkpapa Lakota scholar, concurs, noting that "Our power is obvious. [Women] are primary socializers of our children. Culture is transmitted primarily through the mother. The mother teaches languages, attitudes, beliefs, behavior patterns, etc." Anishinabe writer and activist Winona LaDuke concludes, "Traditionally, American Indian women were never subordinate to men. Or vice versa, for that matter. What native societies have always been about is achieving balance in all things, gender relations no less than any other. Nobody needs to tell us how to do it. We've had that all worked out for thousands of years. And, left to our own devices, that's exactly how we'd be living right now." Or, as Priscilla K. Buffalohead, another Anishinabe scholar has put it, "[We] stem from egalitarian cultural traditions. These traditions are concerned less with equality of the sexes and more with the dignity of the individual and their inherent right--whether they be women, men or children--to make their own choices and decisions."

Disempowerment

The reduction of the status held by women within indigenous nations was a first priority for European colonizers eager to weaken and destabilize target societies. With regard to the Montagnais and Naskapi of the St. Lawrence River Valley, for example, the French, who first entered the area in the 1550's, encountered a people among whom "women have great power...A man may promise you something and if he does not keep his promise, he thinks he is sufficiently excused when he tells you that his wife did not wish him to do it." They responded, beginning in 1633, by sending Jesuit missionaries to show the natives a "better and more enlightened way" of comporting themselves, a matter well-chronicled by the priest, Paul Le Jeune:

Though some observers saw women as drudges, Le Jeune saw women as holding "great power" and having "in every instance...the choice of plans, of undertakings, of journeys, of winterings." Indeed, independence of women was considered a problem by the Jesuits, who lectured the men about "allowing" their wives sexual and other freedom and sought to introduce European principles of obedience.

Most likely the Jesuit program would have gone nowhere had the sharp end of colonization not undercut the Montagnais-Naskapi traditional economy, replacing it with a system far more reliant upon fur trapping and traders by the latter part of the 17th century. As their dependence upon their colonizers increased, the Indians were compelled to accept more and more of the European brand of "morality." The Jesuits imposed a form of monogamy in which divorce was forbidden, implemented a system of compulsory Catholic education, and refused to deal with anyone other than selected male "representatives" of the Montagnais and Naskapi in political or economic affairs (thus deforming the Inddian structure of governance beyond recognition).

Positions of formal power such as political leadership [spiritual leadership], and matrilocality, which placed the economic dependence of a woman with children in the hands of her mother's family...shifted. [Spiritual and political leadership were male [by 1750], and matrilocality had become patrilocality. This is not so strange given the economics of the situation and the fact that over the years the Montagnais became entirely Catholicized.

Among the Haudenosaunee, who were not militarily defeated until after the American Revolution, such changes took much longer. It was not until the early 19th century that, in an attempt to adjust to the new circumstances of subordination to the United States, the Seneca prophet Handsome Lake promulgated a new code of law and social organization which replaced their old "petticoat government" with a male-centered model more acceptable to the colonizers. In attempting to shift power from "the meddling old women" of Iroquois society,

Handsome Lake advocated that young women cleave to their husbands rather than to their mothers and abandon the clan-mother controlled Longhouse in favor of a patriarchal, nuclear family arrangement...While the shift was never complete, it was sufficient. Under the Code of Handsome Lake, which was the tribal version of the white man's way, the Longhouse declined in importance, and eventually Iroquois women were firmly under the thumb of Christian patriarchy.

To the south, "the British worked hard to lessen the power of women in Cherokee affairs. They took Cherokee men to England and educated them in European ways. These men returned to Cherokee country and exerted great influence on behalf of the British in the region." Intermarriage was also encouraged, with markedly privileged treatment accorded mixed-blood offspring of such unions with English colonialists, In time, when combined with increasing

Cherokee dependence on the British trade economy, these advantages resulted in a situation where "men with little Cherokee blood [and even less loyalty] wielded considerable power over the nation's policies." Aping the English, this new male leadership set out to establish a plantation economy devoted to the growing of cotton and tobacco.

The male leadership bought and sold not only black men and women but men and women from neighboring tribes, the women of the leadership retreated to Bible classes, sewing circles, and petticoats that rivaled those of their white sisters. Many of these upper-strata Cherokee women married white ministers and other opportunists, as the men of their class married white women, often the daughters of white ministers...Cherokee society became rigid and modeled on Christian white social organization of upper, middle, and impoverished classes usually composed of very traditional clans.

This situation, of course, greatly weakened the Cherokee Nation, creating sharp divisions within it which have not completely heeled even to the present day. Moreover, it caused Euroamericans in surrounding areas to covet not only Cherokee land *per se*, but the lucrative farming enterprises built up by the mixed-blood male caste. This was a powerful incentive for the U.S. to undertake the compulsory removal of the Cherokees and other indigenous nations from east of the Mississippi to points west during the first half of the 19th century. The reaction of assimilated Cherokees was an attempt to show their "worth" by becoming even more ostentatiously Europeanized.

In an effort to stave off removal, the Cherokee in the early 1800's, under the leadership of men such as Elias Boudinot, Major Ridge, and John Ross (later Principal Chief of the Cherokee in Oklahoma Territory), and others, drafted a constitution that disenfranchised women and blacks. Modeled after the Constitution of the United States, whose favor they were attempting to curry, and in conjunction with Christian sympathizers to the Cherokee cause, the new Cherokee constitution relegated women to the position of chattel...[Under such conditions], the last Beloved Woman, Nancy Ward, resigned her office in 1817, sending her cane and her vote on important questions to the Cherokee Council.

Despite much groveling by the "sellouts," Andrew Jackson ordered removal of the Cherokees--as well as the Creeks, Choctaws, Chickasaws and Seminoles—to begin in 1832. By 1839, the Trail of Tears" was complete, with catastrophic population for the indigenous nations involved. By the later stage, traditionalist Cherokees had overcome sanctions against killing other tribal members in a desperate attempt to restore some semblance of order within their nation: Major Ridge, his eldest son, John, and Elias Boudinot were assassinated on June 22, 1839. Attempts were made to eliminate other members of the "Ridge Faction" such as Stand Watie, John A. Bell, James Starr, and George W. Adair, but these failed, and the assimilationist faction continued to do substantial damage to Cherokee sovereignty. Although John Rollin Ridge, the Major's grandson, was forced to flee to California in 1850 and was unable to return to Cherokee Country until after the Civil War, Stand Watie (Boudinot's younger brother) managed to lead a portion of the Cherokees into a disastrous alliance with the Confederacy from which the nation never recovered.

Across the continent, the story was the same in every case. In *not one* of the more than 370 ratified and perhaps 300 unratified treaties negotiated by the United States with indigenous nations was the federal government willing to allow participation by native women. In *none* of the several thousand non-treaty agreements reached between the United States and these same nations were federal representatives prepared to discuss anything at all with women. In *no* instance was the United States open to recognizing a female as representing her people's interest when it came to administering the reservations onto which American Indians were ultimately forced; always, men were required to do what was necessary to secure delivery of rations, argue for water rights, and all the rest. Meanwhile, as Rebecca Robbins points out in Chapter Three, the best and most patriotic of the indigenous male leadership--men like Tecumseh, Osceola, Crazy Horse, and Sitting Bull--were systematically assassinated or sent to far-away prisons for extended periods. The male leadership of the native resistance was then replaced with men selected on the basis of their willingness to cooperate with their oppressors. Exactly how native women coped with this vast alteration of their circumstances, and those of their people more generally, is a bit mysterious:

> If a generalization may be made, it is that female roles of mother, sister, and wife were ongoing because of the continued care they were supposed to provide for the family. But what of the role of women in relationship to agents, to soldiers guarding the '"hostiles," and to their general physical deprivation in societies whose livelihood and way of life had been destroyed along with the bison? We are very nearly bereft of data and statements which could clarify the transitional status of women during this period. The strategies adopted for cultural survival and the means of transmitting these to daughters and nieces are valuable adaptive mechanisms which cannot be even partially reconstructed.

These practical realities, imposed quite uniformly by the conquerors, ware steadily reinforced by officially sponsored missionizing and mandatory education in boarding schools, processes designed to inculcate the notion that such disempowerment of Indian women and liquidation of "recalcitrant" males was "natural, right, and inevitable." As Jorge Noriega notes in Chapter Thirteen, the purpose of the schools in particular was never to "educate" American Indian children, but rather to indoctrinate them into accepting the dissolution of their cultures and the intrinsic "superiority" of the Euroamerican cultural valves for which they were to abandon their own. In certain instances, further instruction was provided to individuals selected to form a permanent "broker class" adminstering native societies on behalf of the United States. "Manifest Destiny," which Euroamerica believed entitled it to undertake such culturally genocidal actions, was unequivocal. As George Ellis, a well-known Euroamerican clergyman and author, put it in 1882, at the very point the United States had completed its wars of conquest against Native America and was setting out to consolidate the manner of its colonial rule:

> We [whites] have a full right, by our own best wisdom, and then even by compulsion, to dictate terms and conditions to them [Indians]; to use constraint and force; to say what we intend to do, and what we must and shall do...This rightful power of ours will relieve us from conforming to, or even consulting to any troublesome extent, the views and inclinations of the Indians whom we are to manage...The Indian must be made to feel he is in the grasp of a superior.

Contemporary Conditions

The disempowerment of native women corresponded precisely with the extension of colonial domination of each indigenous nation. During the first half of the 20th century, federal authorities developed and perfected the mechanisms of control over Indian land, lives, and resources through such legislation as the General Allotment Act (passed in 1887, but very much ongoing through the 1920's), the 1924 Indian citizenship Act, and the Indian Reorganization Act of 1934. All of this was done under the premises of the "Trust" and "Plenary Power" doctrines discussed at length elsewhere in this book, and all of it was done for profits taken at the direct expense of native people. As Cheyenne historian Roxanne Dunbar Ortiz has observed:

> Throughout this century, the United States government has promoted the corporate exploitation of Indian lands and resources by making unequal agreements on behalf of Indian peoples and cooperating closely with transnational corporations in identifying strategic resources and land areas.

Hence, indigenous nations were systematically denied use of and benefits from even those residual lands they nominally retained. Denied their traditional economies, they were compelled to become absolutely dependent upon government subsidies to survive or--where possible--to join the lowest paid sector of the U.S. workforce. Peoples which had been entirely self-sufficient for thousands of years--indeed, many of them had historically been quite wealthy--were reduced to abject poverty. The capstone of this drive to utilize law as "the perfect instrument of empire" came during the 1950's, when the government set out to drive native people from the land altogether. Beginning in 1954, Congress effected statutes unilaterally "terminating" (dissolving, for purposes of federal recognition) entire indigenous peoples such as the Klamath and Menominee, and coercing thousands of others to relocate from their reservations to non-Indian urban centers (see chapters One and Three). In this way, Indian reservations were systematically opened up for greater corporate utilization. Once "urbanized," those Indians who had been able to find subsistence employment on farms or ranches and/or engage in gardening and limited livestock rearing of their own were forced into the most marginal occupations or left unemployed altogether.

As concerns native women in the workforce, where 47.2 percent of them had been employed in agriculture in 1900, only 2.1 percent remained so by 1970. Meanwhile, whereas only 0.1 percent of them had been in low-paying clerical positions on high-cost urban economies at the turn of the century, 25.9 percent held jobs by 1970. For "service occupations" such as waiting tables, the figures were 12.1 percent in 1900, 25.9 percent in 1970. The data for native men was even more dismal, with nearly 65 percent being completely unemployed nationally. By 1969, even the most conservative statistics revealed that more than 40 percent of all American Indians, as compared to 14 percent of the total population, lived below the poverty line. In an effort to compensate,

Native American women's labor force participation rates rose sharply between 1970 and 1980, from 35 percent to 48 percent. Those who held full-time, year-round jobs earned nearly 89 percent as much as white women. Despite these gains, nearly three-quarters of American Indian women were employed in the secondary labor market in 1980, compared to two-thirds of European American women and one-third of European American men. Repressive, inaccessible, and inadequate education bears much of the blame for this low occupation status, along with discrimination by employers and fellow employees and stagnation of the reservation economy. Almost one-quarter of all American Indian women had not completed high school in 1980, compared to 16 percent of white women.

For Native American males, the situation was nearly as bad:

Those men who managed to find full-time jobs earned only three-fourths as much as white men. Moreover, American Indian men have suffered the highest rate of unemployment (17 percent in 1980), the highest rate of part-time work (58 percent), and a high rate of non-participation in the formal labor force (31 percent). A [heavily male-skewed] BIA study of the labor force status of the 635,000 American Indians living on and adjacent to reservations in January 1989 showed that one-third were unemployed and one-third earned less than $7,000.

In 1976, the federal government itself officially acknowledged that American Indians were by far the most impoverished ethnic group in North America, living as a whole in conditions virtually identical to those prevailing in many Third World locales. In Canada, circumstances were much the same, with "unemployment, suicide, school drop-out rates, health problems and housing shortages at epidemic levels on most reserves. With regard to native women in particular, as the Canadian government admitted in 1979:

Indian women likely rank among the most severely disadvantaged in Canadian society. They are worse off economically than both Indian men and Canadian women and although they live longer than Indian men, their life expectancy does not approach that of Canadian women generally.

Such poverty indeed breeds short life-spans--in 1980, a U.S. reservation-based American Indian man could expect to live only slightly over forty-four years, a woman barely two years longer on the average--as North America's highest rates of death from malnutrition, exposure, diabetes, tuberculosis, typhoid, diphtheria, measles, and even bubonic plague took their toll. Infant mortality among reservation-based Native Americans is also seven times the nation average. Under these conditions, the despair experienced by American Indians of both genders has manifested itself in the most pronounced incidence of alcoholism of any ethnic group in the United States. In turn, the cycle of drunkenness results in vastly increased rates of death, not only from ailments like cirrhosis of the liver, but from accidents, often but not always involving automobiles. Extreme social disruption is also caused by alcohol in other ways, such as children born with fetal alcohol syndrome, and child abuse and abandonment, unknown in traditional native societies. The intensity of colonially induced despair also led Native North America as a whole to experience a wave of teen suicide during the 1980's which has run several times the national average.

In 1980, nearly one in four American Indian families was maintained by a woman (over twice the rate for whites and Asians), and 47 percent of these single-mother families were considered poor by federal guidelines. Among women with children under six, the poverty rate stood at a shocking 82 percent.

On balance, the situation breeds frustration and rage of the most volatile sort, especially among native males, who have been at once heaped with a range of responsibilities utterly alien to their tradition--"head of the household," sole "breadwinner," and so forth--while being structurally denied any viable opportunity to act upon them. In perfect Fanonesque fashion, this has led to a perpetual spiral of internalized violence in which Indian men engage in brutal (and all too often lethal) bar fights with ore another, or turn their angry attentions on their wives and children. Battering has become endemic on some reservations, as well as in the Indian ghettos which exist in most U.S. cities, with the result that at least a few Indian women have been forced to kill their spouses in self-defense.

A headline in the *Navajo Times* in the fall of 1979 reported that rape was the number one crime on the Navajo reservation. In a professional mental health journal of the Indian Health Services, Phyllis Old Dog Cross reported that incest and rape are common among the Indian women seeking services and that their incidence [was] increasing. "It is believed that at least 60 percent of the Native Women seen at the psychiatric service center (5 state area) have experienced some sort of sexual assault.

As Paula Gunn Allen has observed,

Often it is said [correctly] that the increase of violence against women is the result of various sociological factors such as oppression, racism, poverty, hopelessness, emasculation of men, and loss of male self-esteem as their place within traditional society has been systematically destroyed by increasing urbanization, industrialization, and institutionalization, but seldom do we notice that for the past forty to fifty years, American popular media have depicted American Indian men as bloodthirsty savages treating women cruelly. While traditional Indian men seldom did any such thing--and in fact amongst most [nations] abuse of women was simply unthinkable, as was abuse of children or the aged--the lie about "usual" male Indian behavior seems to have taken root and now bears its brutal and bitter fruit.

Gunn also goes on to note,

It is true that colonization destroyed roles that had given men their sense of self-esteem and identity, but the significant roles lost were not those of hunter and warrior. Rather, colonization took away the security of office men once derived from their ritual and political relationship to women.

Throughout the 20th century, new federal policies have been formulated to target the power of American Indian women, specifically usually within their traditional capacity as familial anchors. One evidence of this has been the systematic and persistent forced transfer of Indian children into non-Indian custody, a patent violation of The United Nations' 1948 Convention on Punishment and Prevention of the Crime of Genocide. As of 1974, the Association of American Indian Affairs estimated that between 25 and 35 percent of all native youth were either adopted by Euroamericans, placed in non-Indian foster homes, or permanently housed in institutional settings, while another 25 percent were "temporarily" placed in government or church-run boarding schools each year. Although strong agitation, primarily by Indian women and their supporters, forced Congress to partially correct the situation through passage of the Indian Child Welfare Act (P.L. 95-608; 25 U.S.C. 1901 *et seq.*) in 1978, the issue remains a very real one 1991.
Even more grotesque was policy of involuntary surgical sterilization--another blatant breach of the Genocide Convention--imposed upon native women, usually without their knowledge, by

the Bureau of Indian Affairs' so-called Indian Health Service (IHS) during the late 1960's and the first half of the '70s. Existence of the sterilization program was revealed through analysis of secret documents removed by American Indian Movement members from the BIA's Washington, D.C. headquarters during its occupation by the Trail of Broken Treaties in November 1972 (see Chapter Three). A resulting 1974 study by WARN concluded that as many as 42 percent of all Indian women of childbearing age had by that point been sterilized without their consent. The WARN estimates were probably accurate, as is revealed in a subsequent General Accounting Office investigation, restricted to examining only the years 1973-76 and a mere four of the many IHS facilities. The GAO study showed that during the three-year sample period, 3,406 involuntary sterilizations (the equivalent of over a half-million among the general population) had been performed in just these four hospitals. As a result of strong agitation by Indian women and their supporters, the IHS was transferred to the department of Health and Human Services in 1978.

As Gunn Allen has aptly put it,

Currently our struggles are on two fronts: physical survival and cultural survival. For women this means fighting alcoholism and drug abuse (our own and that of our husbands, lovers, parents, children); poverty...rape, incest, battering by Indian [and non-Indian] men; assaults on fertility and other health matters by the Indian Health Service and Public Health Service; high mortality due to substandard medical care, nutrition, and health information; poor educational opportunities or education that takes us away from our traditions, language, and communities; suicide, homicide, or similar expressions of self-hatred; lack of economic opportunities; substandard housing; sometimes violent and often virulent racist attitudes and behaviors directed against us by an entertainment and educational system that wants only one thing from Indians: our silence, our invisibility, and our collective death...To survive culturally, American Indian women must often fight the United States government, the tribal [puppet] governments, women and men of their [nation] who are...threatened by attempts to change...the colonizers' revisions of our lives, values, and histories.

Fighting Back

The patterns of resistance by which American Indians have fought back against the overwhelming oppression of their colonization are actually as old as the colonization itself, occurring in an uninterrupted flow from the early 1500's onward. As with any struggle, however, native resistance has been cyclical in terms of its intensity, and varied in its expression over time. The "modem era" in this regard was perhaps ushered in with the adoption by Indians of written articulation as a mode of political action. Women, beginning with the Northern Paiute writer and activist Sarah Winnemucca Hopkins, have played a decisive role in developing this new tool for indigenous utilization. Winnemucca's autobiographical *Life Among the Piutes: Their Wrongs and Claims*, first published in 1883, laid the groundwork for the subsequent efforts of the Santee Dakota writer Ohiyesa (Charles Eastman), whose early 20th century books and articles yielded a significant effect in terms of altering the assimilationist policies of the federal government.

Winnemucca was hardly alone in her endeavor. Contemporaneous to Ohiyesa--and carrying a much sharper edge in both her writing and her activism--was Zitkala-sa (Gertrude Bonnin), a Lakota who was the first to announce proudly and in print that she considered her own traditions not simply the equal of anything Euroamerica had to offer, but "superior to white ways and values." She was followed by Ella Deloria, another Lakota author relatively unequivocal in her affirmation of "Indianness." Together, these early Indian women writers set in motion a dynamic wherein native women reasserted their traditional role as "voice of the people," albeit through a much different medium than had historically prevailed. By the late 1970's, Native American literature had assumed a critical galvanizing role within indigenous liberation struggles in North America, and women such as Leslie Marmon Silko (Laguna), Wendy Rose (Hopi), Joy Harjo (Creek), Linda Hogan (Chickasaw), and Mary TallMountain (Athabascan) were providing the muscle and sinew of the effort. The female presence in native literature has continued to increase in importance during the late 1980's and early 1990's, with the emergence of work by Louise Erdrich (Turtle Mountain Anishinabe), Chrystos (Menominee), and others.

As noted earlier, translation of these literary sentiments into serious confrontations began to occur in noticeable fashion with the fish-in movement of the Pacific Northwest during the 1960's.

This happened, in the words of Bobbi Lee, a Canadian Metis active in the fishing rights struggle, "when the women just became fed up. They ran out of patience with what was going on and decided it was time to change things. She describes her first demonstration at the Washington state capitol building:

> Most of the militants there at [the] demonstration in Olympia--were women and three of them did most of the speaking...They were traditionalists so there was nothing unusual about women acting as spokes[people] for the group. In fact, they told me they were having trouble getting the men involved. The only man who spoke was Hank Adams, who's been to a university and wasn't traditional.

The same sort of thing happened with the American Indian Movement (AIM), an entity which received much of its early impetus from the fishing rights movement and the examples set by Marie Lego and others engaged in the Pit River land struggle. Mary Jane Wilson, an Anishinabe activist, was--along with Dennis Banks and George Mitchell--a founder of the organization in 1968. As *AIM* began to grow, much of the grassroots membership which made it successful was comprised of women. As was mentioned above, on the Pine Ridge Lakota Reservation, which became the focal point of the movement's pitched battles with federal forces during the mid '70s, the staunchest and most active traditionalist support came from elder Oglala women. Once again, those who established and maintained the *AIM* survival schools during the latter part of the decade were almost exclusively women.

When it came to repression, however, males bore the brunt. Although female leadership had been readily apparent throughout the confrontation at Wounded Knee, the government simply repeated its historical pattern, targeting six Indian men--Russell Means (Oglala), Pedro Bissonette (Oglala), Leonard Crow Dog (Sicangu Lakota), Dennis Banks (Anishinabe). Carter Camp (Ponca), and Stan Holder (Wichita)--to face up to triple-life plus 88 years imprisonment in the so-called Wounded Knee Leadership Trials. To be sure, AIM woman *were* charged, brought to trial and sometimes convicted--Kamook Nichols Banks (Oglala), Joanna LeDeaux (Oglala), and Nilak Butler (Inuit), to name but three examples, served appreciable sentences--but for every woman locked up, there were a dozen or more men. Twenty-one women and two children were also among the minimum of 69 AIM members and supporters killed by government surrogates on Pine Ridge between mid-1973 and mid-1976, the peak period of the U.S. counterinsurgency warfare directed at the organization. The proportionate emphasis placed by federal authorities upon "neutralizing" AIM men is apparent in the fact that the remaining 46 fatalities were adult males. As Madonna Thunderhawk, a Hunkpapa Lakota AIM member and a founder of WARN, described it in 1980:

> Indian women have *had to* be strong because of what this colonialist system has done to our men...alcohol, suicides, car wrecks, the whole thing. And after Wounded Knee, while all that persecution of the men was going on, we women had to keep things going.

During the 1980's, aside from the earlier-mentioned leadership of elder Dine women in the sustained resistance to forced relocation at Big Mountain, a comparable function has been assumed by the western Shoshone sisters Mary and Carrie Dann in Nevada vis-a-vis a federal drive to take their people's homeland. In northern California, it was Abby Abinanti, a Yurok attorney, who led the legal defense against a government/corporate plan to desecrate the "High Country", a locale sacred to her own and several other peoples in the area (see Chapter Nine). Anywhere confrontations over Indian rights are occurring in the United States, native women are playing crucial roles. Moreover, by the early '80s, women had (re)assumed the primary leadership position in sixty-seven of the 304 remaining reservation-based indigenous nations with the forty-eight contiguous states, and the number is growing steadily (see chapter Three for examples).

The struggle has also been sharp in Canada, where, under provision of Section (12) (1) (b) of the 1876 Indian Act (amended in 1951) a particularly virulent form of patrilineage was built into the definition of "Indian-ness." Under the act, a woman who married, not only a non-Indian but anyone outside her "tribe," was herself (along with her children), legally and automatically deprived of her "Indian Status." Such reversal of traditional matrilineage principles--not to mention the overt racism and sexism involved--had been challenged from 1952 onward, notably by Mohawk leader Mary Two-Axe Early of the Caughnawaga Reserve in Quebec. After losing several cases on the issue in Canadian courts during the early '70s, a group of Maliseet women from the Tobique Reserve in New Brunswick decided to place the situation of one of their number, Sandra Lovelace Sappier, before the United Nations.

The Tobique women's strategy of going the United Nations did exert tremendous pressure on the [Ottawa] government to change the Indian Act. On December 29, 1977 the complaint of Sandra Lovelace against the Canadian government was communicated to the United Nations Human Rights Committee in Geneva, Switzerland. Because of delays by the Canadian government in responding to the Human Rights Committee's requests for information, the final verdict was not made until July 30, 1981. The decision found that Canada was in violation of the International Covenant on Civil and Political Rights. Canada was in breach of the Covenant because the Indian Act denied Sandra Lovelace the *legal* right to live in the community of her birth.

As a result of the Lovelace case, the Canadian government was forced to make a further revision to the Indian Act in 1985 which eliminated discrimination against women, opening the way for resumption of traditional matrilineal/matrilocal expression among indigenous societies across the country. Along the way, the "Tobique Women's Political Action Group" was forced to confront the broker class of their own male population--placed in positions of "leadership" by the Canadian rather than their own governing system, and thus threatened by the women's actions--physically occupying tribal office buildings and effectively evicting the men, beginning in September 1977. Their actions had considerable ramifications, as is witnessed by the fact that at the present time, native women in Canada often serve as chief spokespersons for their peoples. One example is that of Sharon Venne, a Cree attorney selected during the '80s to represent the Treaty Six nations of Alberta in international forums. Another illustration is Norma Kassi, official spokesperson for the Swich'in Nation, elected member of the Yukon Legislative Assembly, and organizer of a broad coalition to oppose oil and gas development on the North Slope of Alaska.

Thus, both north and south of the Euroamerican border separating the United States and Canada, intense struggles have been waged by indigenous people over the past three decades against the sorts of conditions depicted in the preceding section. While it is obvious that the problems confronted have not been solved, it is equally plain that substantial gains have been made in terms of positioning Native North America to change these circumstances through decolonization and reassertion of its self-determining, self-defining, and self-sufficient existence. In each instance, native women--as *Indians*, first, last, and always--have asserted their traditional right and assumed their traditional responsibility of standing at the very center of the fray.

Native American Women and Feminism

Given the reality that Native Americans today comprise only about 0.6 percent of the North American population, and the magnitude of the problems we face, it would seem imperative that we attract support from non-Indian groups, forming alliances and coalitions where possible on the basis of some mutually recognized common ground. Many efforts in this regard, some of them described elsewhere in this book, have been attempted by native activists with varying degrees of success. On the face of it, both the "matriarchal" aspects of indigenous traditions and the nature of many of the struggles engaged in by contemporary native women appear to lend themselves to such a union with what the broader population has come to describe as "feminism." Accordingly, a number of prominent native women activists such as Shirley Hill Witt, Rayna Green (Cherokee), Annie Wauneka (Dine), and Suzan Shown Harjo (Lakota/Creek) have, at least at times, adopted the feminist descriptor to define their own perspectives. American Indian women's organizations of this persuasion, such as OHOYO, have also made appearances. Paula Gunn Allen has gone farther in her attempts to make the link, arguing that indigenous tradition represents the "red roots" of the feminist impulse among all people in North America, whether its various adherents and opponents realize it or not.

It should be noted, however, that those who have most openly identified themselves in this fashion have tended to be among the more assimilated of Indian women activists, generally accepting of the colonialist ideology that indigenous nations are now legitimate sub-parts of the U.S. geopolitical corpus rather than separate nations, that Indian people are now a minority within the overall population rather than the citizenry of their own distinct nations. Such Indian women

46

activists are therefore usually more devoted to "civil rights" than to liberation *per se*. Native American women who are more genuinely sovereigntist in their outlook have proven themselves far more dubious about the potentials offered by feminist politics and alliances: "At the present time, American Indians in general are not comfortable with feminist analysis or action within reservation or urban Indian enclaves. Many Indian women are uncomfortable because they perceive it (correctly) as white-dominated." What this has meant in practice is, as Lorelei Means has put it:

> White women, most of them very middle class and, for whatever they think their personal oppression is, as a group they're obviously the material beneficiaries of the colonial exploitation their society has imposed upon ours...they come and they look at the deformity of our societies produced by colonization, and then they criticize the deformity. They tell us we have to move "beyond" our culture in order to be "liberated" like them. It's just amazing...They virtually demand that we give up our own traditions in favor of what they imagine their own to be, just like the missionaries and the government and all the rest of the colonizers. It was being forced *away* from our own traditions that deformed us--that made the men sexists and things like that--in the first place. What we need to be is *more*, not less Indian. But every time we try to explain this to our self-proclaimed "white sisters," we either get told were missing the point--we're just dumb Indians, after all--or we're accused of "self-hatred" as women. A few experiences with this sort of arrogance and you start to get the idea maybe all this feminism business is just another extension of the same old racist, colonialist mentality.

Janet McCloud explains that, "Many Anglo women try, I expect in all sincerity, to tell us that our most pressing problem is male supremacy. To this, I have to say, with all due respect, *bullshit*. Our problems are what they've been for the past several hundred years: white supremacism and colonialism. And that's a supremacism and a colonialism of which white feminists are still very much apart." Pam Colorado, an Oneida scholar working in Canada. Observes:

It seems to me the feminist agenda is basically one of rearranging social relations within the society which is occupying our land and utilizing our resources for its own benefit. Nothing I've encountered in feminist theory addresses the fact of our colonization, or the wrongness of white women's stake in it. To the contrary, there seems to be a presumption among feminist writers that the colonization of Native America will, even *should*, continue permanently. At least there's no indication any feminist theorist has actively advocated pulling out of Indian Country, should a "transformation of social relations" actually occur. Instead, feminists appear to share a presumption in common with the patriarchs they oppose, that they have some sort of inalienable right to simply go on occupying our land and exploiting our resources for as long as they like. Hence, I can only conclude that, like marxism, which arrives at the same outcome through class rather than gender theory, feminism is essentially a Euro-supremacist ideology and is therefore quite imperialist in its implications.

Evidence of the colonialist content of much Euroamerican feminist practice has advanced, not just at the material level, but in terms of cultural imperialism. Andrea Smith, a Makah writing in *Indigenous Woman*, recently denounced feminism of the "New Age" persuasion for "ripping off" native ceremonies for their own purposes, putting them on notice that "as long as they take part in Indian spiritual abuse, either by being consumers of it, or by refusing to take a stand on [the matter], Indian women will consider white 'feminists' to be nothing more than agents in the genocide of [native] people. Another increasingly volatile issue in this connection has been the appropriation and distortion of indigenous traditions concerning homosexuality by both "radical" or lesbian feminists and gay male activists. Particularly offensive have been non-Indian efforts to convert the indigenous custom of treating homosexuals (often termed "berdache" by anthropologists) as persons endowed with special spiritual powers into a polemic for mass organizing within the dominant society.

Although the special and deeply revered status accorded homosexuals by native societies derived precisely from their being relatively rare, the desire of non-Indian gays and lesbians to legitimate their preferences within the context of their own much more repressive society, and to do so in ways which reinforce an imagined superiority of these preferences, has led many of them to insist upon the reality of a traditional Native North America in which nearly *everyone* was homosexual. Unfortunately, Paula Gunn Allen, in pandering to the needs and tastes of non-Indian gay and lesbian organizers, has done much to reinforce their willful misimpressions of indigenous tradition:

> [L]esbiansim and homosexuality were probably commonplace. Indeed, same-sex relation-ships may have been the norm for primary pair-bonding. There were clans and bands or villages, but the primary personal unit tended to include members of one's own sex rather than members of the opposite sex.

Although Gunn Allen hurriedly goes on to note that it "is questionable whether these practices would be recognized as lesbian by the politically radical lesbian community of today," her sweeping exaggeration has been seized upon by those seeking to deploy their own version of "noble savage" mythology for political purposes. To paraphrase an Inuit lesbian poet who wishes not to be further identified, "I've always been very well accepted and supported within my community for who I am. But now comes this idea, brought in from the outside for reasons that really have noting to do with us, that Indianness and homosexuality are somehow fused, that you can't 'really' be Indian unless you're gay or lesbian, or at least bisexual. The implication is that I'm assessed as being more traditional, and my heterosexual friends less traditional, on the basis of sexual preference. This is not an Indian idea. It's absurd, and it's deeply resented by all of us. But the danger is that it could eventually cause divisions among us Indians that never existed before, and right at the paint when we're most in need of unity." Or, as Chrystos, also a lesbian, has put it:

> This is just another myth imposed by white people for their own purposes, at our expense. And while I may consider it to be more pleasant, its really no better than the myth of us being savage scalpers and torturers, stone age hunter-gatherers, and all the rest. We have all come to the point where we must pull ourselves together in our common humanity if we are to survive. That can only happen on the basis of *truth*, not the projection of still another white fantasy.

For their efforts at lending a native voice to discussions of homosexuality in indigenous tradition, and leading things in a positive contemporary direction, both women have often been called "homophobic." Non-lesbian Indian women who have attempted to make the same points have often been labeled "heterosexist," a designation which prompted at least one of them to respond that "a very vocal part of the white women's movement seems to be afflicted with what you could call *homo* sexism." Janet McCloud has concluded that, under such circumstances, there is little, if anything, to be gained by Indian women making a direct link-up with feminism.

Other, less "radical," native women have arrived at essentially the same conclusion. Laura Waterman Wittstock, a Seneca leader, went on record early with the message that "tribalism, not feminism, is the correct route" for native women to follow. Similarly, Blackfeet traditional Beverly Hungry Wolf in her autobiography, is quite clear that only adherence to "the ways of [her] grandmothers" allowed her to remain unconfused in her cultural-sexual identity throughout her life. They are joined by younger women like Anishinabe-Choctaw scholar Clara Sue Kidwell, who has explored the problems of communicating a coherent indigenous female cultural-sexual identity in the colonial context and determined that recovery of traditional forms is more than ever called for. Even some Euroamerican feminist researchers who have applied analysis rather than "sisterhood is powerul"-style sloganeering to their understanding of Native North America concede that the "social and economic positions of Indian women make them more like Indian men" than like white women (conversely, of course, this makes Euroamerican women more like white men then like Indian women, a factor left conspicuously unremarked).

The Road Ahead

Interestingly, women of other nonwhite sectors of the North American population have shared many native women's criticisms of the Euroamerican feminist phenomenon. African American women in particular have been outspoken in this regard. As Gloria Joseph argues:

> The White women's movement has had its own explicit forms of racism in the way it has given high priority to certain aspects of struggles and neglected others...because of the inherently racist assumptions and perspectives brought to bear in the first articulations by the white women's movement...The Black movement scorns feminism partially on the basis of misinformation, and partially due to a valid perception of the White middle class nature of the movement. An additional reason is due to the myopic ways that white feminists have generalized their sexual-political analysis and have confirmed their racism in the forms their feminism has assumed.

The "self-righteous indignation" and defensiveness that Joseph discerns as experienced by most Euroamerican feminists when confronted with such critiques is elsewhere explained by bell hooks as a response resting in the vested interest of those who feel it:

> [F]eminist emphasis on "common oppression" in the United States was less a strategy for politicization than an appropriation by conservative and liberal women of a radical political vocabulary that masked the extent to which they shaped the movement so that it addressed and promoted their class interests...White women who dominate feminist discourse, who for the most part make and articulate feminist theory, have little or no understanding of white supremacy as a racial politic, of the psychological impact of class, of their [own] political status within a racist, sexist, capitalist state.

"I was struck," hooks says in her book, *Ain't I A Woman*, "by the fact that the ideology of feminism, with its emphasis on transforming and changing the social structure of the U.S., in no way resembled the reality of American feminism. Largely because [white] feminists themselves, as they attempted to take feminism beyond the realm of radical rhetoric into the sphere of American life, revealed that they remained imprisoned in the very structures they hoped to change. Consequently, the sisterhood we all talked about has not become a reality." It is time to "talk back" to white feminists, hooks argues, "spoiling their celebration, their 'sister-hood,' their 'togetherness.'" This must be done because in adhering to feminism in its present form:

> We learn to look to those empowered by the very systems of domination that wound and hurt us for some understanding of who we are that will be liberating and we never find that. It is necessary for [women of color] to do the work ourselves if we want to know more about our experience, if we want to see that experience from perspectives not shaped by domination.

Asian American women, Chicanas, and Latinas have agreed in substantial part with such assessments. Woman of color in general tend not to favor the notion of a "politics" which would divide and weaken their communities by defining "male energy" as "the enemy." It is not for nothing that no community of color in North America has ever produced a counterpart to white feminism's SCUM (Society for Cutting Up Men). Women's liberation, in the view of most "minority" women in the United States and Canada, cannot occur in any context other than the wider liberation, from Eeroamerican colonial domination of the peoples of which women of color are a part. Our sense of priorities is therefore radically and irrevocably different from those espoused by the "mainstream" women's movement.

Within this alienation from feminism lies the potential for the sorts of alliances which may in the end prove most truly beneficial to American Indian people. By forging links to organizations composed of other women of color, founded not merely to fight gender oppression, but also to struggle against racial and cultural oppression, native women can prove instrumental in creating an alternative movement of women in North America, one which is mutually respect-ful of the rights, needs cultural particularities, and historical divergences of each sector of its membership, and which is therefore free of the adherence to white supremacist hegemony previously marring feminist thinking and practice. Any such movement of women--including those Euroamerican women who see its thrust as corresponding to their own values and interests as human beings--cannot help but be of crucial importance within the liberation struggles waged by peoples of color to dismantle the apparatus of Eurocentric power in every area of the continent. The greater the extent to which these struggles succeed, the closer the core agenda of Native North America--recovery of land and resources, reassertion of self-determining forms of government, and reconstitution of traditional social relations within our nations--will come to realization.

European American Women

The material included in this section consists of the "Letters of John and Abigail Adams," "Legal Disabilities of Women, 1838" by Sarah Grimke, "The Marriage Contract of Lucy Stone and Theodore Weld," "The Utilization of Women in City Government" by Jane Addams, "Feminist New Style" by Dorothy Bromley, and "Dust Bowl Diary" by Ann Marie Low. The involvement of women in World War II is included in "Women in the Armed Forces" and "Letter to the Office of War Information." The last articles, "The Problem That Has No Name" from the landmark *The Feminine Mystique* by Betty Friedan and an excerpt from Susan Faludi's "Backlash," are two important articles which I consider vital to the understanding of women's rights.

Abigail Adams, *Letters to John Adams and His Reply* (1776)

Abigail Adams' (1744-1818) plea that her husband "remember the ladies" was an initial appeal for a more equitable distribution of power. Feminists of a later era would spell out in detail Adams' statement on the potential of mate tyranny. On what basis do you think Adams alleged that "all Men would be tyrants if they could?" How did the revolutionary spirit influence her request and the argument of her May 7th letter? How did John Adams deal with the situation? What did he mean by the statement "we know better than to repeal our masculine systems"?*

Abigail Adams to John Adams

Braintree March 31 1776

--I long to hear that you have declared an independency--and by the way in the new Code or Laws which I suppose it will be necessary for you to make, I desire you would Remember the Ladies, and be more generous and favourable to them than your ancestors. Do not put such unlimited power into the hands of the Husbands. Remember all Men would be tyrants if they could. If particular care and attention is not paid to the Ladies we are determined to foment a rebellion, and will not hold ourselves bound by any Laws in which we have no voice, or Representation.

That your Sex are Naturally Tyrannical is a Truth also thoroughly established as to admit of no dispute, but such of you as wish to be happy willingly give up the harsh title of Master for the more tender and endearing one of Friend. Why then, not put it out of the power of the vicious and the Lawless to use us with cruelty and indignity with impunity. Men of Sense in all Ages abhor those customs which treat us only as the vassals of your Sex. Regard us then as Being placed by providence under your protection and in imitation of the Supreme Being make use of that power only for our happiness.

John Adams to Abigail Adams
Ap. 14 1776

As to Declarations of Independency, be patient. Read our Privateering Laws, and our Commercial Laws. What signifies a Word.

As to your extraordinary Code of Laws, I cannot but laugh. We have been told that our Struggle has loosened the bands of Government everywhere. That Children and Apprentices were disobedient--that schools and Colleges were grown turbulent--that Indians slighted their Guardians and Negroes grew insolent to their Masters. But your Letter was the first Intimation that another Tribe more numerous and powerful than all the rest were grown discontented.—This is rather too coarse a Compliment but you are so saucy, I wont blot it out.

Depend upon it, We know better than to repeal our Masculine systems. Altho they are in full Force, you know they are little more than Theory. We dare not exert our Power in its full Latitude. We are obliged to go fair, and softly, and in Practice you know We are the subjects. We have only the Name of Masters, and rather than give up this, which would compleatly subject Us to the Despotism of the Petticoat, I hope General Washington, and all our brave Heroes would fight. I am sure every good Politician would plot, as long as he would against Despotism, Empire, Monarchy, Aristocracy, Oligarchy, or Ochlocracy.

Abigail Adams to John Adams
B[raintree]e May 7 1776

I can not say that you are very generous to the Ladies, for whilst you are proclaiming peace and good will to Men, Emancipating all Nations, you insist upon retaining an absolute power over Wives. But you must remember that Arbitrary power is like other things which are very hard, very liable to be broken--and notwithstanding all your wise Laws and Maxims we have it in our power not only to free ourselves but to subdue our Masters, and without violence throw both your natural and legal authority at our feet--

> "Charm by accepting, by submitting sway
> Yet have our Humour most when we obey."

*From *Adams Family Correspondence* ed. L.H. Butterfield, (Cambridge Mass.: Harvard University Press, 1963), 76-402.

Sarah Grimke, *Legal Disabilities of Women*, 1838

Sarah Grimke, a South Carolina Quaker, and her sister, Angelina, were active and outspoken abolitionists and proponents of women's rights (American History 361-2).

In the following excerpt from the twelfth of her Letters on the Equality of the Sexes, Sarah urges that the laws discriminating against women and denying her "political existence" be repealed. The references to Blackstone in this document (and the one to follow) refer to the eighteenth-century English jurist whose commentaries on the English law exerted enormous influence on jurists and lawmakers on both sides of the Atlantic.

There are few things which present greater obstacles to the improvement and elevation of woman to her appropriate sphere of usefulness and duty, than the laws which have been enacted to destroy her independence, and crush her individuality; laws which, although they are framed for her government, she has had no voice in establishing, and which rob her of some of her *essential rights*. Woman has no political existence. With the single exception of presenting a petition to the legislative body, she is a cipher in the nation; or, if not actually so in representative governments, she is only counted, like the slaves of the South, to swell the number of law-makers who form decrees for her government, with little reference to her benefit, except so far as her good may promote their own...

Blackstone, in the chapter entitled 'Of husband and wife,' says:

By marriage, the husband and wife are one person in law; that is, *the very being, or legal existence of the woman* is suspended during the marriage, or at least is incorporated and consolidated into that of the husband under whose wing, protection and cover she performs everything...

Here now, the very being of a woman, like that of a slave, is absorbed in her master. All contracts made with her, like those made with slaves by their owners, are a mere nullity. Our kind defenders have legislated away almost all our legal right, and in the true spirit of such injustice and oppression, have kept us in ignorance of those very laws by which we are governed. They have persuaded us, that we have no right to investigate the laws, and that, if we did, we could not comprehend them; they alone are capable of understanding the mysteries of Blackstone, &c. But they are not backward to make us feel the practical operation of their power over our actions.

The husband is bound to provide his wife with necessaries by law, as much as himself; and if she contracts debts for them, he is obliged to pay for them; but for anything besides necessaries, he is not chargeable.

Yet a man may spend the property he has acquired by marriage at the ale-house, the gambling table, or in any other way that he pleases. Many instances of this kind have come to my knowledge; and women, who have brought their husbands handsome fortunes, have been left, in consequence of the wasteful and dissolute habits of their husbands, in straitened circumstances and compelled to toil for the support of their families...

The husband, by the old law, might give his wife moderate correction, as he is to answer for her misbehavior. The law thought it reasonable to entrust him with this power of restraining her by domestic chastisement. The courts of law will still permit a husband to restrain a wife of her liberty, in case of any gross misbehavior.

What a mortifying proof this law affords, of the estimation is which woman is held! She is placed completely in the hands of a being subject like herself to the outbursts of passion, and therefore unworthy to be trusted with power. Perhaps I may be told respecting this law, that it is a dead letter, as I am sometimes told about the slave laws; but this is not true in either case. The slave-holder does kill his slave by moderate correction, as the law allows; and many a husband, among the poor, exercises the right given him by the law, of degrading women by personal chastisement. And among the higher ranks, if actual imprisonment is not resorted to, women are not unfrequently restrained of the liberty of going to places of worship by irreligious husbands, and of doing many other things about which, as moral and responsible beings, *they* should be the *sole* judges…

And further, all the avails of her labor are absolutely in the power of her husband. All that she acquires by her industry is his; so that she cannot, with her own honest earnings, become the legal purchaser of any property. If she expends her money for articles of furniture, to contribute to the comfort of her family, they are liable to be seized for her husband's debts: and I know an instance of a woman, who by labor and economy had scraped together a little maintenance for herself and do-little husband, who was left, at his death, by virtue of his last will and testament, to be supported by charity. I knew another woman, who by great industry had acquired a little money which she deposited in a bank for safe keeping. She has saved this pittance whilst able to work, in hopes that when age or sickness disqualified her for exertion, she might have something to render life comfortable, without being a burden to her friends. Her husband, a worthless, idle man, discovered this hid treasure, drew her little stock from the bank, and expended it all in extravagance and vicious indulgence…

As these abuses do exist, and women suffer intensely from them, our brethren are intensely called upon in this enlightened age, by every sentiment of honor, religion and justice, to repeal these unjust and unequal laws, and restore to woman those rights which they have wrested from her. Such laws approximate too nearly to the laws enacted by slaveholders for the government of their slaves, and must tend to debase and depress the mind of that being, whom God created as a help meet for man, or 'helper like unto himself,' and designed to be his equal and his companion. Until such laws are annulled, woman never can occupy that exalted station for which she was intended by her Maker.

Questions

1. What does Grimke mean when she says "Woman has no political existence"?
2. Why does Grimke continually compare the position of women to that of slaves, and men to slaveholders? Do you agree with her?

The Marriage of Lucy Stone Under Protest (1855)

Lucy Stone & Henry B. Blackwell

While acknowledging our mutual affection by publicly assuming the relationship of husband and wife, yet in justice to ourselves and a great principle, we deem it a duty to declare that this act on our part implies no sanction of, nor promise of voluntary obedience to such of the present laws of marriage, as refuse to recognize the wife as an independent, rational being, while they confer upon the husband an injurious and unnatural superiority, investing him with legal powers which no honorable man would exercise, and which no man should possess. We protest especially against the laws which give to the husband:

1. The custody of the wife's person.
2. The exclusive control and guardianship of their children.
3. The sole ownership of her personal, and use of her real estate, unless previously settled upon her, or placed in the hands of trustees as in the case of minors, lunatics, and idiots.
4. The absolute right to the product of her industry.
5. Also against laws which give to the widower so much larger and more permanent an interest in the property of his deceased wife, than they give to the widow in that of the deceased husband.
6. Finally, against the whole system by which "the legal existence of the wife is suspended during marriage," so that in most States, she neither has a legal part in the choice of her residence, nor can she make a will, nor sue or be sued in her own name, nor inherit property.

We believe that personal independence and equal human rights can never be forfeited, except for crime; that marriage should be an equal and permanent partnership, and so recognized by law; that until it is so recognized, married partners should provide against the radical injustice of present laws, by every means in their power.

We believe that where domestic difficulties arise, no appeal should be made to legal tribunals under existing laws, but that all difficulties should be submitted to the equitable adjustment of arbitrators mutually chosen.

Thus reverencing law, we enter our protest against rules and customs which are unworthy of the name, since they violate justice, the essence of law.

From *History of Woman Suffrage, Vol. 1, 1848-1861*, ed., Elizabeth Cady Stanton, Susan B. Anthony, and Matilda Joslyn Gage (New York: Fowler and Wells, 1881), 260-61.

Jane Addams, *Utilization of Women in City Government*, 1907

Jane Addams was not only a leader in the settlement house movement and progressive causes, she was also an outspoken advocate of women's suffrage.

In the following selection, Addams presents what your textbook refers to as the "conservative justification for suffrage." She argues that women should be given the vote because "as mothers and wives and homemakers they had special experiences and special sensitivities to bring to public life" (American History, 635).

It has been well said that the modern city is a stronghold of industrialism, quite as the feudal city was a stronghold of militarism, but the modern city fears no enemies, and rivals from without and its problems of government are solely internal. Affairs for the most part are going badly in these great new centres in which the quickly congregated population has not yet learned to arrange its affairs satisfactorily, insanitary housing, poisonous sewage, contaminated water, infant mortality, the spread of contagion, adulterated food, impure milk, smoke-laden air, illventilated factories, dangerous occupations, juvenile crime, unwholesome crowding, prostitution, and drunkenness are the enemies which the modern city must face and overcome would it survive. Logically, its electorate should be made up of those who can bear a valiant part in this arduous contest, of those who in the past have at least attempted to care for children, to clean houses, to prepare foods, to isolate the family from moral dangers, of those who have traditionally taken care of that side of life which, as soon as the population is congested, inevitably becomes the subject of municipal consideration and control…demands the help of minds accustomed to detail and variety of work, to a sense of obligation for the health and welfare of young children, and to a responsibility for the cleanliness and comfort of others.

Because all these things have traditionally been in the hands of women, if they take no part in them now, they are not only missing the education which the natural participation in civic life would bring to them, but they are losing what they have always had. From the beginning of tribal life women have been held responsible for the health of the community, a function which is now represented by the health department; from days of the cave dwellers, so far as the home was clean and wholesome, it was due to their efforts, which are now represented by the bureau of tenement-house inspection; from the period of the primitive village, the only public sweeping performed was what they undertook in their own dooryards, that which is now represented by the bureau of street cleaning. Most of the departments in a modern city can be traced to a women's traditional activity, but in spite of this, so soon as these old affairs were turned over to the care of the city, they slipped from woman's hands, apparently because they then became matters for collective action and implied the use of the franchise. Because the franchise had in the first instance been given to the man who could fight, because in the beginning he alone could vote who could carry a weapon, the franchise was considered an improper thing for a woman to possess.

Is it quite public spirited for women to say, "We will take care of these affairs so long as they stay in our own houses, but if they go outside and concern so many people that they cannot be carried on without the mechanism of the vote, we will drop them. It is true that these activities which women have always had, are not at present being carried on very well by the men in most of the great American cities, but because we do not consider it 'ladylike' to vote shall we ignore their failure?"

Because women consider the government men's affair and something which concerns itself with elections and alarms, they have become so confused in regard to their traditional business in life, the rearing of children, that they hear with complacency a statement made by…sanitary reformers, that one-half of the tiny lives which makeup the city's death rate each year might be saved by a more thorough application of sanitary science. Because it implies the use of the suffrage, they do not consider it women's business to save these lives. Are we going to lose ourselves in the old circle of convention and add to that sum of wrong-doing which is continually committed in the world because we do not look at things as they really are? Old-fashioned ways which no longer apply to changed conditions are a snare in which the feet of women have always become readily entangled…

Why is it that women do not vote upon the matters which concern them so intimately? Why do they not follow these vital affairs and feel responsible for their proper administration, even though they have become municipalized? What would the result have been could women have regarded the suffrage, not as a right or a privilege, but as a mere piece of governmental machinery without which they could not perform their traditional functions under the changed conditions of city life? Could we view the whole situation as a matter of obligation and of normal development, it would be much simplified. We are at the beginning of a prolonged effort to incorporate a progressive developing life founded upon a response to the needs of all the people, into the requisite legal enactments and civic institutions. To be in any measure successful, this effort will require all the intelligent powers of observation, all the sympathy, all the common sense which may be gained from the whole adult population…

QUESTIONS

1. What is "conservative" about Addams' argument for women's suffrage?
2. What was Adams predicting would be the result of giving women the vote? Was she correct?

Dorothy Bromley, *Feminist--New Style*

Although she represented only a small minority of working women, the "new professional woman" (American History, 708) of the 1920's was a distinct and highly publicized social type. One of them was the journalist, Dorothy Bromley. In 1927 she published an essay in Harper's Magazine entitled "Feminist--New Style." This essay is a jaunty declaration of independence from an older style of feminism, the adherents of which Bromley characterizes as "fighting feminists who wore flat heels and had very little feminine charm."

The Queen is dead. Long live the Queen!

Is it not high time that we laid the ghost of the so-called feminist?

"Feminism" has become a term of opprobrium to the modern young woman. For the word suggests either the old school of fighting feminists who wore flat heels and had very little feminine charm, or the current species who antagonize men with their constant clamor about maiden names, equal rights, woman's place in the world, and many another cause... *ad infinitum.* Indeed, if a blundering male assumes that a young woman is a feminist simply because she happens to have a job or a profession of her own, she will be highly--and quite justifiably insulted: for the word evokes the antithesis of what she flatters herself to be. Yet she and her kind can hardly be dubbed "old-fashioned" women. What *are* they, then?

The pioneer feminists were hard-hitting individuals, and the modern young woman admires them for their courage while she judges them for their zealotry and their inartistic methods. Furthermore, she pays all honor to them, for they fought her battle. But *she* does not want to wear their mantle (indeed, she thinks they should have been buried in it), and she has to smile at those women who wear it today-with the battle-cry still on their lips. The worst of the fight is over, yet this second generation of feminists are still throwing hand grenades. They bear a grudge against men, either secretly or openly; they make an issue of little things as well as big; they exploit their sex for the sake of publicity; they rant about equality when they might better prove their ability. Yet it is these women--the ones who do more talking than acting—on whom the average man focuses his microscope when he sits down to dissect the "new woman." For like his less educated brethren, he labors under the delusion that there are only two types of women, the creature of instinct who is content to be a "home-maker" and the "sterile intellectual" who cares solely about "expressing herself"--home and children be damned.

But what of the constantly increasing group of young women in their twenties and thirties who are the truly modern ones, those who admit that a full life calls for marriage and children as well as a career? These women if they launch upon marriage are keen to make a success of it and an art of child-rearing. But *at the same time* they are moved by an inescapable inner compulsion to be individuals in their own right. And in this era of simplified housekeeping they see their opportunity, for it is obvious that a woman who plans intelligently can salvage some time for her own pursuits. Furthermore, they are convinced that they will be better wives and mothers for the breadth they gain from functioning outside the home. In short, they are highly conscious creatures who feel obliged to plumb their own resources to the very depths, despite the fact that they are under no delusions as to the present inferior status of their sex in most fields of endeavor.

Numbers of these honest, spirited young women have made themselves heard in article and story. But since men must have things pointed out to them in black and white, we beg leave to enunciate the tenets of the modern woman's credo. Let us call her "Feminist--New Style."...

In brief, Feminist--New Style reasons that if she is economically independent, and if she has, to boot, a vital interest in some work of her own she will have given as few hostages to Fate as it is humanly possible to give. Love may die, and children may grow up, but one's work goes on forever.

She will not, however, live for her job alone, for she considers that a woman who talks and thinks only shop has just as narrow a horizon as the housewife who talks and thinks only husband and children--perhaps more so, for the latter may have a deeper understanding of human nature. She will therefore refuse to give up all of her personal interests, year in and year out, for the sake of her work. In this respect she no doubt will fall short of the masculine idea of commercial success, for the simple reason that she has never felt the economic compulsion which drives men on to build up fortunes for the sake of their growing families.

Yet she is not one of the many women who look upon their jobs as tolerable meal-tickets or as interesting pastimes to be dropped whenever they may wish. On the contrary, she takes great pride in becoming a vital factor in whatever enterprise she has chosen, and she therefore expects to work long hours when the occasion demands.

But rather than make the mistake that some women do of domesticating their jobs, *i.e.*, burying all of their affections and interests in them, or the mistake that many men make of milking their youth dry for the sake of building up a fortune to be spent in a fatigued middle-age, she will proceed on the principle that a person of intelligence and energy can attain a fair amount of success--perhaps even a high degree of success--by the very virtue of living a well-balanced life, as well as by working with concentration.

Nor has she become hostile to the other sex in the course of her struggle to orient herself. On the contrary, she frankly likes men and is grateful to more than a few for the encouragement and help they have given her.

QUESTIONS

1. What is the center of gravity in the life of the "new-style feminist"? How does Bromley think it makes her secure against the traditional cycle of life?
2. What does Bromley mean by "a well-balanced life"?
3. How does Bromley set her "feminist" off not only against the "old-style feminist" but against most of her female contemporaries?

Ann Marie Low, *Dust Bowl Diary*

Ann Marie Low grew up on a farm in the Badlands of North Dakota. When the droughts of the 1930's brought on the nightmare of the dust bowl (American History, 730, 819-22), she was in her twenties. She kept a diary, in which she recorded her own and her family's struggles to cope with the combined difficulties of hard times and ecological disaster.

[*April 25, 1934, Wednesday*] Last weekend was the worst dust storm we ever had. We've been having quite a bit of blowing dirt every year since the drought started, not only here, but all over the Great Plains. Many days this spring the air is just full of dirt coming, literally, for hundreds of miles. It sifts into everything. After we wash the dishes and put them away, so much dust sifts into the cupboards we must wash them again before the next meal. Clothes in the closets are covered with dust.

Last weekend no one was taking an automobile out for fear of ruining the motor. I rode Roany to Frank's place to return a gear. To find my way I had to ride right beside the fence, scarcely able to see from one fence post to the next.

Newspapers say the deaths of many babies and old people are attributed to breathing in so much dirt.

[*May 7, 1934, Monday*] The dirt is still blowing. Last weekend Bud [her brother] and I helped with the cattle and had fun gathering weeds. Weeds give us greens for salad long before anything in the garden is ready. We use dandelions, lamb's quarter and sheep sorrel. I like sheep sorrel best. Also, the leaves of sheep sorrel, pounded and boiled down to a paste, make a good salve.

Still no job. I'm trying to persuade Dad I should apply for rural school # 3 out here where we went to school. I don't see a chance of getting a job in a high school when so many experienced teachers are out of work.

He argues that the pay is only $60.00 a month out here, while even in a grade school in town I might get $75.00. Extra expenses in town would probably eat up that extra $15.00. Miss Eston, the practice teaching supervisor, told me her salary has been cut to $75.00 after all the years she has been teaching in Jamestown. She wants to get married. School boards will not hire married women teachers in these hard times because they have husbands to support them. Her fiance is the sole support of his widowed mother and can't support a wife, too. So she is just stuck in her job, hoping she won't get another salary cut because she can scarcely live on what she makes and dress the way she is expected to.

Dad argues the patrons always stir up so much trouble for a teacher at # 3 some teachers have quit in mid-term. The teacher is also the janitor, so the hours are long.

I figure I can handle the work, kids, and patrons. My argument is that by teaching here I can work for my room and board at home, would not need new clothes, and so could send most of my pay to Ethel [her sister] and Bud.

In April, Ethel had quit college, saying she did not feel well.

[*May 21, 1934, Monday*] Ethel has been having stomach trouble. Dad has been taking her to doctors though suspecting her trouble is the fact that she often goes on a diet that may affect her heath. The local doctor said he thought it might be chronic appendicitis, so Mama took Ethel by train to Valley City last week to have a surgeon there remove her appendix.

Saturday Dad, Bud, and I planted an acre of potatoes. There was so much dirt in the air I couldn't see Bud only a few feet in front of me. Even the air in the house was just a haze. In the evening the wind died down, and Cap came to take me to the movie. We joked about how hard it is to get cleaned up enough to go anywhere.

The newspapers report that on May 10 there was such a strong wind the experts in Chicago estimated 12,000,000 tons of Plains soil was dumped on that city. By the next day the sun was obscured in Washington, D.C., and ships 300 miles out at sea reported dust settling on their decks.

Sunday the dust wasn't so bad. Dad and I drove cattle to the Big Pasture. Then I churned butter and baked a ham, bread, and cookies for the men, as no telling when Mama will be back.

[*May 30, 1934, Wednesday*] Ethel got along fine, so Mama left her at the hospital and came to Jamestown by train Friday. Dad took us both home.

The mess was incredible! Dirt had blown into the house all week and lay inches deep on everything. Every towel and curtain was just black. There wasn't a clean dish or cooking utensil. There was no food. Oh, there were eggs and milk and one loaf left of the bread I baked the weekend before. I looked in the cooler box down the well (our refrigerator) and found a little ham and butter. It was late, so Mama and I cooked some ham and eggs for the men's supper because that was all we could fix in a hurry. It turned out they had been living on ham and eggs for two days.

Mama was very tired. After she had fixed starter for bread, I insisted she go to bed and I'd do all the dishes.

It took until 10 o'clock to wash all the dirty dishes. That's not wiping them-- just washing them. The cupboards had to be washed out to have a clean place to put them.

QUESTIONS

1. What were the advantages of working in a town school instead of a rural school? Why did Low prefer the rural school?
2. Does the diary contain any evidence to indicate whether the Lows had electricity in their home?
3. On what principle were school boards refusing to hire married women as teachers?

Women in the Armed Forces

Marion Stegeman

Of the more than fifteen million Americans who entered the armed services during World War II, approximately 350,000 were women. Like the Rosie the Riveters, women who joined the armed forces experienced new challenges, greater geographical mobility, and increased respons-ibility. The largest number served in the Women's Army Corps (WACS)--140,000--followed by 100,000 volunteers for the WAVES (Women Appointed for Volunteer Emergency Service) in the Navy. There were women's branches of the Marines and Coast Guard, and one thousand WASPs (Women's Airforce Service Pilots) did stateside and noncombat air duty.

Avenger Field in Sweetwater, Texas, was the place to be if you were a woman and a pilot in World War II. The letters that Marion Stegeman wrote home convey the excitement of being a WASP, a thrill that was part patriotism but mainly the sheer joy of flying. They also convey the disappointments, like a friend "washing out" (being asked to leave) or, worse, the death of classmates in training exercises. In all, thirty-eight WASPs lost their lives during the war.

Marion Stegeman had learned to fly in a Civilian Pilot Training Program while a student at the University of Georgia, from which she graduated with a degree in journalism and art in 1941. She became a WASP because she "wanted to be part of the action." After her training at Sweetwater, she was stationed at Love Field in Dallas. But, as her last letter shows, she realized that there was no future for women as pilots in the armed services and in 1944 she resigned to marry her boyfriend Ned Hodgson, a Marine stationed in Texas. After the war, they settled in Fort Worth to raise a family, both their lives dramatically and irrevocably affected by their service during World War II.

Sweetwater, Texas
April 24, 1943

Dearest Mother,

The gods must envy me! This is just too, *too* to be true. (By now you realize I had a good day as regards flying. Nothing is such a gauge to the spirits as how well or how poorly one has flown.) Where was I? Oh, yes, I'm far too happy. The law of compensation must be waiting to catch up with me somewhere. Oh, God, how I love it! Honestly, Mother, you haven't *lived* until you get way *up* there--all alone--just you and that big beautiful plane humming under your control. I just sit there and sing at the top of my lungs while I'm climbing up to 4,000 feet--or however high I want to go. Of course, I'm too busy to sing while in the middle of aerobatics--but you ought to hear me let loose when I'm "clearing my area" between maneuvers. (We always clear the area first to make sure there are no planes underneath or close by--safety foist!)

The only thing that I know that's going to happen that I won't like is that they are changing my instructors some day soon. Mine is going on to the B.T.'s (Basic trainers--one step ahead of primary trainers) but maybe I'll get him again when I get to the B.T.'s. Hope so! I have no idea who my new instructor will be--I hope I'll like him as much as I do this one. He'll have to be pretty good and mighty nice though, to beat Mr. Wade's time....

Smackers and much love to John, Janet, Joanna and you--M.

Mother, Darling--

Get set! Prepare yourself! Because here comes another one of those slap-happy, nonsensical (??) ecstatic letters! OOOOOOO, Mom. I'm so happy I could die.

By now you know I've either (1) had a good day at flying or (2) passed a check ride. It just so happens that both are correct!

Honestly, mother, I was so scared when I climbed into that cockpit to take my first civilian check ride on the B.T. that I thought I'd vomit all over the controls. I had been running to the johnny for a nervous B.M. every ten minutes. One girl, seeing me dash in to the john for the fourth or fifth time (prior to my check ride) said to me, "You either are about to have a check ride or you're going on a cross country. Which is it?" It seems that it affects us gals the same way!

Anyway, I gave the check pilot a good ride and he told my instructor he might have an H.P. (hot pilot) on his hands. But since the only H.P.'s are dead pilots--proved by experience, he got his terminology mixed, but anyway, he meant it as a compliment. Happy day!

Then I went up for a ride with my instructor, and he told me to climb in the *back* seat which meant I was to do instrument (under the hood) flying--which is a very great compliment, since you aren't supposed to get instrument instruction until you are either qualified to solo or have already soloed! So he must think I'm ready to handle it alone as soon as I have the required eight hours, which makes me veddy, veddy happy indeed! I can hardly wait. He told me he thought I had the feel of the airplane now, and that I was cooking on the front burner! Also, he let me do a few slow rolls in the *B.T.* from the *back seat*--and he said they were *perfect*. Of course I came out from under the hood to do the slow rolls...

While I was still under the hood, later, he said, "O.K. I'll take it, then you come out from under the hood when I tell you to." So he messed around awhile, then said, "All right, Come out!" So I came out from under the hood and *I was still under the hood!* He had flown right into the middle of a huge white cloud. More fun! So he flew the instruments until we were out of the cloud and could see again...

So you see, your baby chile is enjoying life to the fullest. I have *everything* I want: my family loves me (and I'm sorta fond of it); I've got wonderful roommates--real *friends*; I'm doing what I love better than anything in the world; I'm so healthy and feel so good that it's revolting; and the men love me and I love the men! EEEEEEEEE, law! What a life!...

I love you all--M.

*   *   *

Mother, Dear,

I went on my fourth solo cross-country ("X-C") yesterday and at last something happened to break the monotony. Each trip is around 400 miles and takes about three hours, and they really get boring. But yesterday a strong wind blew me off course and made me temporarily uncertain. I decided to head out for home anyway, but things started looking *wrong,* and the checkpoints didn't jibe with the map. I buzzed a couple of towns but couldn't find the names of them anywhere, so I turned around and went back to a town I had just passed over that had an airport. I knew it was either Ballinger or another town north of Ballinger, both of which had army airports. The roads leading out of each town made a similar pattern and the fields were located in the same place in relation to the towns. So I entered the traffic pattern with a bunch of P.T.'s and landed. I could've tried to get on home, but I didn't have a heck of a lot of gas and I was bored with it all anyway, and didn't want to waste tine. The Army cadets and instructors nearly fell out of their planes when they saw a *girl* taxiing by in *B.T.!* I beamed at them all and got out at a hangar where I telephoned our squadron commander, after I had found it was Ballinger, after all.

While I was waiting for the call to go through, some Lt. came up and said, "You're from Sweetwater?" I said, yace, and he went on: "Have you seen Major McConnell?" I said, "No, he's not at Sweetwater any more." (He was our commanding officer before being transferred.) The Lieutenant grinned and said, "I know. He's the C.O. here, and I bet you knew it all along." His last remark was untrue, though I *had* heard that he was at Ballinger, but had forgotten it. He's a young, attractive bachelor, so I don't blame the Lt. for thinking I had stopped over on purpose for a visit with the Major. (It turned out one girl had preceded me thereby about a half hour, having secretly planned deliberately to stop over and see him. Sh-H-H! No one knows) Anyway, I nearly fainted from the news and trucked on over to see the Commanding Officer.

Meanwhile I had gotten Avenger Field on the phone. I forgot to tell you: when I taxied up and brought the plane to a stop, I dropped my map on the bottom of the cockpit and I thought: Ah! I'll just pretend this happened while I was in the air, and then I will have had a good excuse to land. (They tell us always to put the airplane down if we lose our air map.) So that was my story after I realized that Ballinger was almost directly on course and if I didn't have some alibi they'd never believe I didn't have an ulterior motive in landing. So everyone but my roommates think I lost my map in the bottom of the plane and landed to retrieve it.

The Sqn. Cmdr. here (when I got him on the phone) told me I had done the right thing and to come on home if I could get clearance to take off from Ballinger. So I sacheted over to Major McConnell's office and got the most cordial greeting I've ever had. He said, "Sure I'll clear you, but I refuse to do it for a couple of hours." So he took me to the PX for cokes and cigarettes and showed me around the post. He devoted his entire time to me, and then--and then!--flew formation home with me! I had a wonderful time and the girls were really impressed and refuse to believe it wasn't all planned. The major's parting words, before he took off for Ballinger after delivering me here safely, were: "Next time make it late in the afternoon!"...

Darling, I do miss you so! Please don't worry about me when you miss me, though, because, honestly, I'm so happy and having so much fun it's worth any chance in the world I could take. And, actually, I'm not doing anything dangerous at all. I fly well-kept-up planes in a country where no one will shoot me down, so I'm not really brave at all, though you may keep on thinking so if you like!

LOVE YA, M.

Mother dear,

...Mother, the most heart-breaking thing has happened. Jane...the older roommate--washed out yesterday. The check pilots said the B.T. was just too much for her to handle, that it was no reflection on her flying...Some people just aren't capable of handling the faster, heavier ships and still they make good pilots on lighter planes. Poor Jane, though! Next to Shirley and Sandy she was my favorite, and I'll sure miss her and her inimitable sense of humor. She was loads of fun and it just about broke my heart to watch what she was going through while waiting for what she knew was to be her last ride. Of course, this doesn't hit her as hard as it would someone like the other roommates because Jane has a husband and daughter--but, as she put it, that didn't keep her "from being heartsick." Poor gal cried for two days, and I cried right with her most of the time...

Love you *deely*. M.

*   *   *

Sweetwater, Texas
[Late Summer, 1943]

Dear Mom,

... Mother, this was to be a short letter, but now something has happened that I must tell you about.

You may just as well get used to hearing about these things, Mom, because so long as I'm in the flying racket they are bound to happen. Two of my classmates and their instructor were killed yesterday afternoon near Big Spring....

This is no doubt another of those undetermined causes that brings about crashes, and no one will ever know what it was. Maybe it was one of those rare structural failure cases--no one knows. It seems likely, since the instructor was in the plane it could have been that the girls were changing seats in mid air and one of them could've grabbed the wheel for support, thus stalling the plane. There are endless possibilities. Most of them things that *could* have been avoided, as most crashes seem to be...

Don't worry about it though, Mom, because it's very unusual for anything so mysterious to happen (especially *here)* and they're inspecting all the airplanes before we go up in them again.

As I've told you before, we *do* take chances, but they are small compared to those that thousands take every day all over the world. And we could fall down in our bathtubs at home and be killed, or get in a car and meet death. It's just not up to us to say where or when. You believe that, don't you? We'll talk about it more when I get home...

I love you, Marion

Tallahassee, Florida
March 30, 1944

Mother, dear:

(1) General Arnold [Henry H. "Hap" Arnold, Chief of the Army Air Forces] says openly that the Army Air Forces has more than enough pilots.

(2) There are experienced instructors now being forced into the foot army--and others out of jobs.

(3) If I go into the Army, they could chain me to a typewriter for the duration plus six months, in spite of anything they might promise.

(4) I can't see myself running around saluting and kow-towing and obeying orders from [those who] ...will really dish out the works to those of us who have been in only a year and will be mere Second Lieutenants. I can do what I'm told gracefully now only because--underneath it all--I know I don't *have* to.

Summary: All this adds up to a great deal of rationalization that has been taking place since I last saw my love. I want to marry him--now! Of course, though, I'd stay on the job indefinitely as a civilian, because I owe so much, but since the Army is forcing me to become a puppet or resign, I'm tempted to go my own way--mine and Ned's.

I don't think the airplane will replace the man, do you?

It may be days, weeks, or months before it is necessary for me to decide. How's about a long letter of advice from you--and also please ask Aunt Helvig and Grannie what they think.

I love you, M.

Source: From *We're in This War, Too: World War II Letters from American Women in Uniform* edited by Judy Barrett Litoff and David C. Smith, pp. 115-118, 119, 1201 Copyright 1994 by Judy Barrett Litoff and David C. Smith. Reprinted by permission of Oxford University Press, Inc.

Norma Yerger Queen, Letter to Office of War Information, 1944

As your textbook makes clear, the "Rosie the Riveter" image of women workers during World War II tended "to obscure the significant limits that remained on the ability of women to participate fully in the workplace" (American History, 805-07).

In response to a request for information from the Office of War Information, Norma Yerger Queen of Utah wrote the following letter detailing her observations of women workers in Utah.

The people of this community all respect women who work regardless of the type of work. Women from the best families & many officers' wives work at our hospital. It is not at all uncommon to meet at evening parties in town women who work in the kitchens or offices of our hospital (Army-Bushnel-large general). The city mayor's wife too works there.

The church disapproves of women working who have small children. The church has a strong influence in our county.

For the canning season in our county men's & women's clubs & the church all recruited vigorously for women for the canneries. It was "the thing to do" to work so many hrs. a week at the canneries.

I personally have encouraged officers' wives who have no children to get out and work. Those of us who have done so have been highly respected by the others and we have not lost social standing. In fact many of the social affairs are arranged at our convenience.

Some husbands do not approve of wives working & this has kept home some who do not have small children. Some of the women just do not wish to put forth the effort.

The financial incentive has been the strongest influence among most economic groups but especially among those families who were on relief for many years. Patriotic motivation is sometimes present but sometimes it really is a front for the financial one. A few women work to keep their minds from worrying about sons or husbands in the service.

In this county, the hospital is the chief employer of women. A few go to Ogden (20 miles away) to work in an arsenal, the depot, or the air field. When these Ogden plants first opened quite a few women started to work there, but the long commuting plus the labor at the plants plus their housework proved too much.

Many women thoroughly enjoy working & getting away from the home. They seem to get much more satisfaction out of it than out of housework or bringing up children. Those who quit have done so because of lack of good care for their children, or of inability to do the housework & the job...

I am convinced that if women could work 4 days a week instead of 5 ½ or 6 that more could take jobs. I found it impossible to work 5 ½ days & do my housework but when I arranged for 4 days I could manage both. These days one has to do everything--one cannot buy services as formerly. For instance--laundry. I'm lucky. I can send out much of our laundry to the hospital but even so there is a goodly amount that must be done at home--all the ironing of summer dresses is very tiring. I even have to press my husband's trousers--a thing I never did all my married life.

The weekly housecleaning--shoe shining--all things we formerly had done by others. Now we also do home canning. I never in the 14 yrs. of my married life canned 1 jar. Last summer I put up dozens of quarts per instructions of Uncle Sam. I'm only one among many who is now doing a lot of manual labor foreign to our usual custom. I just could not take on all that & an outside job too. It is no fun to eat out--you wait so long for service & the restaurants cannot be immaculately kept--therefore it is more pleasant & quicker to cook & eat at home even after a long day's work. I've talked with the personnel manager at the hospital & he agrees that fewer days a week would be better. The canneries finally took women for as little as 3 hrs. a day.

This is a farming area & many farm wives could not under any arrangements take a war job. They have too much to do at their farm jobs & many now have to go into the fields, run tractors & do other jobs formerly done by men. I marvel at all these women are able to do & feel very inadequate next to them. Some do work in Ogden or Brigham during the winter months.

Here is the difference between a man working & a woman as seen in our home--while I prepare the evening meal, my husband reads the evening paper. We then do the dishes together after which he reads his medical journal or cogitates over some lecture he is to give or some problem at his lab. I have to make up grocery lists, mend, straighten up a drawer, clean out the ice box, press clothes, put away anything strewn about the house, wash bric a brac, or do several of hundreds of small "woman's work is never done stuff." This consumes from 1 to 2 hrs. each evening after which I'm too weary to read any professional social work literature & think I'm lucky if I can keep up with the daily paper, Time Life or Reader's Digest. All this while my husband is relaxing & resting. When I worked full time, we tried doing the housecleaning together but it just didn't click. He is responsible for introducing penicillin into Bushnell and thus into the army & there were so many visiting brass hats & night conferences he couldn't give even one night a week to the house. Then came a mess of lectures of all kinds of medical meetings--he had to prepare those at home. I got so worn out it was either quit work or do it part time.

This has been a lot of personal experience but I'm sure we are no exception. I thought I was through working in 1938. My husband urged me to help out for the war effort--he's all out for getting the war work done & he agreed to do his share of the housework. He is not lazy but he found we could not do it. I hope this personal experience will help to give you an idea of some of the problems.

QUESTIONS

1. What is the major incentive for women going to work? What are some of the other incentives?
2. Did the women appear to enjoy their work outside the home?
3. What suggestions does Queen make for increasing the number of women working outside the home?

Betty Friedan on *The Problem That Has No Name, 1963*

The problem lay buried, unspoken, for many years in the minds of American women. It was a strange stirring, a sense of dissatisfaction, a yearning that women suffered in the middle of the twentieth century in the United States. Each suburban wife struggled with it alone. As she made the beds, shopped for groceries, matched slipcover material, ate peanut butter sandwiches with her children, chauffeured Cub Scouts and Brownies, lay beside her husband at night—she was afraid to ask even of herself the silent question--"Is this all?"

For over fifteen years there was no word of this yearning in the millions of words written about women, for women, in all the columns, books and articles by experts telling women their role was to seek fulfillment as wives and mothers. Over and over women heard voices of tradition and of Freudian sophistication that they could desire no greater destiny than to glory in their own femininity. Experts told them how to catch a man and keep him, how to breastfeed children and handle their toilet training, how to cope with sibling rivalry and adolescent rebellion; how to buy a dishwasher, bake bread, cook gourmet snails, and build a swimming pool with their own hands; how to dress, look, and act more feminine and make marriage more exciting; how to keep their husbands from dying young and their sons from growing into delinquents. They were taught to pity the neurotic, unfeminine, unhappy women who wanted to be poets or physicists or presidents. They learned that truly feminine women do not want careers, higher education, political rights--the independence and the opportunities that the old-fashioned feminists fought for. Some women, in their forties and fifties, still remembered painfully giving up those dreams, but most of the younger women no longer even thought about them. A thousand expert voices applauded their femininity, their adjustment, their new maturity. All they had to do was devote their lives from earliest girlhood to finding a husband and bearing children...

The suburban housewife--she was the dream image of the young American women and the envy, it was said, of women all over the world. The American housewife--freed by science and labor-saving appliances from the drudgery, the dangers of childbirth and the illnesses of her grandmother. She was healthy, beautiful, educated, concerned only about her husband, her children, her home. She had found true feminine fulfillment. As a housewife and mother, she was respected as a full and equal partner to man in his world. She was free to choose automobiles, clothes, appliances, supermarkets; she had everything that women ever dreamed of.

In the fifteen years after World War II, this mystique of feminine fulfillment became the cherished and self-perpetuating core of contemporary American culture. Millions of women lived their lives in the image of those pretty pictures of the American suburban housewife, kissing their husbands goodbye in front of the picture window, depositing their stationwagonsful of children at school, and smiling as they ran the new electric waxer over the spotless kitchen floor. They baked their own bread, sewed their own and their children's clothes, kept their new washing machines and dryers running all day. They changed the sheets on the beds twice a week instead of once, took the rug-hooking class in adult education, and pitied their poor frustrated mothers, who had dreamed of having a career. Their only dream was to be perfect wives and mothers; their highest ambition to have five children and a beautiful house, their only fight to get and keep their husbands. They had no thought for the unfeminine problems of the world outside the home; they wanted the men to make the major decisions. They gloried in their role as women, and wrote proudly on the census blank: "Occupation: housewife."

For over fifteen years, the words written for women, and the words women used when they talked to each other, while their husbands sat on the other side of the room and talked shop or politics or septic tanks, were about problems with their children, or how to keep their husbands happy, or improve their children's school, or cook chicken or make slipcovers. Nobody argued whether women were inferior or superior to men; they were simply different. Words like "emancipation" and "career" sounded strange and embarrassing; no one had used them for years. When a Frenchwoman named Simone de Beauvoir wrote a book called *The Second Sex*, an American critic commented that she obviously "didn't know what life was all about," and besides, she was talking about French women. The "woman problem" in America no longer existed.

If a woman had a problem in the 1950's and 1960's, she knew that something must be wrong with her marriage, or with herself. Other women were satisfied with their lives, she thought. What kind of woman was she if she did not feel this mysterious fulfillment waxing the kitchen floor? She was so ashamed to admit her dissatisfaction that she never knew how many other women shared it. If she tried to tell her husband, he didn't understand what she was talking about. She did not really understand it herself. For over fifteen years women in America found it harder to talk about this problem than about sex. Even the psychoanalysts had no name for it. When a woman went to a psychiatrist for help, as many women did, she would say, "I'm so ashamed," or "I must be hopelessly neurotic." "I don't know what's wrong with women today," a suburban psychiatrist said uneasily. "I only know something is wrong because most of my patients happen to be women. And their problem isn't sexual." Most women with this problem did not go to see a psychoanalyst, however. "There's nothing wrong really," they kept telling themselves. "There isn't any problem."

But on an April morning in 1959, I heard a mother four, having coffee with four other mothers in a suburban development fifteen miles from New York, say in a tone of quiet desperation, "the problem." And the others knew, without words, that she was not talking about a problem with her husband, or her children, or her home. Suddenly they realized they all shared the same problem, the problem that has no name. They began, hesitantly, to talk about it. Later, after they had picked up their children at nursery school and taken them home to nap, two of the women cried, in sheer relief, just to know they were not alone.

Gradually I came to realize that the problem that has no name was shared by countless women in America. As a magazine writer I often interviewed women about problems with their children, or their marriages, or their houses, or their communities. But after a while I began to recognize the telltale signs of this other problem. I saw the same signs in suburban ranch houses and split-levels on Long Island and in New Jersey and Westchester County; in colonial houses in a small Massachusetts town; on patios in

Memphis; in suburban and city apartments; in living rooms in the Midwest. Sometimes I sensed the problem, not as a reporter, but as a suburban housewife, for during this time I was also bringing up my own three children in Rockland County, New York. I heard echoes of the problem in college dormitories and semi-private maternity wards, at PTA meetings and luncheons of the League of Women Voters, at suburban cocktail parties, in stationwagons waiting for trains, and in snatches of conversation overheard at Schrafft's. The groping words I heard from other women, on quiet afternoons when children were at school or on quiet evenings when husbands worked late, I think I understood first as a woman long before I understood their larger social and psychological implications.

Just what was this problem that has no name? What were the words women used when they tried to express it? Sometimes a woman would say "I feel empty somehow... incomplete." Or she would say, "I feel as if I don't exist." Sometimes she blotted out the feeling with a tranquilizer. Sometimes she though the problem was with her husband, or her children, or that what she really needed was to redecorate her house, or move to a better neighborhood, or have an affair, or another baby. Sometimes, she went to a doctor with symptoms she could hardly describe; "A tired feeling...I get so angry with the children it scares me...I feel like crying without any reason." (A Cleveland doctor called it "the housewife's syndrome.")...

Most men, and some women, still did not know that this problem was real. But those who had faced it honestly knew that all the superficial remedies, the sympathetic advice, the scolding words and the cheering words were somehow drowning the problem in unreality. A bitter laugh was beginning to be heard from American women. They were admired, envied, pitied, theorized over until they were sick of it, offered drastic solutions or silly choices that no one could take seriously. They got all kinds of advice from the growing armies of marriage and child-guidance counselors, psychotherapists, and armchair psychologists, on how to adjust to their role as housewives. No other road to fulfillment was offered to American women in the middle of the twentieth century. Most adjusted to their role and suffered or ignored the problem that has no name. It can be less painful for a woman, not to hear the strange, dissatisfied voice stirring within her.

It is no longer possible to ignore that voice, to dismiss the desperation of so many American women. This is not what being a woman means, no matter what the experts say. For human suffering there is a reason; perhaps the reason has not been found because the right questions have not been asked, or pressed far enough. I do not accept the answer that there is no problem because American women have luxuries that women in other times and lands never dreamed of; part of the strange newness of the problem is that it cannot be understood in terms of the age-old material problems of man; poverty, sickness, hunger, cold. The women who suffer this problem have a hunger that food cannot fill. It persists in women whose husbands are struggling interns and law clerks, or prosperous doctors and lawyers; in wives of workers and executives who make $5,000 a year or $50,000. It is not caused by lack of material advantages; it may not even be felt by women preoccupied with desperate problems of hunger, poverty or illness. And women who think it will be solved by more money, a bigger house, a second car, moving to a better suburb, often discover it gets worse.

It is no longer possible today to blame the problem on loss of femininity; to say that education and independence and equality with men have made American women unfeminine. I have heard so many women try to deny this dissatisfied voice within themselves because it does not fit the pretty picture of femininity the experts have given them. I think, in fact, that this is the first clue to the mystery: the problem cannot be understood in the generally accepted terms by which scientists have studied women, doctors have treated them, counselors have advised them, and writers have written about them. Women who suffer this problem, in whom this voice is stirring, have lived their whole lives in the pursuit of feminine fulfillment. They are not career women (although career women may have other problems); they are women whose greatest ambition has been marriage and children. For the oldest of these women, these daughters of the American middle class, no other dream was possible. The ones in their forties and fifties who once had other dreams gave them up and threw themselves joyously into life as housewives. For the youngest, the new wives and mothers, this was the only dream. They are the ones who quit high school and college to marry, or marked time in some job in which they had no real interest until they married. These women are very "feminine" in the usual sense, and yet they still suffer the problem...

If I am right, the problem that has no name stirring in the minds of so many American women today is not a matter of loss of femininity or too much education, or the demands of domesticity. It is far more important than anyone recognizes. It is the key to these other new and old problems which have been torturing women and their husbands and children, and puzzling their doctors and educators for years. It may well be the key to our future as a nation and a culture. We can no longer ignore that voice within women that says: "I want something more than my husband and my children and my home."

Excerpts from "The Problem That Has No Name" from *The Feminine Mystique* by Betty Friedan, pp. 11-16, 21-22, 27, with the permission of W. W. Norton & Company, Inc. Copyright 1983, 1974,1973,1963 and renewed 1991 by Betty Friedan.

Susan Faludi, *Backlash* (1992)

Susan Faludi wrote that the "backlash" against women involved media distortions of feminism, as well as governmental denial of vital support necessary to sustain working mothers. In this excerpt from her book she describes the 1980 election in terms of a gender gap over women's rights Why does Faludi believe that some white men "feared and reviled feminism"?*

But what exactly is it about women's equality that even its slightest shadow threatens to erase male identity? What is it about the way we frame manhood that even today, it still depends so on "feminine" dependence for its survival? A little-noted finding by the Yankelovich Monitor survey, a large nationwide poll that has tracked social attitudes for the last two decades, takes us a good way toward a possible answer. For twenty years, the Monitor's pollsters have asked its subjects to define masculinity. And for twenty years, the leading definition, ahead by a huge margin, has never changed. It isn't being a leader, athlete, lothario, decision maker, or even just being "born male." It is simply this: being a "good provider for his family."

If establishing masculinity depends most of all an succeeding as the prime breadwinner, then it is hard to imagine a force more directly threatening to fragile American manhood than the feminist drive for economic equality. And if supporting a family epitomizes what it means to be a man, then it is little wonder that the backlash erupted when it did--against the backdrop of the '80s economy. In this period, the "traditional" man's real wage shrank dramatically (a 22 percent free-fall in households where white men were the sole breadwinners), and the traditional male breadwinner himself became an endangered species (representing less than 8 percent of all households). That the ruling definition of masculinity remains so economically based helps to explain, too, why the backlash has been voiced most bitterly by two groups of men: blue-collar workers, devastated by the shift to a service economy, and younger baby boomers, denied the comparative riches their fathers and elder brothers enjoyed. The '80s was the decade in which plant closings put blue-collar men out of work by the millions, and only 60 percent found new jobs--about half at lower pay. It was a time when, of all men losing earning power, the younger baby boom men were losing the most. The average man under thirty was earning 25 to 30 percent less than his counterpart in the early '70s. Worst off was the average young man with only a high-school education: he was making only $18,000, half the earnings of his counterpart a decade earlier. As pollster Louis Harris observed, economic polarization spawned the most dramatic attitudinal change recorded in the last decade and a half: a spectacular doubling in the proportion of Americans who describe themselves as feeling "powerless."

When analysts at Yankelovich reviewed the Monitor survey's annual attitudinal data in 1986, they had to create a new category to describe a large segment of the population that had suddenly emerged, espousing a distinct set of values. This segment, now representing a remarkable one-fifth of the study's national sample, was dominated by young men, median age thirty-three, disproportionately single, who were slipping down the income ladder--and furious about it. They were the younger, poorer brothers of the baby boomers, the ones who weren't so celebrated in '80s media and advertising tributes to that generation. The Yankelovich report assigned the angry young men the euphemistic label of "the Contenders."

The men who belonged to this group had one other distinguishing trait: they feared and reviled feminism. "It's these downscale men, the ones who can't earn as much as their fathers, who we find are the most threatened by the women's movement," Susan Hayward, senior vice president at Yankelovich, observes. They represent 20 percent of the population that cannot handle the changes in women's roles. They were not well employed, they were the first ones laid off, they had no savings and not very much in the way of prospects for the future. By the late '80s, the American Male Opinion Index found that the *largest* of its seven demographic groups was now the "Change Resisters," a 24-percent segment of the population that was disproportionately underemployed, "resentful," convinced that they were "being left behind" by a changing society, and most hostile to feminism.

To single out these men alone for blame, however, would be unfair. The backlash's public agenda has been framed and promoted by men of far more affluence and influence than the Contenders, men at the helm in the media, business, and politics. Poorer or less-educated men have not so much been the creators of the antifeminist thesis as its receptors. Most vulnerable to its message, they have picked up and played back the backlash at distortingly high volume. The Contenders have dominated the ranks of the militant wing of the '80s antiabortion movement, the list of plaintiffs filing reverse-discrimination and "men's rights" lawsuits, the steadily mounting police rolls of rapists and sexual assailants. They are men like the notorious Charles Stuart, the struggling fur salesman in Boston who murdered his pregnant wife, a lawyer, because he feared that she--better educated, more successful--was gaining the "upper hand."

African American Women

"Female Slaves: Sex Roles and Status in the Antebellum Plantation South" tells the story of these courageous sisters as they struggle within their slave community for status and against exploitation by the master. Sojourner Truth took a stand against exploitation when she gave her now famous "Ain't I A Woman" speech in Akron, Ohio in 1851. The last two articles in this section deal with the role of African American Women within the Civil Rights Movement. Daisy Bates in "Long Shadow of Little Rock, 1962" describes the frenzy of racial confrontation during desegregation. Anne Standley in "The Role of Black Women in the Civil Rights Movement" discusses the many issues that Black women had to confront along with racism.

Female Slaves: Sex Roles and Status in the Antebellum Plantation South

Deborah Gray White

In his study of the black family in America, sociologist E. Franklin Frazier theorized that in slave family and marriage relations, women played the dominant role. Specifically, Frazier wrote that "the Negro woman as wife or mother was the mistress of her cabin, and, save for the interference of master and overseer, her wishes in regard to mating and family matters were paramount." He also insisted that slavery had schooled the black woman in self-reliance and self-sufficiency and that "neither economic necessity nor tradition had instilled in her the spirit of subordination to masculine authority" (1939:125). The Frazier thesis received support from other social scientists, including historians Kenneth Stampp (1956:344) and Stanley Elkins (1959:130), both of whom held that slave men had been emasculated and stripped of their paternity rights by slave masters who left control of slave households to slave women. In his infamous 1965 national report, Daniel Patrick Moynihan (1965:31) lent further confirmation to the Frazier thesis when he alleged that the fundamental problem with the modern black family was the "often reversed roles of husband and wife" and then traced the origin of the problem back to slavery.

Partly in response to the criticism spawned by the Moynihan Report, historians reanalyzed antebellum source material, and the matriarchy thesis was debunked. For better or worse, said historians Robert Fogel and Stanley Engerman (1974:141), the "dominant" role in slave society was played by men. Men were dominant, they said, because men occupied all managerial and artisan slots, and because masters recognized the male head of the family group. From historian John Blassingame we learned that by building furnishings and providing extra food for their families, men found indirect ways of gaining status. If a garden plot was to be cultivated, the husband "led" his wife in the family undertaking (1972:92). After a very thoughtful appraisal of male slave activities, historian Eugene Genovese concluded that "slaves from their own experience had come to value a two parent, male-centered household, no matter how much difficulty they had in realizing the ideal" (1974:491-492). Further tipping the scales toward patriarchal slave households, historian Herbert Gutman argued that the belief that matrifocal households prevailed among slaves was a misconception. He demonstrated that children were more likely to be named after their fathers than mothers, and that during the Civil War slave men acted like fathers and husbands by fighting for their freedom and by protecting their wives and children when they were threatened by Union troops or angry slave holders (1976:188-191, 369-386).

With the reinterpretation of male roles came a revision of female roles. Once considered dominant, slave women were now characterized as subordinated and sometimes submissive. Fogel and Engerman found proof of their subordinated status in the fact that they were excluded from working in plow gangs and did all of the household chores (1974:141-142). Genovese maintained that slave women's "attitude toward housework, especially cooking, and toward their own femininty," belied the conventional wisdom "according to which women unwittingly helped ruin their men by asserting themselves in the home, protecting their children, and assuming other

79

normally masculine responsibilities (1974:500). Gutman found one Sea Island slave community where the black church imposed a submissive role upon married slave women (1976:72).

In current interpretations of the contemporary black family the woman's role has not been "feminized" as much as it has been "deemphasized." The stress in studies like those done by Carol Stack (1974) and Theodore Kennedy (1980), is not on roles per se but on the black family's ability to survive in flexible kinship networks that are viable bulwarks against discrimination and racism. These interpretations also make the point that black kinship patterns are not based exclusively on consanguineous relationships but are also determined by social contacts that sometimes have their basis in economic support.

Clearly then, the pendulum has swung away from the idea that women ruled slave households, and that their dominance during the slave era formed the foundation of the modern day matriarchal black family. But how far should that pendulum swing? This paper suggests that we should tread the road that leads to the patriarchal slave household and the contemporary amorphous black family with great caution. It suggests that, at least in relation to the slave family, too much emphasis has been placed on what men could not do rather than on what women could do and did. What follows is not a comprehensive study of female slavery, but an attempt to reassess Frazier's claim that slave women were self-reliant and self-sufficient through an examination of some of their activities, specifically their work, their control of particular resources, their contribution to their households and their ability to cooperate with each other on a daily basis. Further, this paper will examine some of the implications of these activities, and their probable impact on the slave woman's status in slave society, and the black family.

At the outset a few points must be made about the subject matter and the source material used to research it. Obviously, a study that concentrates solely on females runs the risk of overstating woman's roles and their importance in society. One must therefore keep in mind that this is only one aspect, although a very critical one, of slave family and community life. In addition, what follows is a synthesis of the probable sex role of the average slave woman on plantations with at least twenty slaves. In the process of constructing this synthesis I have taken into account such variables as plantation size, crop, region of the South, and the personal idiosyncrasies of slave masters. Finally, in drawing conclusions about the sex role and status of slave women, I have detailed their activities and analyzed them in terms of what anthropologists know about women who do similar things in analogous settings. I took this approach for two reasons. First, information about female slaves cannot be garnered from sources left by slave women because they left few narratives, diaries or letters. The dearth of source material makes it impossible to draw conclusions about the slave woman's feelings. Second, even given the ex-slave interviews, a rich source material for this subject, it is almost impossible to draw conclusions about female slave status from an analysis of their individual personalities. Comments such as that made by the slave woman. Fannie, to her husband Bob, "I don't want no sorry nigger around me," perhaps says something about Fannie, but not about all slave women (Egypt et al., 1945:184). Similarly, for every mother who grieved over the sale of her children there was probably a father whose heart was also broken. Here, only the activities of the slave woman will be examined in an effort to discern her status in black society

Turning first to the work done by slave women, it appears that they did a variety of heavy and dirty labor, work which was also done by men. In 1853, Frederick Olmsted saw South Carolina slaves of both sexes carting manure on their heads to the cotton fields where they spread it with their hands between the ridges in which cotton was planted. In Fayetteville, North

Carolina, he noticed that women not only hoed and shovelled but they also cut down trees and drew wood (Olmsted, 1971:67, 81). The use of women as lumberjacks occurred quite frequently, especially in the lower South and Southwest, areas which retained a frontier quality during the antebellum era. Solomon Northrup, a kidnapped slave, knew women who wielded the ax so perfectly that the largest oak or sycamore fell before their well-directed blows. An Arkansas ex-slave remembered that her mother used to carry logs (Osofsky, 1969:308-309; Rawick, 1972, vol. 10, pt. 5:54). On Southwestern plantations women did all kinds of work. In the region of the Bayou Boeuf women were expected to "plough, drag, drive team, clear wild lands, work on the highway," and do any other type of work required of them (Osofsky, 1969:313). In short, full female hands frequently did the same kind of work as male hands.

It is difficult, however, to say how often they did the same kind of field work, and it would be a mistake to say that there was no differentiation of field labor on Southern farms and plantations. The most common form of differentiation was that women hoed while men plowed. Yet, the exceptions to the rule were so numerous as to make a mockery of it. Many men hoed on a regular basis. Similarly, if a field had to be plowed and there were not enough male hands to do it, then it was not unusual for an overseer to command a strong woman to plow. This could happen on a plantation of twenty slaves or a farm of five.

It is likely, however, that women were more often called to do the heavy labor usually assigned to men after their childbearing years. Pregnant women, and sometimes women breastfeeding infants, were usually given less physically demanding work. If, as recent studies indicate (see Dunn, 1977:58; Gutman, 1976:50, 74, 124, 171; Trussell, 1978:504), slave women began childbearing when about twenty years of age and had children at approximately two and a half year intervals, at least until age thirty-five, slave women probably spent a considerable amount of time doing tasks which men did not do. Pregnant and nursing women were classified as half-bands or three-quarters hands and such workers did only some of the work that was also done by full hands. For instance, it was not unusual for them to pick cotton or even hoe, work done on a regular basis by both sexes. But frequently, they were assigned to "light work" like raking stubble or pulling weeds, which was often given to children and the elderly.

Slave women might have preferred to be exempt from such labor, but they might also have gained some intangibles from doing the same work as men. Anthropologists (Mullings, 1976:243-244; Sacks, 1974:213-222) have demonstrated that in societies where men and women are engaged in the production of the same kinds of goods and where widespread private property is not a factor, participation in production gives women freedom and independence. Since neither slave men nor women had access to, or control over, the products of their labor, parity in the field may have encouraged egalitarianism in the slave quarters. In Southern Togo, for instance, where women work alongside their husbands in the field because men do not alone produce goods which are highly valued, democracy prevails in relationships between men and women (Rocher et al., 1962:151-152).

But bondswomen did do a lot of traditional "female work" and one has to wonder whether this work, as well as the work done as a "half-hand," tallied on the side of female subordination. In the case of the female slave, domestic work was not always confined to the home, and often "woman's work" required skills that were highly valued and even coveted because of the place it could purchase in the higher social echelons of the slave world. For example, cooking was definitely "female work" but it was also a skilled occupation. Good cooks were highly respected by both blacks and whites, and their occupation was raised in status because the masses of slave women did not cook on a regular basis. Since field work occupied the time of most women, meals were often served communally. Female slaves therefore, were, for the most part, relieved of this traditional chore, and the occupation of "cook" became specialized.

Sewing too was often raised above the level of inferior "woman's work." All females at one time or another had to spin and weave. Occasionally each woman was given cloth and told to make her family's clothes, but this was unusual and more likely to happen on small farms than on plantations. During slack seasons women probably did more than during planting and harvesting seasons, and pregnant women were often put to work spinning, weaving and sewing. Nevertheless, sewing could be raised to the level of a skilled art, especially if a woman sewed well enough to make the white family's clothes. Such women were sometimes hired out and allowed to keep a portion of the profit they brought their master and mistress (Rawick, 1972, vol. 17, 158; SHC, White Hill Plantation Books:13; Rawick, 1972, vol. 2, pt. 2:114),

Other occupations which were solidly anchored in the female domain, and which increased a woman's prestige, were midwifery and doctoring. The length of time and extent of training it took to become a midwife is indicated by the testimony of Clara Walker, a former stave interviewed in Arkansas, who remembered that she trained for five years under a doctor who became so lazy after she had mastered the job that he would sit down and let her do all the work After her "apprenticeship" ended she delivered babies for both slave and free, black and white (Rawick, 1972, vol. 10, pt. 5:21). Other midwives learned the trade from a female relative, often their mother, and they in turn passed the skill on to another female relative.

A midwife's duty often extended beyond delivering babies, and they sometimes became known as "doctor women." In this capacity they cared for men, women, and children. Old women, some with a history of midwifery and some without, also gained respect as "doctor women." They "knowed a heap about yarbs [herbs]," recalled a Georgia ex-slave (Rawick, 1972, vol. 2, pt. 2:112). Old women had innumerable cures, especially for children's diseases, and since plantation "nurseries" were usually under their supervision, they had ample opportunity to practice their art. In sum, a good portion of the slave's medical care, particularly that of women and children, was supervised by slave women.

Of course, not all women were hired-out seamstresses, cooks, or midwives; a good deal of "female work" was laborious and mundane. An important aspect of this work, as well as of the field work done by women, was that it was frequently done in female groups. As previously noted, women often hoed while men plowed. In addition, when women sewed they usually did so with other women. Quilts were made by women at gatherings called, naturally enough, "quiltins." Such gatherings were attended only by women and many former slaves had vivid recollections of them. The "quiltin's and spinnin' frolics dat de women folks had" were the most outstanding remembrances of Hattie Anne Nettles, an Alabama ex-slave (Rawick, 1972, vol. 6:297, 360). Women also gathered, independent of male slaves, on Saturday afternoons to do washing. Said one ex-slave, "they all had a regular picnic of it as they would work and spread the clothes on the bushes and low branches of the tree to dry. They would get to spend the day together" (Rawick, 1972, vol. 7:315).

In addition, when pregnant women did field work they sometimes did it together. On large plantations the group they worked in was sometimes known as the "trash gang." This gang, made up of pregnant women, women with nursing infants, children and old slaves, was primarily a female work gang. Since it was the group that young girls worked with when just being initiated into the work world of the plantation, one must assume that it served some kind of socialization function. Most likely, many lessons about life were learned by twelve-year-old girls from this group of women who were either pregnant or breastfeeding, or who were grandmothers many times over.

It has been noted that women frequently depended on slave midwives to bring children into the world; their dependence on other slave women did not end with childbirth but continued through the early life of their children. Sometimes women with infants took their children to the fields with them. Some worked with their children wrapped to their backs, others laid them under a tree. Frequently, however, an elderly woman watched slave children during the day while their mothers worked in the field. Sometimes the cook supervised young children at the master's house. Mothers who were absent from their children most of the day, indeed most of the week, depended on these surrogate mothers to assist them in child socialization. Many ex-slaves remember these women affectionately. Said one South Carolinian: "De old lady, she looked after every blessed thing for us all day long en cooked for us right along wid de mindin'" (Rawick, 1972, vol. 2, pt. 1:99).

Looking at the work done by female slaves in the antebellum South, therefore, we find that sex role differentiation in field labor was not absolute but that there was differentiation in other kinds of work. Domestic chores were usually done exclusively by women, and certain "professional" occupations were reserved for females. It would be a mistake to infer from this differentiation that it was the basis of male dominance. A less culturally biased conclusion would be that women's roles were different or complementary. For example, in her overview of African societies, Denise Paulme notes that in almost all African societies, women do most of the domestic chores, yet they lead lives that are quite independent of men. Indeed, according to Paulme, in Africa, "a wife's contribution to the needs of the household is direct and indispensable, and her husband is just as much in need of her as she of him" (1963:4). Other anthropologists have suggested that we should not evaluate women's roles in terms of men's roles because in a given society, women may not perceive the world in the same way that men do (Rogers, 1978:152-162). In other words, men and women may share a common culture but on different terms, and when this is the case, questions of dominance and subservience are irrelevant. The degree to which male and female ideologies are different is often suggested by the degree to which men and women are independently able to rank and order themselves and cooperate with members of their sex in the performance of their duties. In societies where women are not isolated from one another and placed under a man's authority, where women cooperate in the performance of household tasks, where women form groups or associations, women's roles are usually complementary to those of men, and the female world exists independently of the male world. Because women control what goes on in their world, they rank and order themselves vis a vis other women, not men, and they are able to influence decisions made by their society because they exert pressure as a group. Ethnographic studies of the Igbo women of Eastern Nigeria (Tanner, 1974:146-15O), the Ga women of Central Accra in Ghana (Robertson, 1976:115-132), and the Patani of Southern Nigeria (Leis, 1974, 221-242) confirm these generalizations. Elements of female slave society--the chores done in and by groups, the intrasex cooperation and dependency in the areas of child care and medical care, the existence of high echelon female slave occupation--may be an indication, not that slave women were inferior to slave men, but that the roles were complementary and that the female slave world allowed women the opportunity to rank and order themselves and obtain a sense of self which was quite apart from the men of their race and even the men of the master class.

That bondswomen were able to rank and order themselves is further suggested by evidence indicating that in the community of the slave quarters certain women were looked to for leadership. Leadership was based on either one or a combination of factors, including occupation, association with the master class, age, or number of children. It was manifested in all aspects of female slave life. For instance, Louis Hughes, an escaped slave, noted that each plantation had a "forewoman who...had charge of the female slaves and also the boys and girls from twelve to sixteen years of age, and all the old people that were feeble" (Hughes, 1897:22). Bennett H. Barrow repeatedly lamented the fact that Big Lucy, one of his oldest slaves, had more control over his female slaves than he did: "Anica, Center, Cook Jane, the better you treat them the worse they are. Big Lucy, the Leader, corrupts every young negro in her power" (Davis, 1941:191). When Elizabeth Botume went to the Sea Islands after the Civil War, she had a house servant, a young woman named Amy who performed her tasks slowly and sullenly until Aunt Mary arrived from Beaufort. In Aunt Mary's presence the obstreperous Amy was "quiet, orderly, helpful and painstaking" (Botume, 1893:132).

Another important feature of female life, bearing on the ability of women to rank and order themselves independently of men, was the control women exercised over each other by quarreling. In all kinds of sources there are indications that women were given to fighting and irritating each other. From Jesse Belflowers, the overseer of the Allston rice plantation in South Carolina, Adele Petigru Allston learned that "mostly mongst the Woman," there was "goodeal of quarling and disputing and telling lies" (Easterby, 1945:291). Harriet Ware, a northern missionary, writing from the Sea Islands in 1863 blamed the turmoil she found in black community life on the "tongues of the women" (Pearson, 1906:210). The evidence of excessive quarreling among women hints at the existence of a gossip network among female slaves. Anthropologists (Rosaldo, 1974:10-11, 38; Stack, 1974:109-115; Wolfe, 1974:162) have found gossip to be a principal strategy used by women to control other women as well as men. Significantly, the female gossip network, the means by which community members are praised, shamed, and coerced, is usually found in societies where women are highly dependent on each other and where women work in groups or form female associations.

In summary, when the activities of female slaves are compared to those of women in other societies a clearer picture of the female slave sex role emerges. It seems that slave women were schooled in self-reliance and self-sufficiency but the "self" was more likely the female slave collective than the individual slave woman. On the other hand, if the female world was highly stratified and if women cooperated with each other to a great extent, odds are that the same can be said of men, in which case neither sex can be said to have been dominant or subordinate.

There are other aspects of the female slave's life that suggest that her world was independent of the male slave's and that slave women were rather self-reliant. It has long been recognized (Bassingame, 1972:77-101) that slave women did not derive traditional benefits from the marriage relationship, that there was no property to share and essential needs like food, clothing, and shelter were not provided by slave men. Since in almost all societies where men consistently control women, that control is based on male ownership and distribution of property and/or control of certain culturally valued subsistence goods, these realities of slave life had to contribute to female slave self-sufficiency and independence from slave men. The practice of "marrying abroad," having a spouse on a different plantation, could only have reinforced this tendency, for as ethnographers (Noon, 1949:30-31; Rosaldo, 1974:36, 39) have found, when men live apart from women, they cannot control them. We have yet to learn what kind of obligations brothers, uncles, and male cousins fulfilled for their female kin, but it is improbable that wives were controlled by husbands whom they saw only once or twice a week. Indeed, "abroad marriages" may have intensified female intradependency.

The fact that marriage did not yield traditional benefits for women, and that "abroad marriages" existed, does not mean that women did not depend on slave men for foodstuffs beyond the weekly rations, but since additional food was not guaranteed, it probably meant that women along with men had to take initiatives in supplementing slave diets. So much has been made of the activities of slave men in this sphere (Blassingame, 1972:92; Genovese, 1974:486) that the role of slave women has been overlooked. Female house slaves, in particular, were especially able to supplement their family's diet. Mary Chesnut's maid, Molly, made no secret of the fact that she fed her offspring and other slave children in the Confederate politician's house. "Dey gets a little of all dat's going," she once told Chesnut (Chesnut, 1905:348). Frederick Douglass remembered that his grandmother was not only a good nurse but a "capital hand at catching fish and making the nets she caught them in" (1855:27). Eliza Overton, an ex-slave, remembered how her mother stole, slaughtered, and cooked one of her master's hogs. Another ex-slave was not too bashful to admit that her mother "could hunt good ez any man." (Rawick, 1972, vol. 11:53, 267.) Women, as well as men, were sometimes given the opportunity to earn money. Women often sold baskets they had woven, but they also earned money by burning charcoal for blacksmiths and cutting cordwood (Olmsted, 1971:26; Rawick, 1972, vol. 7; 23). Thus, procuring extra provisions for the family was sometimes a male and sometimes a female responsibility, one that probably fostered a self-reliant and independent spirit.

The high degree of female cooperation, the ability of slave women to rank and order themselves, the independence women derived from the absence of property considerations in the conjugal relationship, "abroad marriages," and the female slave's ability to provide supplementary foodstuffs are factors which should not be ignored in considerations of the character of the slave family. In fact, they conform to the criteria most anthropologists (Gonzalez, 1970:231-243; Smith, 1956; 257-260, 1973:125; Tanner, 1974:129-156) list for that most misunderstood concept--matrifocality. Matrifocality is a term used to convey the fact that women *in their role as mothers* are the focus of familial relationships. It does not mean that fathers are absent; indeed two-parent households can be matrifocal. Nor does it stress a power relationship where women rule men. When *mothers* become the focal point of family activity, they are just more central than are fathers to a family's continuity and survival as a unit. While there is not set model for matrifocality, Smith (1973:125) has noted that in societies as diverse as Java, Jamaica, and the Igbo of eastern Nigeria, societies recognized as matrifocal, certain elements are constant. Among these elements are female solidarity, particularly in regard to their cooperation within the domestic sphere. Another factor is the economic activity of women which enables them to support their children independent of fathers *if they desire to do so or are forced to do so.* The most important factor is the supremacy of the mother-child bond over all other relationships (Smith, 1973:139-142).

Female solidarity and the "economic" contribution of bondswomen in the form of medical care, foodstuffs, and money has already been discussed; what can be said of the mother-child bond? We know from previous works on slavery (Bassett, 1925:31, 139, 141; Kemble, 1961:95, 127, 179; Phillips, 1909:I, 109, 312) that certain, slaveholder practices encouraged the primacy of the mother-child relationship. These included the tendency to sell mothers and small children as family units, and to accord special treatment to pregnant and nursing women and women who were exceptionally prolific. We also know (Gutman, 1976:76) that a husband and wife secured themselves somewhat from sale and separation when they had children. Perhaps what has not been emphasized enough is the fact that it was the wife's childbearing and her ability to keep a child alive that were the crucial factors in the security achieved in this way. As such, the insurance against sale which husbands and wives received once women had borne and nurtured children heads the list of female contributions to slave households.

In addition to slaveowner encouragement of close mother-child bonds there are indications that slave women themselves considered this their most important relationship. Much has been made of the fact that slave women were not ostracized by slave society when they had children out of "wedlock" (Genovese, 1974:465-66; Gutman, 1976:74, 117-118). Historians have usually explained this aspect of slave life in the context of slave sexual norms which allowed a good deal of freedom to young unmarried slave women. However, the slave attitude concerning "illegitimacy" might also reveal the importance that women, and slave society as a whole, placed on the mother role and the mother-child dyad. For instance, in the Alabama community studied by Charles S. Johnson (1934:29, 66-70) in the 1930's, most black women felt no guilt and suffered no loss of status when they bore children out of wedlock. This was also a community in which, according to Johnson, the role of the mother was "of much greater importance than in the more familiar American family group." Similarly, in his 1956 study of the black family in British Guyana, Smith (1956:109, 158, 250-251) found the mother-child bond to be the strongest in the whole matrix of social relationships, and it was manifested in a lack of condemnation of women who bore children out of legal marriage. If slave women were not ostracized for having children without husbands, it could mean that the mother-child relationship took precedence over the husband-wife relationships.

The mystique which shrouded conception and childbirth is perhaps another indication of the high value slave women placed on motherhood and childbirth. Many female slaves claimed that they were kept ignorant of the details of conception and childbirth. For instance, a female slave interviewed in Nashville, noted that at age twelve or thirteen she and an older girl went around to parsley beds and hollow logs looking for newborn babies. "They didn't tell you a thing," she said (Egypt et al., 1945:10; Rawick, 1972, vol. 16:15). Another ex-slave testified that her mother told her that doctors brought babies, and another Virginia ex-slave remembered that "people was very particular in them days. They wouldn't let children know anything." (Egypt et al., 1945:8; Rawick, 1972, vol. 16:25. See also Rawick, 1972, vol. 7:3-24 and vol. 2:51-52). The alleged naivete can perhaps be understood if examined in the context of motherhood as a *rite de passage*. Sociologist Joyce Ladner (1971:177-263) found that many black girls growing up in a ghetto area of St. Louis in the late 1960's were equally ignorant of the facts concerning conception and childbirth. Their mothers had related only "old wives tales" about sex and childbirth even though the community as one where the mother-child bond took precedence over both the husband-wife bond and the father-child bond. In this St. Louis area, having a child was considered the most important turning point in a black girl's life, a more important *rite de passage* than marriage. Once a female had a child all sorts of privileges were bestowed upon her. That conception and childbirth were cloaked in mystery in antebellum slave society is perhaps an indication of the sacredness of motherhood. When considered in tandem with the slave attitude toward "illegitimacy," the mother-child relationship emerges as the most important familial relationship in the slave family.

Finally, any consideration of the slave's attitude about motherhood and the expectations which the slave community had of childbearing women must consider the slave's African heritage. In many West African tribes the mother-child relationship is and has always been the most important of all human relationships. To cite one of many possible examples, while studying the role of women in Ibo society, Sylvia Leith-Ross (1939:127) asked an Ibo woman how many of ten husbands would love their wives and how many of ten sons would love their mothers. The answer she received demonstrated the precedence which the mother-child tie took: "Three husbands would love their wives but seven sons would love their mothers."

When E. Franklin Frazier (1939:125) wrote that slave women were self-reliant and that they were strangers to male slave authority he evoked an image of an overbearing, even brawny woman. In all probability visions of Sapphire danced in our heads as we learned from Frazier that the female slave played the dominant role in courtship, marriage and family relationships, and later from Elkins (1959:130) that male slaves were reduced to childlike dependency on the slave master. Both the Frazier and Elkins theses have been overturned by historians who have found that male slaves were more than just visitors to their wives' cabins, and women something other than unwitting allies in the degradation of their men. Sambo and Sapphire may continue to find refuge in American folklore but they will never again be legitimized by social scientists.

However, beyond the image evoked by Frazier is the stark reality that slave women did not play the traditional female role as it was defined in nineteenth-century America, and regardless of how hard we try to cast her in a subordinate or submissive role in relation to slave men, we will have difficulty reconciling that role with the plantation realities. When we consider the work done by women in groups, the existence of upper echelon female slave jobs, the intradependence of women in childcare and medical care; if we presume that the quarreling or "fighting and disputing" among slave women is evidence of a gossip network and that certain women were elevated by their peers to positions of respect, then what we are confronted with are slave women who are able, within the limits set by slaveowners, to rank and order their female world, women who identified and cooperated more with other slave women than with slave men. There is nothing abnormal about this. It is a feature of many societies around the world, especially where strict sex role differentiation is the rule.

Added to these elements of female interdependence and cooperation were the realities of chattel slavery that decreased the bondsman's leverage over the bondswoman, made female self-reliance a necessity, and encouraged the retention of the African tradition which made the mother-child bond more sacred than the husband-wife bond. To say that this amounted to a matrifocal family is not to say a bad word. It is not to say that it precluded male-female cooperation, or mutual respect, or traditional romance and courtship. It does, however, help to explain how African-American men and women survived chattel slavery.

Questions

1. Describe the work of female slaves in the south.
2. Why were the occupations of cook, seamstress, midwife and doctor so prestigious for female slaves?
3. How did female slaves attain leadership and respect from other female slaves?

Sojourner Truth, *A'n't I a Woman?* Address to the Woman's Rights Convention in Akron (1851)

Wall, chilern, whar dar is so much racket dar must be somethin' out o' kilter. I tink dat 'twixt de niggers of de Souf and de womin at de Norf, all talkin' 'bout rights, de white men will be in a fix pretty soon. But what's all dis here talkin' 'bout?

Dat man ober dar say dat womin needs to be helped into carriages, and lifted ober ditches, and to hab de best place everywhar. Nobody eber helps me into carriages, or ober mud-puddles, or gibs me any best place!...And a'n't I a woman? Look at me! Look at my arm! (and she bared her right arm to the shoulder, showing her tremendous muscular power). I have ploughed, and planted, and gathered into barns, and no man could head me! And a'n't I a woman? I could work as much and eat as much as a man--when I could get it--and bear de lash as well! And a'n't I a woman? I have borne thirteen children, and seen 'em mos' all sold off to slavery, and when I cried out with my mother's grief, none but Jesus heard me! And a'n't I a woman?

Den dey talks 'bout dis ting in de head; what dis dey call it? ("Intellect," whispered some one near.) Dat's it, honey. What's dat got to do wid womin's rights or nigger's rights? If my cup won't hold but a pint, and yourn holds a quart, wouldn't ye be mean not to let me have my little half-measure full?...

Den dat little man in black dar, he say women can't have as much rights as men, 'cause Christ wan't a woman! Whar did your Christ come from?...Whar did your Christ come from? From God and a woman! Man had nothin' to do wid Him...

If de fust woman God ever made was strong enough to turn de world upside down all alone, dese women togedder (and she glanced her eye over the platform) ought to be able to turn it back, and get it right side up again! And now dey is asking to do it, de men better let 'em...'Bleeged to ye for hearin' on me, and now ole Sojourner han't got nothin' more to say.

From *History of Woman Sufrage, Vol. 1, 1848-1861*, ed., Elizabeth Cady Stanton, Susan B. Anthony, and Matilda Joslyn Gage (New York: Fowler and Wells, 1881), 116.

Rosie the Riveter

Fanny Christina Hill

No image captured the popular view of women's contributions to the war effort better than Norman Rockwell's Saturday Evening Post cover of "Rosie the Riveter": a patriotic housewife who dons overalls and goes to work in a defense plant "for the duration." Yet there was no one Rosie the Riveter: she was a recent high school graduate taking her first job or a mother with a son in the service; she had been working before the war or was taking her first full-time job after years of homemaking; she was single or married, white or black or Latina, middle- or working-class. What unified the experiences of these women was that they proved to themselves (and the country) that they could do a "man's job," and could do it well.

The experiences of black women in the defense industry are especially instructive. World War II's labor shortage opened up skilled work in industry, providing better working conditions and dramatic increases in pay over black women's previous concentration in domestic service or farm labor. The jobs opened to blacks, however, were always less desirable than those available to whites. But the process of whites working alongside blacks, (and, to a lesser degree, Latinas) encouraged a breaking down of social barriers and a healthy recognition of diversity.

The oral history of Fanny Christina (Tina) Hill illuminates these broader trends. A black woman who was born in Texas but migrated to California, she had been trapped in domestic service until at age 24 she got a job at North American Aircraft. Her memoir balances excitement at the opportunity with an awareness of the discrimination blacks faced on the job. Her story also confirms the need to look beyond just the war years to understand the life cycles of the Rosie the Riveters. After quitting work near war's end to have a child, she returned to North American Aircraft in 1946 (one of the minority of wartime women who got their jobs back), remaining there until her retirement in 1980. As her final comment underscores, Tina Hill realizes that World War II had a positive impact on her life.

I don't remember what day of the week it was, but I guess I must have started out pretty early that morning. When I went there, the man didn't hire me. They had a school down here on Figueroa and he told me to go to the school. I went down and it was almost four o'clock and they told me they'd hire me. You had to fill out a form. They didn't bother too much about your experience because they knew you didn't have any experience in aircraft. Then they give you some kind of little test where you put the pegs in the right hole.

There were other people in there, kinda mixed. I assume it was more women than men. Most of the men was gone, and they weren't hiring too many men unless they had a good excuse. Most of the women was in my bracket, five or six years younger or older. I was twenty-four. There was a black girl that hired in with me. I went to work the next day, sixty cents an hour.

I think I stayed at the school for about four weeks. They only taught you shooting and bucking rivets and how to drill the holes and to file. You had to use a hammer for certain things. After a couple of whiles, you worked on the real thing. But you were supervised so you didn't make a mess.

When we went into the plant, it wasn't too much different than down at the school. It was the same amount of noise; it was the same routine. One difference was there was just so many more people, and when you went in the door you had a badge to show and they looked at your lunch. I had gotten accustomed to a lot of people and I knew if it was a lot of people, it always meant something was going on. I got carried away: "As long as there's a lot of people here, I'll be making money." That was all I could ever see.

I was a good student, if I do say so myself. But I have found out through life, sometimes even if you're good, you just don't get the breaks if the color's not right. I could see where they made a difference in placing you in certain jobs. They had fifteen or twenty departments, but all the Negroes went to Department 17 because there was nothing but shooting and bucking rivets. You stood on one side of the panel and your partner stood on this side, and he would shoot the rivets with a gun and you'd buck them with the bar. That was about the size of it. I just didn't like it. I didn't think I could stay there with all this shooting and a'bucking and a'jumping and a'bumping. I stayed in it about two or three weeks and then I just decided I did *not* like that. I went and told my foreman and he didn't do anything about it, so I decided I'd leave.

While I was standing out on the railroad track, I ran into somebody else out there fussing also. I went over to the union and they told me what to do. I went back inside and they sent me to another department where you did bench work and I liked that much better. You had a little small jig that you would work on and you just drilled out holes. Sometimes you would rout them or you would scribe them and then you'd cut them with a cutters.

I must have stayed there nearly a year, and then they put me over in another department, "Plastics." It was the tail section of the B-Bomber, the Billy Mitchell Bomber. I put. a little part in the gun sight. You had a little ratchet set and you would screw it in there. Then I cleaned the top of the glass off and put a piece of paper over it to seal it off to go to the next section. I worked over there until the end of the war. Well, not quite the end, because I got pregnant, and while I was off having the baby the war was over...

Negroes rented rooms quite a bit. It was a wonderful thing, 'cause it made it possible for you to come and stay without a problem. My sister and I was rooming with this lady and we was paying six dollars a week, which was good money, because she was renting the house for only twenty-six dollars a month. She had another girl living on the back porch and she was charging her three dollars. So you get the idea.

We were accustomed to shacking up with each other. We had to live like that because that was the only way to survive. Negroes, as a rule, are accustomed to a lot of people around. They have lived like that from slavery time on. We figured out how to get along with each other. In the kitchen everybody had a little place where he kept his food. You had a spot in the icebox: one shelf was yours. You bought one type of milk and the other ones bought another type of milk, so it didn't get tangled up. But you didn't buy too much to have on hand. You didn't overstock like I do today. Of course, we had rationing, but that didn't bother me. It just taught me a few things that I still do today. It taught me there's a lot of things you can get along without. I liked cornbread a lot--and we had to use Cream of Wheat, grits, to make cornbread. I found out I liked that just as well. So, strange as it may seem, I didn't suffer from the war thing.

I started working in April and before Thanksgiving, my sister and I decided we'd buy a house instead of renting this room. The people was getting a little hanky-panky with you; they was going up on the rent. So she bought the house in her name and I loaned her some money. The house only cost four thousand dollars with four hundred dollars down. It was two houses on the lot, and we stayed in the little small one-bedroom house in the back. I stayed in the living room part before my husband came home and she stayed in the bedroom. I bought the furniture to go in the house, which was the stove and refrigerator, and we had our old bedroom sets shipped from Texas. I worked the day shift and my sister worked the night shift. I worked ten hours a day for five days a week. Or did I work on a Saturday? I don't remember, but I know it was ten hours a day. I'd get up in the morning, take a bath, come to the kitchen, fix my lunch--I always liked a fresh fixed lunch--get my breakfast, and then stand outside for the ride to come by. I always managed to get someone that liked to go work slightly early. I carried my crocheting and knitting with me.

You had a spot where you always stayed around, close to where you worked, because when the whistle blew, you wanted to be ready to get up and go to where you worked. The leadman always come by and give you a job to do or you already had one that was a hangover from the day before. So you had a general idea what you was going to do each day.

Then we'd work and come home. I was married when I started working in the war plant, so I wasn't looking for a boyfriend and that made me come home in the evening. Sometimes you'd stop on the way home and shop for groceries. Then you'd come home and clean house and get ready for bed so you can go back the next morning. Write letters or what have you. I really wasn't physically tired.

Recreation was Saturday and Sunday. But my sister worked the swing shift and that made her get up late on Saturday morning, so we didn't do nothing but piddle around the house. We'd work in the garden, and we'd just go for little rides on the streetcar. We'd go to the parks, and then we'd go to the picture show downtown and look at the newsreel: "Where it happens, you see it happen." We enjoyed going to do that on a Sunday, since we was both off together.

We had our little cliques going; our little parties. Before they decided to break into the white nightclubs, we had our own out here on Central Avenue. There were a ton of good little nightclubs that kept you entertained fairly well. I don't know when these things began to turn, because I remember when I first came to Los Angeles, we used to go down to a theater called the Orpheum and that's where all the Negro entertainers as well as whites went. We had those clip joints over on the east side. And the funniest thing about it, it would always be in our nightclubs that a white woman would come in with a Negro man, eventually. The white man would very seldom come out in the open with a black woman. Even today. But the white woman has always come out in the open, even though I'm sure she gets tromped on and told about it...

Some weeks I brought home twenty-six dollars, some weeks sixteen dollars. Then it gradually went up to thirty dollars, then it went up a little bit more and a little bit more. And I learned somewhere along the line that in order to make a good move you gotta make some money. You don't make the same amount everyday. You have some days good, sometimes bad. Whatever you make you're supposed to save some. I was also getting that fifty dollars a month from my husband and that was just saved right away. I was planning on buying a home and a car. And I was going to go back to school. My husband came back, but I never was laid off, so just never found it necessary to look for another job or to go to school for another job.

I was still living over on Compton Avenue with my sister in this small little back house when my husband got home. Then, when Beverly was born, my sister moved in the front house and we stayed in the back house. When he came back, he looked for a job in the cleaning and pressing place, which was just plentiful. All the people had left these cleaning and pressing jobs and every other job; they was going to the defense plant to work because they was paying good. But in the meantime he was getting the same thing the people out there was getting, $1.25 an hour. That's why he didn't bother to go out to North American. But what we both weren't thinking about was that they did have better benefits because they did have an insurance plan and a union to back you up. Later he did come to work there, in 1951 or 1952.

I worked up until the end of March and then I took off. Beverly was born the twenty-first of June. I'd planned to come back somewhere in the last of August.. I went to verify the fact that I did comeback, so that did go on my record that I didn't just quit. But they laid off a lot of people, most of them, because the war was over.

It didn't bother me much--not thinking about it jobwise. I was just glad that the war was over. I didn't feel bad because my husband had a job and he also was eligible to go to school with his GI bill. So I really didn't have too many plans--which I wish I had had. I would have tore out page one and fixed it differently; put my version of page one in there.

I went and got me a job doing day work. That means you go to a person's house and clean up for one day out of the week and then you go to the next one and clean up. I did that a couple of times and I discovered I didn't like that so hot. Then I got me a job downtown working in a little factory where you do weaving--burned clothes and stuff like that. I learned to do that real good. It didn't pay too much but it paid enough to get me going, seventy-five cents or about like that.

When North American called me back, was I a happy soul! I dropped that job and went back. That was a dollar an hour. So, from sixty cents an hour, when I first hired in there, up to one dollar. That wasn't traveling fast, but it was better than anything else because you had hours to work by and you had benefits and you come home at night with your family. So it was a good deal.

It made me live better. I really did. We always say that Lincoln took the bale off of the Negroes. I think there is a statue up there in Washington, D.C., where he's lifting something off the Negro. Well, my sister always said—that's why you can't interview her because she's so radical--"Hitler was the one that got us out of the white folks' kitchen."

Source: Reprinted with permission of Twayne Publishers, an imprint of Simon & Schuster Macmillan, from *Rosie the Riveter Revisited*, by Sherna Berger Gluck, pp. 37-42. Copyright 1987 by Sherna Berger Gluck.

Daisy Bates, *The Long Shadow of Little Rock, 1962*

In 1957, three years after the Court had ruled that segregation was unconstitutional, the Courts ordered the desegregation of Central High School in Little Rock, Arkansas.

The following excerpt is from a book by Daisy Bates, newspaper editor who was president of the Arkansas State NAACP in 1957. It describes what occurred when Elizabeth Eckford, one of the nine black students who desegregated Central High School, arrived at school in September of 1957 (American History, 869).

DR. BENJAMIN FINE was then education editor of *The New York Times*. He had years before won for his newspaper a Pulitzer prize. He was among the first reporters on the scene to cover the Little Rock story.

A few days after the National Guard blocked the Negro children's entrance to the school, Ben showed up at my house. He paced the floor nervously, rubbing his hands together as he talked.

"Daisy, they spat in my face. They called me a 'dirty Jew.' I've been a marked man ever since the day Elizabeth tried to enter Central. I never told you what happened that day. I tried not to think about it. Maybe I was ashamed to admit to you or to myself that white men and women could be so beastly cruel."

"I was standing in front of the school that day. Suddenly there was a shout--'They're here! The niggers are coming!' I saw a sweet little girl who looked about fifteen, walking alone. She tried several times to pass through the guards. The last time she tried, they put their bayonets in front of her. When they did this, she became panicky. For a moment she just stood there trembling. Then she seemed to calm down and started walking toward the bus stop with the mob baying at her heels like a pack of hounds. The women were shouting, 'Get her! Lynch her!' The men were yelling 'Go home, you bastard of a black bitch!' She finally made it to the bus stop and sat down on the bench. I sat down beside her and said, 'I'm a reporter from *The New York Times*, may I have your name?' She just sat there, her head down. Tears were streaming down her cheeks from under her sun glasses. Daisy, I don't know what made me put my arm around her; lifting her chin, saying, 'Don't let them see you cry.' Maybe she reminded me of my fifteen-year-old daughter, Jill."

"There must have been five hundred around us by this time. I vaguely remember someone hollering 'Get a rope and drag her over to this tree.' Suddenly I saw a white-haired, kind-faced woman fighting her way through the mob. She looked at Elizabeth, and then screamed at the mob, 'Leave this child alone! Why are you tormenting her? Six months from now, you will hang your heads in shame.' The mob shouted, 'Another nigger lover. Get out of here!' The woman, who I found out later was Mrs. Grace Lorch, the wife of Dr. Lee Lorch, professor at Philander Smith College, turned to me and said, 'We have to do something. Let's try to get a cab.'"

"We took Elizabeth across the street to the drugstore. I remained on the sidewalk with Elizabeth while Mrs. Lorch tried to enter the drugstore to call a cab. But the hoodlums slammed the door in her face and wouldn't let her in. She pleaded with them to call a cab for the child. They closed in on her saying, 'Get out of here, you bitch!' Just then the city bus came. Mrs. Lorch and Elizabeth got on. Elizabeth must have been in a state of shock. She never uttered a word. When the bus pulled away, the mob closed in around me. 'We saw you put your arm around that little bitch. Now its your turn.' A drab, middle-aged woman said viciously, 'Grab him and kick him in the balls!' A girl I had seen hustling in one of the local bars screamed, 'A dirty New York Jew! Get him!' A man asked me, 'Are you a Jew?' I said, 'Yes.' He then said to the mob, 'Let him be! We'll take care of him later.'"

"The irony of it all, Daisy, is that during all this time the National Guardsmen made no effort to protect Elizabeth or to help me. Instead, they threatened to have me arrested for inciting to riot."

Source: "Daisy Bates, *The Long Shadow of Little Rock.*" Copyright 1962 by Daisy Bates. Used by permission of David McKay Co., a division of Random House, Inc.

QUESTIONS

1. How do you account for the violence and hostility that greeted Elizabeth as she attempted to gain admission to Central High School?
2. What did the National Guard do?
3. Do you think Mrs. Grace Lorch was correct when she told the mob, "Six months from now, you will hang your heads in shame"?

The Role of Black Women in the Civil Rights Movement

Anne Standley

The role of black women in the civil rights movement has received scant attention from historians. Most studies of the movement have examined such organizations as the Southern Christian Leadership Conference, the Student Nonviolent Coordinating Committee, the Congress of Racial Equality, and the National Association for the Advancement of Colored People, and accordingly have focused on the black ministers who served as officers in those organizations, all of whom were men. Harvard Sitkoff's list of the leaders of the movement, for example, consisted exclusively of men--Martin Luther King, Jr., of SCLC, James Forman and John Lewis of SNCC, James Farmer of CORE, Roy Wilkins of the NAACP, and Whitney Young of the National Urban League. The accounts of other historians, such as Aldon Morris, Clayborne Carson, and August Meier, also showed male preachers spearheading the various protests--boycotts of bus companies and white-owned businesses, voter registration drives, and marches--that constituted the movement. Likewise, the vast majority of students leading the sit-ins and freedom rides named by Sitkoff were men. He cited only two of the many women who held positions of leadership in the movement--Fannie Lou Hamer, who was elected delegate to the Democratic National Convention by the Mississippi Freedom Democratic Party in 1964, and Ella Baker, executive secretary of SCLC--and understated their influence...

The argument that men were the principal leaders of the civil rights movement is not wholly inaccurate. According to women who achieved prominence within the movement, such as Septima Clark, who trained teachers of citizenship schools for SCLC, or Ella Baker, and historians Jacqueline Jones and Paula Giddings, the ministers' sexism and authoritarian views of leadership prevented women from assuming command of any of the movement organizations. Indeed, in light of the advantages men possessed in establishing themselves as leaders of the movement-- the preachers' virtual monopoly on political power within the black community and the exclusion of women from the ministry in many black churches--it is remarkable that any women achieved positions of authority.

Yet, in fact, woman exerted an enormous influence, both formally, as members of the upper echelon of SNCC, SCLC, and the Mississippi Freedom Democratic Party, and informally, as spontaneous leaders and dedicated participants. Many of the protests that historians describe as led by ministers were initiated by women. For example, Martin Luther King, Jr., is usually cited as the leader of the Montgomery Bus Boycott, since it was King who was appointed director of the organization that coordinated the boycott, the Montgomery Improvement Association. Yet the boycott was started by a woman, Jo Ann Robinson, and by the women's group that she headed, the Women's Political Council. Black women directed voter registration drives, taught in freedom schools, and provided food and housing for movement volunteers. As members of the MFDP, women won positions as delegates to the national Democratic convention in 1964 and as representatives to Congress. They demonstrated a heroism no less than that of men. They suffered the same physical abuse, loss of employment, destruction of property, and risk to their lives.

Back women also deserve credit for the refusal within the movement to accept halfway measures towards eradicating Jim Crow practices. Fannie Lou Hamer's rejection of the compromise offered the MFDP delegation at the Democratic National Convention in 1964 typified the courage of black women, who formed the majority of the preachers' congregations and whose pressure forced the ministers in SCLC, CORE, and the other movement associations to persist in the face of white opposition to their demands. Paula Giddings reported that when the ministers of Montgomery met after the first day of the bus boycott to discuss whether to continue the boycott, they agreed on the condition that their names not be publicized as the boycott leaders. E. D. Nixon, former head of the Montgomery NAACP, shamed them into giving their public endorsement by reminding them of the women to whom they were accountable: "How you gonna have a mass meeting, gonna boycott a city bus line without the white folks knowing about it? You guys have went around here and lived off these poor washerwomen all your lives and ain't never done nothing for 'em. Now you got a chance to do something for 'em, you talking about you don't want the White folks to know about it."

As well, black women were responsible for the movement's success in generating popular support for the movement among rural blacks. Ella Baker convinced SCLC to jettison plans to take control of SNCC, allowing the student-run group to remain independent of the other movement organizations and to adopt, with Baker's encouragement, an egalitarian approach to decision making. Because SNCC workers formulated the organization's objectives by soliciting the views of members of black communities in which the volunteers worked, they were able to build considerable grass-roots support for the movement.

Despite the exclusion of black women from top positions in movement organizations and the little recognition they received from either blacks or whites for their contributions, the published accounts of black women activists suggest that the movement gave women as well as men a sense of empowerment...Yet these women differed in their analyses of the cause of the racial oppression that they combatted. Two of the older women leaders--Daisy Bates, who was president of the NAACP State Conference of Branches, and who led the integration of Central High School in Little Rock, Arkansas, and Jo Ann Robinson--and a younger leader Diane Nash, who organized sit-ins and freedom rides for SNCC, viewed racism as politically motivated. They believed that if blacks could obtain the vote, white politicians would be forced to act against racial discrimination at the polls, segregated schools, and the varied forms of extralegal violence carried out against blacks. Blacks could use their political influence to improve their economic status, which in turn would enhance their image among whites.

Because they saw themselves as having to convince whites to support the movement, and because they identified so completely with the struggle for civil rights, Bates, Robinson, and Nash refrained from making critical judgments about the movement or their roles within it...Consequently their behavior showed contradictions--on the one hand a boldness in initiating protests and applying pressure on whites in power, while at the same time a submissiveness in their acceptance of the authority of the black male clergy.

Jo Anne Robinson was born in 1916 in Colloden, Georgia, twenty-five miles from Macon. She was the youngest of twelve children. Her family subsequently moved to Macon, where she graduated first in her class from an all black high school. Robinson received a bachelor's degree from Georgia State College in Fort Valley, taught for five years at a public school in Macon, and earned a master's degree in English literature from Atlanta University. In 1949, after teaching for a year at Mary Allen College in Crockett, Texas, she moved to Montgomery to join the faculty at

Alabama State University. Robinson chaired the Women's Political Council in Montgomery, an organization of professional women that sought to raise the status of blacks by working with juvenile and adult delinquents and organizing voter registration. She also served on the Executive Board of the Montgomery Improvement Association and edited the MIA newsletter.

Rohinson declared that in publishing her memoir, she hoped to improve whites' image of blacks by demonstrating blacks' courage, dedication, and self-discipline in their fight for their rights. Robinson saw the movement as blacks' attempt to overcome the circumstances that degraded them--to secure the same living conditions and opportunities as whites--so as to live decently and thereby prove their equality with whites...

Robinson's view of the movement as the first step towards blacks' redemption in the eyes of whites, and the role she assumed as the movement's publicist, left little room for a candid evaluation of the male leadership or for challenging its authority. She briefly criticized the ministers in Montgomery for their timidity, stating that only when they read a circular advertising the bus boycott and realized that "all the city's black congregations were quite intelligent on the matter and were planning to support the one-day boycott with or without the ministers' leadership" did they endorse it. She offset this reproach, however, with praise for the preachers' work, and attributed the boycott's success to the clergymen.

> Had it not been for the ministers and the support they received from their wonderful congregations, the outcome of the boycott might have been different. The ministers gave themselves, their time...and their leadership...which set examples for the laymen to follow. They gave us confidence, faith in ourselves, faith in them and their leadership, that helped the congregations to support the movement every foot of the way.

In her memoir, *The Long Shadow of Little Rock*, Daisy Bates displayed similar contradictions between her readiness to confront her white oppressors, which she demonstrated both as a child and as an adult, and her acceptance of what she regarded as a flawed black leadership. Bates grew up in southern Arkansas, in a town controlled by a sawmill company. She first experienced discrimination at the age of eight, when a white grocer refused to serve her until he had waited on all of the white customers...

Bates not only challenged whites while growing up; she also defied the authority of her parents and members of the black community...Bates' narrative showed that as an adult, she continued to challenge those in power. She met with the governor of Arkansas and the U.S. Attorney to urge them, unsuccessfully, to respond to the whites' violence. In contrast, however, she appears to have deferred to the male leadership in the black community. She made only a passing reference to her irritation at the black ministers' silence in the face of the whites' terrorism carried out against the black students, suggesting that she suppressed her frustration. In her conclusion, she assailed Congress and the Eisenhower administration for their lackluster support of desegregation, but like Robinson, refrained from placing any blame for the movement's slow progress on its leadership.

One can see similar inconsistencies in the actions of Diane Nash, a SNCC volunteer. Nash grew up in Chicago and came to Nashville to attend Fisk University. Nash's shock at the segregation of restaurants, water fountains, and other public facilities in the south prompted her to join SNCC. In 1965, Nash wrote an article for *Ebony* that implied that she accepted the prevailing view that the civil rights movement, and specifically SCLC, should be led primarily by men. Nash's article, "The Men Behind Martin Luther King" profiled the male staff members of

SCLC. She depicted the women on the staff who numbered three out of a total of twelve, as important but peripheral figures...At no point did Nash question the women's secondary status within SCLC.

Nash's prominence in protest efforts, however, seemed to contradict the unspoken assumption of her article that men should lead the movement. Nash chaired the central committee of the sit-in movement in Nashville. She also assembled a second group of freedom riders to continue the journey when harassment forced the first group to disperse in Birmingham before they reached their destination of New Orleans...

While Bates, Robinson, and Nash attributed racism to blacks' lack of representation in the political process, the majority of black women leaders who left accounts of their experiences regarded racial oppression as symptomatic of a structurally flawed society. Disheartened by the movement's fragmentation in the late sixties and by what they regarded as its limited success, they concluded that racial oppression formed part of a larger system of inequities that characterized American society and that could not be eradicated without addressing the other injustices to which it was connected. One activist who became disillusioned was Jean Smith, a student at Howard University who registered voters for SNCC in 1963 and who organized the MFDP meetings that elected an integrated delegation to the Democratic National Convention in 1964. Smith maintained that the right to vote, while unifying the black community and giving blacks the confidence to assert themselves and challenge racist laws or customs, had proved ineffectual in diminishing white hegemony and improving the living conditions of blacks.

> The best way to understand is to look at what the Negro people who cast their lot with the Movement believed. They believed, I think, that their participation in the drive for voting rights would ultimately result in the relief of their poverty and hopelessness. They thought with the right to vote they could end the exploitation of their labor by the plantation owners. They thought they could get better schools for their children; they could get sewers dug and sidewalks paved. They thought they could get adequate public-health facilities for their communities. And of course they got none of these...They believed there was a link between representation in government and making that government work for you. What they--and I-- discovered was that for some people, this link does not exist...

This disenchantment with the civil rights movement led some activists to temporarily embrace separatism. Smith, for example, in 1968 argued for a self-sufficient black community as the solution to blacks' political impotence...Two years earlier, in 1966, [Joyce] Ladner [a SNCC volunteer] had also abandoned integration as a goal, convinced by the unrelenting brutality of whites that black power offered the most effective means of improving the status of blacks.

> When Vernon Dahmier [Ladner's mentor] was killed, my faith in integration was shaken. I found myself trying to justify my belief that "Black and white together" was still the solution to the race problem...What Blacks needed to do, I thought, was to unite as a group and develop their own institutions and communities. What they needed was Black power!...

In addition to embracing separatism, Ladner turned to marxism for a diagnosis and a solution to racial oppression, along with Frances Beale, a former SNCC activist. Ladner asserted that in aspiring to middle-class goals of upward mobility and wealth, blacks condoned a structure of economic inequality. For Ladner, it was not blacks' lowly position in the hierarchy, but their acceptance of a capitalist economy which required a hierarchy, in which the fortunes of a few came from the exploitation of many, that oppressed them. Similarly, Frances Beale claimed that the feminists who sought only to improve their own position, demanding, for example, equal pay for equal work, failed to attack capitalism as the root of inequality and thus perpetuated an unjust system...

Robinson, Bates and Nash sought to present a united front to white authorities. Consequently, they suppressed their differences with the male leadership. In contrast, the other activists aired their disagreements with the men managing the movement organizations, although most did so only in hindsight.

Only two of the women, Ella Baker and Septima Clark, confronted the male leaders of the movement while working with them to challenge their policies Baker, like Robinson and Bates, belonged to the older generation of women civil rights leaders. She was 57 when SCLC appointed her as executive secretary in 1960. Baker was born in 1903 in Norfolk, Virginia...Baker's father waited on tables for the Norfolk-Washington ferry; her mother tended to the sick in the community. After graduating from Shaw University in Raleigh, Baker began a long career of activism. She worked for a WPA [Works Progress Administration] consumer education project in New York City during the depression. The NAACP hired her in 1938 to recruit members and raise money in the south, and five years later named her national director of branches. Baker helped found SNCC in 1960. In 1964 she gave the keynote address at the MFDP convention in Jackson and established the MFDP Washington office.

Baker's readiness to confront the male officers in SCLC may have come in part from her commitment to participatory decision making...Baker's account of the debate within SCLC on a strategy to bring SNCC under SCLC's control showed her opposing SCLC's hierarchical style of management--her efforts to democratize the leadership of the movement by lobbying for an autonomous SNCC, and refusal to defer to King.

> The Southern Christian Leadership Conference felt that they could influence how things went. They were interested in having the students become an arm of SCLC. They were most confident that this would be their baby, because I was their functionary and I had called the meeting. At a discussion called by the Reverend Dr. King, the SCLC leadership made decisions [about] who would speak to whom to influence the students to become part of SCLC. Well, I disagreed. There was no student at Dr. King's meeting. I was the nearest thing to a student, being the advocate, you see. I also knew from the beginning that having a woman be an executive of SCLC was not something that would go over with the male-dominated leadership. And then, of course, my personality wasn't right, in the sense I was not afraid to disagree with the higher authorities. I wasn't one to say, yes, because it came from the Reverend King. So when it was proposed that the leadership could influence the direction by speaking to, let's say, the man from Virginia, he could speak to the leadership of the Virginia student group, and the assumption was that having spoken to so-and-so, so-and-so would do what they wanted done, I was outraged, I walked out.

Septima Clark, the other activist who challenged the male staff of SCLC, was also a member of the older generation of women civil rights leaders. Clark was born in 1898 in Charleston, North Carolina. She taught in the Charleston public schools until she lost her job in 1956 when the legislature passed a law prohibiting state employees from belonging to the NAACP. The Highlander Folk School, which brought blacks and whites together to discuss social issues at a farm in Tennessee, hired Clark to lead workshops training members of rural communities to teach their neighbors to read and to register to vote. In 1961, when the Tennessee legislature moved to close Highlander, SCLC and the United Church of Christ provided the funds to enable Clark to continue organizing citizenship schools, which in 1964 numbered 195.

Clark talked freely about what she saw as the sexism of the SCLC staff.

I was on the executive staff of the SCLC, but the men on it didn't listen to me too well. They like to send me into many places, because I could always make a path in to get people to listen to what I have to say. But those men didn't have any faith in women, none whatsoever. They just thought that women were sex symbols and had no contributions to make. That's why Reverend Abernathy would say continuously, "Why is Mrs. Clark on this staff?" Dr. King would say, "Well she has expanded our program. She has taken it into eleven deep south states." Rev. Abernathy'd [sic] come right back the next time and ask again.

I had a great feeling that Dr. King didn't think much of women either...when I was in Europe with him, when he received the Nobel Peace Prize in 1964, the American Field Service Committee people wanted me to speak. In a sort of casual way he would say "Anything I can't answer, ask Mrs. Clark." But he didn't mean it, because I never did get the chance to do any speaking to the AFS committee in London or to any of the other groups.

Like Baker, Clark communicated to King her differences with his style of leadership, urging him in a letter to run SCLC more democratically by delegating authority. She also attacked other ministers for their dependence on King, in which Lucy assumed that only King could lead the movement, and for their belief that to suggest expanding the leadership of the movement cast doubt on King's own capabilities...

Kathleen Cleaver...reported in 1971 that she joined the women's movement because she observed while working for SNCC, beginning in 1966, that women did most of the work but that few women held positions of authority. Those women who obtained administrative posts, Cleaver noticed, carried the double burden of their jobs and their duties as wives and mothers, and also had to contend with the male staff members' refusal to accept them as their equals. Cleaver attributed the death of Ruby Doris Smith, Executive Secretary of SNCC, to sheer exhaustion from the many demands and from having to fight racism and sexism simultaneously. "What killed Ruby Doris was the constant outpouring of work, work, work, with being married, having a child, the constant conflicts, the constant struggles that she was subjected to because she was a woman."

A letter written in 1977 by Cynthia Washington, who directed a freedom project for SNCC in Mississippi in 1963, suggested that the position of black women in the movement was more ambiguous than the deference of Robinson, Bates, or Nash to the male leadership, or the anger of Baker, Clark, or Cleaver at women's subordinate status indicated...

During the fall of 1964, I had a conversation with Casey Hayden about the role of women in SNCC. She complained that all the women got to do was type, that their role was limited to office work no matter where they were. What she said didn't make any particular sense to me because, at the time, I had my own project in Bolivar County, Mississippi. A number of other black women also directed their own projects. What Casey and other white women seemed to want was an opportunity to prove they could do something other than office work. I assumed that if they could do something else, they'd probably be doing that.

Washington said that while some black men viewed the women as inferior--she quoted Stokely Carmichael's jeer that the only position for women in SNCC was prone--she believed that the authority she enjoyed as project director demonstrated that few shared his view. "Our relative autonomy as projects directors seemed to deny or override his statement. We were proof that what he said wasn't true--or so we thought."...Yet Washington...later concluded that sexism did exist, despite her lack of awareness of it at the time. "In fact, I'm certain that our single-minded focus on the issues of racial discrimination and the black struggle for equality blinded us to other issues."

The ambiguity in the status of women in the movement brought out by Washington's letter paralleled the activists' ambivalence towards the male leaders, in which even those women who criticized the male activists for their condescending attitudes towards women did not hold the men responsible for their sexism. Some, such as Clark, saw the men's treatment of women as reflecting their hostility towards a racially oppressive society that put down black men even more than black women. Clark thought that black men's sexism was a reaction against their overprotective mothers, who tried to shield their sons from the violence of whites to which black men were particularly susceptible...

Other movement workers, such as Beale and Cleaver, blamed capitalism as well as racism for black men's discrimination against women. Sexism, like racism, they argued, was a device by which whites reinforced the exploitation of the masses. Just as racism perpetuated lower-class whites' poverty by preventing them from joining forces with blacks to overthrow their oppressors, so too, by internalizing the sexism of whites, black men contributed to the marginal economic status of blacks. Their complicity in the segregation of jobs by sex, which limited black women's access to all but the lowest paid jobs, and which treated women as a source of surplus labor and as strikebreakers, impoverished blacks as a group.

Cleaver agreed with Clark that black men developed sexist attitudes because they were oppressed, although Cleaver saw their oppression as economic. The black men, according to Cleaver, resented the "strong" role black women had had to assume as breadwinners as well as mothers. They vented their frustration by asserting their power over women--treating them as inferior, abusing them--or by abandoning their families to escape their guilt at their inability to find employment...

All of the women leaders agreed that discrimination against women was of secondary importance to the subjection of all blacks and the inequitable distribution of power in society. Cleaver, for example, insisted that to focus on sexism diverted blacks from attacking the root of all injustice, "colonization," or economic exploitation of white women and minority men and women...

Moreover, these activists held differing views of the relationship between the status of black women and that of blacks as a whole. Cleaver thought that women's equality was a necessary precondition to achieving the equality of all blacks--a means of ensuring the full utilization of blacks' resources...Ladner, on the other hand, feared that the assertiveness of women made black men look relatively weak, ...and hindered the men from proving their equality to whites...

The inconsistencies in the behavior of these women leaders, in which they challenged white authorities but deferred to black ministers, or criticized the male activists, but only in hindsight, or directly challenged the male officers or movement organizations, yet nevertheless accepted their leadership, cannot entirely be explained by their various theories on the source of racism. Indeed, only in the case of three of the activists, Robinson, Bates, and Nash, do their ideologies seem consistent with their actions. A more plausible explanation for their contradictory behavior is that these women, for the reasons given by Washington, did not consider themselves oppressed by black men, either in or out of the movement, and in some respects believed that black men were worse off than black women. Consequently they did not seek to change their roles in the movement. In addition, the women had conflicting feelings about whom to hold responsible for sexism, if they thought that it did exist, and were uncertain as to how the assertion of their rights as women would affect the status of blacks as a group. These women leaders' reflections suggest that the role of black women in the civil rights movement, largely ignored by historians, was complicated by their ambivalence about what it ought to be and defies a definitive answer.

"The Role of Black Women in the Civil Rights Movement" by Anne Standley from *Black Women's History*, ed. Darlene Clark Hine, 10 (1990), pp. 183-201.

Mexican American, Chicana Women

This section consists of stories about real Latina and Mexican American women. In New Mexico women like "La Tules" had to deal with the challenges of territorial conquest by the United States after the Mexican American War in 1846.

Mexican American women have worked in either their home by taking in laundry and sewing, or outside the home as domestics, cannery workers, factory employees and in agricultural fields as pickers. The story of women in the canneries is a moving story of their struggle for good pay and decent working conditions.

Dolores Huerta is the unsung herione of the United Farm Workers unionization movement. In the past, she has served as Vice-President and contract negotiator. Presently she is serving as Treasure of the United Farmworkers Union.

"The Development of the Chicana Feminist Discourse" deals with the controversey within the Chicana movement and its attempt to develop an identity independent of the larger Women's Rights Movement. This article also emphasizes the struggle between Latina women and Latina men because Latinas wanted equality.

La Tules of Image and Reality: Euro-American Attitudes and Legend Formation on a Spanish-Mexican Frontier

Deena F. Gonzalez

In the summer of 1846, Dona Gertrudis Barcelo stood at an important crossroad. Exempted from the hardships and tribulations endured by the women around her, Barcelo had profited enormously from the "gringo" merchants and itinerant retailers who had arrived in Santa Fe after the conquest. The town's leading businesswoman, owner of a gambling house and saloon, and its most unusual character, Barcelo exemplified an ingenious turnaround in the way she and others in her community began resolving the problem of the Euro-American, now lodged more firmly than ever in their midst. Barcelo also epitomized the growing dilemma of dealing with newcomers whose culture and orientation differed from hers.

Since 1821, people like Barcelo had seen traders enter their town and change it. But local shopkeepers and vendors had done more than observe the developing marketplace. They had forged ahead, establishing a partnership with the adventurers who brought manufactured items and textiles to Santa Fe while exporting the products of Nuevo Mexico, including gold, silver, and equally valuable goods, such as Navajo blankets and handwoven rugs.

Barcelo's life and activities were indisputably anchored in a community shaped by a changing economy, as well as by other political, social, and cultural demands. Orthodox interpretations of her life have overlooked the primacy of the surrounding turmoil. Moreover, by 1846, she would become the female object of the easiest, most exaggerated misunderstandings bred by such complicated frontier situations. The exaggerations have been examined from several perspectives; but standard works have failed to assess the role that sex and gender played in discussions of Barcelo's business and personality. The outcome has been the creation of a legend around her, one directly shaped by the disruptions experienced by her generation and focused on her business and her sex.

Gertrudis Barcelo was said to have controlled men and to have dabbled in local politics, but these insinuations do not form the core of her legend. Rather, reporters of her time, professional historians today, and novelists have debated her morals, arguing about her influence over political leaders and speculating about whether she was operating a brothel. These concerns are consistently revealed in early accounts of Barcelo by writers and soldiers recalling their experiences in the "hinterlands" of northern Mexico. The negative images and anti-Mexican stereotypes in these works not only stigmatized Barcelo but also helped legitimize the Euro-Americans' conquest of the region. Absorbed and reiterated by succeeding generations of professional historians and novelists, the legend of Barcelo has obscured the complex reality of cultural accommodation and ongoing resistance.

Moreover, the legend evolving around Barcelo affected the lives of other Spanish-Mexican women. Her supposed moral laxity and outrageous dress were generalized to include all the women of Santa Fe. Susan Shelby Magoffin, the first Euro-American woman to travel down the Santa Fe Trail, observed in 1846 that "These were dressed in the Mexican style; large sleeves, short waists, ruffled skirts, and no bustles--which latter looks exceedingly odd in this day of grass skirts and pillows. All danced and smoked cigarittos, from the old woman with false hair and teeth

[Dona Tula], to the little child."

This was not the first account of La Tules, as Barcelo was affectionately called (in reference either to her slimness or to her plumpness, because *tules* means "reed"). Josiah Gregg, a trader during the 1830's, said that La Tules was a woman of "loose habits," who "roamed" in Taos before she came to Santa Fe. In his widely read *Commerce of the Prairies*, Gregg linked local customs--smoking, gambling, and dancing--to social and moral disintegration. La Tules embodied, for him and others, the extent of Spanish-Mexican decadence.

La Tules's dilemmas predated 1846 and, at a social and economic level, portended a community's difficulties, which were not long in developing. Governing officers in Chihuahua had already sent word of a crackdown on illegal trafficking, Bishop Zubiria in Durango issued a pastoral limiting church holidays and celebrations, in an effort to economize on expenses but also on priests' time. This pastoral gave added emphasis to the regulations descending on New Mexicans, who now became aware that the Catholic church, too, was reconsidering its obligations. In this period, Barcelo and other Spanish-Mexicans experienced the tightening grip of the Mexican state, which was bent on rooting out uncontrolled trading; but they gained a reprieve accidentally. As orders arrived from the church concerning the condition of Christians on the northern frontier, the United States chose to invade, hurling General Stephen Kearny and his troops toward the capital city.

Barcelo's activities and business acumen demonstrated, despite these pressures, the *vecinos'* (residents') proven resilience and the town's characteristic adaptability. But in the 1840's Barcelo also became the object of intense Euro-American scrutiny and harsh ridicule. She was an expert dealer at monte, a card game named after the *monte* (mountain) of cards that accumulated with each hand. She drew hundreds of dollars out of merchants and soldiers alike; it was the former who embellished her name and reputation, imbuing her facetiously with characteristics of superiority and eccentricity.

Josiah Gregg, the trader, first brought Barcelo notoriety because his book described her as a loose woman. But Gregg also argued that money from gambling eventually helped elevate her moral character. A Protestant, and a doctor in failing health, Gregg respected only her gift--the one he understood best--for making money. During her lifetime, she became extraordinarily wealthy, and for that reason as well, Gregg and others would simultaneously admire and disdain her.

In the face of such contradictory attitudes toward her, Barcelo ventured down a trail of her own choosing. Not quite as rebellious as Juana Lopes, who had defied husband and judge alike, she nevertheless achieved personal autonomy. Several times, she appeared before magistrates to pay fines, testifying once against an indicted judge who had pocketed her money. She even involved her family in her pursuits, and they were fined along with her. As early as 1825, she was at the mining camp outside of Santa Fe, Real del Oro, doing a brisk business at monte. By the 1830's, the card dealer was back in town, enticing Euro-Americans to gamble under terms she prescribed. At her saloon, she served the men alcohol as she dealt rounds of cards. Controlling consumption as well as the games, Barcelo accommodated the newcomers, but on her own terms. "Shrewd," Susan Shelby Magoffin, wife of the trader Samuel Magoffin, called Barcelo in 1846.

Barcelo had proven her shrewdness long before that. Since the 1820's, Barcelo had engaged in an extremely profitable enterprise. Gambling, dubbed by observers the national pastime, was ubiquitous, and by the mid-1830's nearly every traveler and merchant felt compelled to describe Barcelo's contributions to the game. Matt Field, an actor and journalist from Missouri, depicted

Barcelo's saloon as a place where her "calm seriousness was alone discernible, and the cards fell from her fingers as steadily as though she were handling only a knitting needle...Again and again the long fingers of Senora Toulous swept off the pile of gold, and again were they replaced by the unsteady fingers of her opponent." By any account, Euro-Americans could understand what drove Barcelo. Because they recognized in her their own hungry search for profit, they embellished their stories and, just as frequently, maligned her.

When Barcelo died in 1852, she was worth over ten thousand dollars, a sum twice as high as most wealthy Spanish-Mexican men possessed and larger than the average worth of Euro-Americans in Santa Fe. Her properties were extensive: she owned the saloon, a long building with large rooms, and she had an even larger home not far from the plaza. She made enough money to give generously to the church and to her relatives, supporting families and adopting children. Military officers claimed that she entertained lavishly and frequently.

Dinners, dances, gambling, and assistance to the poverty-stricken elevated Barcelo to a special place in New Mexican society, where she remained throughout her life. The community respected her, since it tolerated atypical behavior in others and rarely seemed preoccupied with what Barcelo represented. Even her scornful critics were struck by how well received and openly admired the woman with the red hair and heavy jewelry was among Santa Fe's "best society."

What was it about Nuevo Mexico in the two decades after the war that allowed a woman like Barcelo to step outside the accepted boundaries of normal or typical female behavior, make a huge sum of money, undergo excessive scrutiny, primarily by newcomers to Santa Fe, and yet be eulogized by her own people? Some answers lie within her Spanish-Mexican community, which, although beset by persisting problems, had flexibility and an inclination toward change. Others lie in the general position and treatment of women in that society.

Court records and other documents reveal that Santa Fe's women were expected to defer to men but did not, that they were bound by a code of honor and respectability but often manipulated it to their advantage, and that they were restrained by fathers and brothers from venturing too far out of family and household but frequently disobeyed them. One professional historian has argued that social codes in colonial New Mexican society, with their twin emphasis on honor and virtue, were primarily metaphors for expressing hierarchical relationships, but also served to resolve conflict as much as to restrict women. Women's behavior and the espoused social ideals of restraint, respectability, and deference were at cross-purposes, especially in a community that was supremely concerned about the appearance of honor, if not its reality. Separate requirements based on gender--or what the society would label appropriate masculine and feminine virtues--occupied an equally important place in these social codes, and also concerned power and the resolution of conflict.

Barcelo's gambling and drinking violated the rigid codes organizing appropriate female behavior, but such behavior was not the key to her distinctiveness. Rather, her success as a businesswoman and gambler gave her a unique independence ordinarily denied women. Thus, the most hostile comments about her frequently came from Spanish-Mexican women.

In particular, complaints filed against Barcelo reveal the extent of other women's animosity, not men's, and were usually thinly disguised as aspersions on her honor. In 1835, Ana Maria Rendon remonstrated that Barcelo and Lucius Thruston, a migrant from Kentucky, were cohabiting. In fact Barcelo's husband lived in the same house, indicating that Thruston was probably a boarder. Honor lay in the proof, and Barcelo achieved both by defending herself and her husband as well. Another time, Barcelo complained about a slanderous comment made by

Josefa Tenorio and was also exonerated. Spanish-Mexicans of Santa Fe remained a litigious people, and they waged battles on many fronts. The *acalde* court (local court) prevailed as the best place to seek resolution. However, Catholic Spanish-Mexican *vecinos* were generally a forgiving people, especially where slander and gossip were involved. Barcelo forgave Ana Maria Rendon's complaint when Rendon retracted it, and the records are filled with similar recantations in other cases.

At issue, then, were not Barcelo's violations of gender and social codes--she had in part moved beyond that--but the others' violations of her good name and reputation. On one level, their hostility and outright distrust of Barcelo were vendettas directed against a neighbor on the road to wealth and prestige. On another, women upheld the gender code (albeit with some trepidation) because, in complaining about Barcelo, they defended themselves and their society. Even when she was fined for gambling, the amounts were so minuscule that they neither halted Barcelo's gambling nor conveyed a forceful message about modifying social behavior.

Barcelo, a married woman, would not have been able to step outside the boundaries of her society, nor would Manuela Baca or Juana Lopes in the previous decade, if there were no disjunction between the idealized married life and the conditions that stood in the way of its realization--conditions such as taking in boarders or having children out of wedlock. Rallitas Washington, Barcelo's grandniece born out of wedlock, as well as hundreds of other women whose mothers were unmarried, formed a decidedly heterodox, yet devoutly Catholic, community. In relationships as in personal behavior, these women's lack of conformity did not shake the conscience of a community as much as needle it.

Beyond cultural mores and behavioral codes, though, what might go unrecognized is that women of the Far West who defied the rules might have been viewed from the outset as marginal. When not ignored completely, women who have existed outside the boundaries of a society of community--or who have been ostracized for various reasons--have frequently been termed outlaws and burdened with characteristics obscuring their social or economic conditions. That may have been standard procedure for marginal women everywhere.

But marginality signifies not only the transgression of social boundaries but also the aftermath of such transgression; it represents the fate of people who press against those boundaries and afterward must live on the edges of society. Barcelo cleverly crossed social and sexual barriers to gamble, make money, buy property, and influence politicians, but she avoided marginality. She did not regard herself as a marginal woman, nor was she necessarily marginalized, except by Euro-Americans. She was unusual and she was mocked for it, but not by her own people. In fact, her life and legend are interesting precisely because, in the eyes of observers, she came to represent the worst in Spanish-Mexican culture while, as a Spanish-Mexican, she mastered the strategies and methods of the Americanizers; she achieved what they had professed in speeches and reports originally to want for all New Mexicans.

Barcelo's life and her legend contradict orthodox notions of marginality in a situation of conquest. In their writings, conquerors maligned and ostracized her. The opinions they expressed and the images they drew of her sealed her legend in the popular imagination, because their works were distributed throughout the United States. Translated into several languages, Gregg's *Commerce of the Prairies* was reprinted three times between 1844, when it first appeared, and 1857. Thousands of readers learned through him of the "certain female of very loose habits, known as La Tules." What Gregg and the others could not communicate to their audience was that La Tules was adaptable, and that before their eyes, she had begun disproving their notion that

Spanish-Mexicans were "lazy and indolent." She contradicted James Josiah Webb's contention that all Spanish-Mexicans did was "literally dance from the cradle to the grave." Barcelo's busy saloon hosted nightly fandangos, or dances, and their organizer easily became the target of Webb's manipulation of stereotype. Dancing, drinking, and gambling--the order was often changed according to how much the writer wanted to emphasize licentious behavior--gave these Protestant travelers pause, and they quickly made use of the observations to fictionalize Barcelo's, and all women's, lives.

But the tales about La Tules are important in another respect. Fictitious representations marginalized Barcelo because they shrouded her life in mystery and called forth several stereotypes about Mexicans. Yet Barcelo was hardly the excessive woman the travelers depicted. Instead, she became pivotal in the achievement of their conquest. Worth thousands of dollars, supportive of the army, friendly to accommodating politicians, Barcelo was in the right place to win over Spanish-Mexicans for the intruders. Using business and political skills, she made the saloon the hub of the town's social and economic life, and at the hall she kept abreast of the latest political developments. Politicians and military officers alike went there seeking her opinion, or involved her in their discussions about trade or the army. As adviser and confidante, she took on a role few other women could have filled. If she existed on the fringes of a society, it was because she chose to place herself there--a woman with enormous foresight who pushed against her own community's barriers and risked being labeled by the travelers a madam or a whore.

Such caricatures denied her contributions to the economy and the society. Had she not been a gambler, a keeper of a saloon, or a woman, she might have been praised for her industry and resourcefulness, traits that antebellum Americans valued in their own people. But from the point of view of the writers, the admirable qualities of a woman who lived by gambling and who was her own proprietor would have been lost on Protestant, middle-class readers. Furthermore, they could hardly imagine, let alone tolerate, the diversity Santa Fe exhibited. It became easier to reaffirm their guiding values and walk a literary tightrope by making La Tules a symbol of Spanish-Mexican degeneracy or an outcast altogether. Barcelo had exceeded their wildest expectations, and in their eyes she was an outlaw.

Yet the aspersions heaped on Barcelo were not designed solely to obscure her personality and life or to make her activities legendary. They created an image that fit the Euro-Americans' preconceptions about Spanish-Mexicans. Thus described to the readers, the image of Barcelo in the travel documents merely confirmed older, pernicious stereotypes. Many recalled the *leyenda negra* (black legend) of the sixteenth century, when Spaniards were objectified as a fanatical, brutal people. Historians and others have traced another critical stage in the development of anti-Mexican fervor to the antebellum period, when expansionist dreams and sentiments of such politicians as Senator Thomas Hart Benton gave rise to a continued confusion about Spanish-Mexican culture. Not only travelers from the United States but residents in general harbored deep prejudices toward Spanish-Mexicans. The travelers of the nineteenth century thus represented broader racial attitudes arid demonstrated the ethnocentrism of a population back home.

Racial slurs and derogatory comments about Mexicans appeared regularly in the *Congressional Record,* in newspapers, and, not coincidentally, in travel accounts. Speeches and statements consistently equated brown skin with promiscuity, immorality, and decay. Albert Pike, who arrived in New Mexico from New England in 1831, called the area around Santa Fe "bleak, black, and barren;" New Mexicans, he said, were "peculiarly blessed with ugliness." The chronicler of a military expedition to New Mexico in the 1840's, Frank Edwards, said that all

Mexicans were "debased in all moral sense" and amounted to little more than "swarthy thieves and liars." The same judgments were made later, long after the war had ended, and reflect the persistence of the same thinking. The historian Francis Parkman argued that people in the West could be "separated into three divisions, arranged in order of their merits: white men, Indians, and Mexicans; to the latter of whom the honorable title of 'whites' is by no means conceded." In the same period, William H. Emory of the boundary commission declared that the "darker colored" races were inevitably "inferior and syphilitic."

These select references--and there are hundreds of other comments like them--describe a set of racist attitudes and ethnocentric beliefs from the Jacksonian period that carried into Santa Fe. Travelers thus mirrored the intrinsic values of a nation encroaching on Mexican territory, and were fueled by the heightened fervor over destiny and superiority.

Scholars have assessed the genre of travel guides and recollections as contributions to literature and have debated its special characteristics of construction, organization, and distortion. But the books had something besides literary appeal; they sold rapidly in a country hungry for information about the West. Many planned visits and escapes to the healthier climates of the Southwest, while others intended to live in warmer areas and to find markets for their goods: such motives had inspired Gregg to leave Missouri for Santa Fe. Although he and his fellow adventurers were genuinely curious about Mexicans and about what the West had to offer, one important consequence of their visits, vacations, and reports, at least for Barcelo, was that the migrants also brought capital to Santa Fe. The accounts cannot, therefore, be considered only as travel literature; they do not, as some have argued, simply unveil anti-Mexican, anti-Catholic sentiment. Rather, they describe--from the outside in, from the perspective of the colonizer--the systematic movement of an ethnocentric people to Santa Fe and reveal the interest in the promise of continued prosperity in the Southwest.

Travel writers of the nineteenth century, however, were also conscious of the desires and proclivities of their readers. Hence, these writers described the unsavory material culture (Matt Field gazed upon the adobe buildings and labeled Santa Fe's houses a testament to "the power of mud") and the miserable conditions because they thought the objectionable portraits would suit their audience. Assessed today, the writers and their reflections continue to convey the overwhelmingly persistent attitudes, values, and ideas of a conquering group interpreting others. Except for a government official, Brantz Mayer, whose book indicted United States travelers by citing their prejudices against Mexicans, these writers mainly exhibited condescension and an implied, if not outspoken, sense of superiority.

This uniformity in outlook is not the only characteristic binding these works and suggesting their significance in conquest. Many of the writers patterned their books after previously published accounts, such as Zebulon Pike's narrative of his reconnaissance trips in the early nineteenth century. Imitating his organization and style, such writers as Gregg exaggerated La Tules's appearance, blamed her for the ruin of many "wayward youth," and imitated previous travelogues in other ways to portray and dismiss the wretched condition of the Spanish-Mexicans. Barcelo's smoking and gambling were but two of the most widely reported vices. George Brewerton, writing for *Harper's Magazine* in the 1850's, continued the tradition. To the growing list of those at fault, he added the duplicitous New Mexican priests, for stifling individuality and stunting well-being:

Here were the men, women, and children--the strong man, the mother, and the lisping child--all engaged in the most debasing of vices, gambling, the entire devotion to which is the besetting sin of the whole Mexican people...What better could you have expected from an ignorant, priest-ridden peasantry, when those whom they are taught to reverence and respect, and who should have been their prompters to better things, not only allow, but openly practice this and all other iniquities?

The popularity of gambling and drinking among all people prompted Brewerton and his predecessors to decry the pervasive debauchery--which, it seemed, only they, as Americans, could relieve. They failed to understand that Spanish-Mexicans loved celebration and socializing. The church organized parties, pageants, and social affairs on varied occasions; yet even officially sanctioned church holidays or the days when patron saints were honored did not escape Euro-American comments. Brewerton found "rude engravings" of saints everywhere, among rich and poor, which he said would be "decked out by the females of the family with all sorts of tawdry ornaments." He wondered about people who would use a doll to represent the Virgin Mary. Brewerton failed, his rigid anti-Catholic viewpoint, to understand the beauty and intricacy of the *bultos* and *retablos* (icons and altarpieces). Catholicism, in Brewerton's opinion, did nothing but give Spanish-Mexicans occasion to revel in superstition, or to drink and dance. A community's way of celebrating--even the pious processions when the Virgin and the saints were paraded through town for all to worship in the annual outpouring of public devotion--was lost on Protestants: During this whole time the city exhibited a scene of universal carousing and revelry. All classes abandoned themselves to the most reckless dissipation and profligacy... I never saw a people so infatuated with the passion for gaming. Whether commemorating saints or gathering for entertainment and diversion, Spanish-Mexicans appeared lascivious.

To the Protestant mind, nothing short of the complete elimination of gambling would lift New Mexicans out of their servility and make them worthy of United States citizenship. The Jacksonian Americans wanted to replace gambling with industry and enterprise. To them, gambling stemmed from a fundamental lack of faith in the individual, and it was risky besides. Travelers called monte a game of chance; they said that it required no particular skills and brought undeserved wealth. By that logic, La Tules, a dealer par excellence, was not an entrepreneur; her wealth was undeserved because it sprang from "unbridled passions." Her gravest sin against Protestant ethics became not the unskilled nature of her trade or her undeserved success, but her lack of restraint: her wealth was uncontrolled. Yet initial misgivings about Barcelo and the games passed after many entertaining evenings at the gambling house. Once soldiers and others began going there, they lingered, and returned often. Deep-seated anti-Mexican feelings and moralistic judgments gave way to the profits that awaited them if they won at monte, or the pleasures to be savored each evening in Santa Fe even if they lost.

At the numerous tables that lined Barcelo's establishment, men who could not speak Spanish and people who did not understand English learned a new language. Card games required the deciphering of gestures and facial expressions but did not depend on any verbal communication. Soldiers and travelers new to Santa Fe understood easily enough what was important at the gaming table. Over cards, the men and women exchanged gold or currency in a ritual that emblazoned their meetings with new intentions. Drinking, cursing, and smoking, the soldiers and others unloaded their money at the table; if Barcelo profited, they lost. But the game was such a diversion for the lonely soldiers that they hardly seemed to mind. The stakes grew larger at every turn, and many dropped away from the table to stand at the bar. Barcelo's saloon took care of those who did not gamble as well as those who lost. Sometimes a group of musicians arrived and began playing. Sometimes women--who, if not gambling, had been observing the scene--cleared a space in the long room, and dancing began.

Barcelo did more than accommodate men by inviting them to gamble. She furthered their adjustment to Santa Fe by bringing them into a setting that required their presence and money. At the saloon, the men were introduced to Spanish-Mexican music, habits, and humor. They could judge the locals firsthand, and could observe a community's values and habits through this single activity. After they had a few drinks, their initial fears and prejudices gradually yielded to the relaxed, sociable atmosphere of the gambling hall.

In the spring of 1847, Lieutenant Alexander Dyer first visited the saloon. By June, his journal listed attendance at no fewer than forty fandangos and described numerous visits to La Tules's saloon. Frequently, cryptic citations indicated his rush to abandon the journal for the card games: "at the Me. House tonight" meant a visit to the monte house, and it appeared dozens of times in any given month. Dyer's "Mexican War Journal" leaves the distinct impression that a soldier's life, for those of his stripe, involved a constant round of entertainment; visits and parties at Barcelo's hall were part of an officer's busy social life.

Thus, rhetoric about gambling or cavorting lessened with tine. If visitors did not entirely accept the sociable atmosphere, they were sufficiently lonely for Euro-American women and companionship to go to Barcelo's saloon and attend other events to which they were invited. When Kearny and his officers went to Mass on their first Sunday in town, they endeared themselves to Spanish-Mexicans. Some soldiers at the fort, like Dyer, had little choice but to adapt, because they were assigned to Santa Fe for two years. Other newcomers, however, were shocked into submission.

Finding much to upset them, visitors were nevertheless impressed by the scenic grandeur of Santa Fe and the environs. James Ohio Pattie remained as awed by Taos Mountain, stretching fifteen thousand feet high, as he was intrigued by the native life below it. He puzzled over differences: "I had expected to find no difference between these people and our own, but their language. I was never so mistaken. The men and women were not clothed in our fashion."

Nine days later, Pattie reached Santa Fe, and this time his tone grew prosaic:

The town contains between four and five thousand inhabitants. It is situated on a large plain. A handsome stream runs through it, adding life and beauty to a scene striking and agreeable from the union of amenity and cultivation around, with the distant view of snow clad mountains. It is pleasant to walk on the flat roofs of the houses in the evening, and look on the town and plain spread below.

In a few weeks, Pattie had reached Chihuahua City, traveling the considerable distance in a short time. He described it as the "largest and handsomest town I had ever seen." The trek across treacherous deserts, the long unbroken plain, and probably the fact that Spanish-Mexicans were much friendlier to him than Indians (whom he feared and loathed) changed Pattie's original reservations.

But travel records contain an underlying difficulty: they tend to freeze their author's thoughts in time, and do not reveal the extent of the adaptations or changes a writer might have experienced. Many travelers evidently did not find anything to admire or enjoy in Santa Fe, but some did. Although locked into a particular time and a special setting, the men, after consistent reflection and observation, relaxed their worst fears. Pattie's descriptions might not have been atypical in that regard.

Court cases offer other impressions of how sojourning Euro-Americans changed their organizing concepts and values. The evidence is especially suggestive for those who began making a transition to becoming settlers. In the 1820's, Julian Green was fined for gambling at monte; on the same day, the judge assessed a fine against Barcelo. In 1850, the census lists Green, with a woman named Maria, in a household containing six children; all have Spanish first names. Another *vecino*, Marcelo Pacheco, sued William Messervy for slander in the 1840's, calling the merchant "a trespasser who thinks he owns everything." He won his case, and Messervy had to pay a fine. Perhaps Green and Messervy were perplexed about Santa Fe's ways, as many migrants had been, but because they paid their fines and stayed in Santa Fe, they changed.

Investigations in these records delineate the onset of the newcomers' accommodation. Barcelo was not the only one practicing accommodation; it worked in two directions. Whether obeying the community's laws or breaking them, new men were adjusting to life away from home. Santa Fe modified the settling Euro-Americans, at times even the sojourning ones, and Barcelo had begun to socialize them in the traditions of an older settlement. The people of the Dancing Ground continued their practice of accepting newcomers, particularly those who seemed able to tolerate, if not embrace, the community's religious and secular values.

At the same time, the conquering soldiers were armed, as the merchants Gregg and Webb were, with purpose and commitment. Military men brought plans and realized them: a fort above the town was begun the day after Kearny marched into Santa Fe. Soldiers built a two-story-high flagstaff, and the imposing structure on the plaza attracted visitors from the Dancing Ground, who supposedly came to admire it, but probably also were there to assess the military's strength. What better symbol than a new garrison and an obtrusive monument rising high for all the people to notice? Soldiers hailed these crowning achievements as signs of blessings from God to a nation destined to control the hemisphere, but locals were not so pleased.

A new wave of resistance derailed Barcelo's efforts to help resettle Euro-Americans in Santa Fe. Nevertheless, even after her death in 1852, Barcelo's legend continued to indicate that her role extended beyond the immediate helping hand she had lent Euro-Americans. No documents written by her, except a will, have survived to tell whether she even recognized her accomplishment, or if she read much into the assistance she had given the American cause. Her wealth would suggest that she might have harbored an understanding of her influential status in the process of colonization. One fact remains, whether she realized it or not: beginning with her, the accommodation of Euro-Americans proceeded on several levels. Barcelo had inaugurated the first, at the gambling hall, and she set the stage as well for the second, when women began marrying the newcomers.

But as one retraces the original surrounding tensions--deriving from the steady and continuing presence of traders, merchants, and soldiers--and juxtaposes them against Barcelo's achievement as an architect of a plan that reconciled the Euro-American to Santa Fe, the realities of displacement and encroachment must not be forgotten. Lieutenant Dyer reported problems as he observed them, and he commented a year after his arrival in Santa Fe: "Still it began to be apparent that the people generally were dissatisfied with the change." In January 1847, resisters in Taos caught and scalped Governor Charles Bent, leaving him to die. In the spring, a lieutenant who had been pursuing horse thieves was murdered, and forty-three Spanish-Mexicans were brought to Santa Fe to stand trial for the crime. In October of the same year, some months after several revolts had been suppressed and their instigators hanged, Dyer reported "a large meeting of citizens at the Palace," where speakers expressed disaffection at the course of the commissioned officers.

Local dissatisfaction and political troubles had not subsided, in spite of Barcelo's work. In the late 1840's, Navajos and Apaches stepped up their raids, and reports filtered in of surrounding mayhem. The garrisoned soldiers grew impatient and acted rashly, and Dyer reported that "a Mexican was unfortunately shot last night by the sentinel at my store house. Tonight we have a rumor that the Mexicans are to rise and attack us." The government in Santa Fe was being forced again to come to terms with each new case of racial and cultural conflict, because it was still charged with trying murders and treason, and it had now become the seat for initiating solutions. Problems no longer brewed outside; they had been brought home by accommodated Euro-Americans.

But Barcelo should not be blamed here, as she has been by some, for so many problems. She symbolized the transformations plaguing her people. She symbolized as well how an older community had handled the arrival of men from a new, young nation still seeking to tap markets and find a route to the Pacific. Moreover, she exemplified contact and conflict between independent female Catholics and westering male Protestants. The political and social constraints within which she existed had not disappeared as a community contemplated what to do with the strangers among them.

The people of Santa Fe did not kill any newcomers as residents of Taos had. Surrounding the Dancing Ground, stories and legends of other people resisting Americanization were about to begin, and these no longer emphasized accommodation. Barcelo was unusual in that way as well. She was of a particular time and a special place. The famed resister to American encroachment, Padre Antonio Jose Martinez of Taos, opposed (in his separatist plans and principles) all that Barcelo had exemplified. A legend developed around him that stands in interesting contrast to La Tules's.

Yet, in New Mexico and throughout the West, resistance was giving way to Euro-American encroachment. Richard Henry Dana, traveling in California during the 1830's, mourned the seemingly wasted opportunity presented by land still in the possession of Spanish-Mexicans: "In the hands of an enterprising people, what a country this might be!" His fellow sojourners to New Mexico concurred. What Dana and the other Euro-Americans failed to see was that the land and its communities were already in the hands of such enterprising persons as Barcelo. But rather than acknowledge the truth, they disparaged her; their conquerors' minds could not comprehend her intellect, enterprise, and success. Barcelo, they believed, had erred. Yet in giving herself to the conquest, but not the conquerors, she survived and succeeded. She drew betting clients to her saloon; they played but lost, she gambled and won. In the end, the saloon that attracted conquerors released men who had been conquered.

Questions

1. Describe the physical appearance of "La Tules" and how her appearance encouraged speculation about her morals.

2. Discuss the skills that La Tules had which allowed her to be financially independent in Sante Fe, New Mexico.

3. Speculate about the effect that travel writers descriptions about the Southwest had on European American ethnocentrism.

A PROMISE FULFILLED:
MEXICAN CANNERY WORKERS
IN SOUTHERN CALIFORNIA

Vicki L. Ruiz

Since 1930 approximately one-quarter of all Mexican women wage earners in the Southwest have found employment as blue collar industrial workers (25.3% (1930), 25.6% (1980)).These women have been overwhelmingly segregated into semi-skilled, assembly line positions. Garment and food processing firms historically have hired Mexicanas for seasonal line tasks. Whether sewing slacks or canning peaches, these workers have generally been separated from the year-round, higher paid male employees. This ghettoization by job and gender has in many instances facilitated labor activism among Mexican women. An examination of a rank and file union within a Los Angeles cannery from 1939 to 1945 illuminates the transformation of women's networks into channels for change.

On August 31, 1939, during a record-breaking heat wave, nearly all of the four hundred and thirty workers at the California Sanitary Canning Company (popularly known as Cal San), one of the largest food processing plants in Los Angeles, staged a massive walk-out and established a twenty-four hour picket line in front of the plant. The primary goals of these employees, mostly Mexican women, concerned not only higher wages and better working conditions, but also recognition of their union--The United Cannery, Agricultural, Packing and Allied Workers of America, Local 75--and a closed shop.

The Cal San strike marked the beginning of labor activism by Mexicana cannery and racking workers in Los Angeles. This essay steps beyond a straight narrative, chronicling the rise and fall of UCAPAWA locals in California. It provides a glimpse of cannery life--the formal, as well as the. informal, social structures governing the shop floor. An awareness of the varying lifestyles and attitudes of women food processing workers will be developed in these pages. No single model representing either the typical female or typical Mexicana industrial worker exists. Contrary to the stereotype of the Hispanic woman tied to the kitchen, most Mexican women, at some point in their lives, have been wage laborers. Since 1880, food processing has meant employment for Spanish-speaking women living in California, attracted to the industry because of seasonal schedules and extended family networks within the plants.

During the 1930's, the canning labor force included young daughters, newly-married women, middle-aged wives, and widows. Occasionally, three generations worked at a particular cannery--daughter, mother, and grandmother. These Mexicanas entered the job market as members of a family wage economy. They pooled their resources to put food on the table. "My father was a busboy," one former Cal San employee recalled, "and to keep the family going ... in order to bring in a little more money...my mother, my grandmother, my mother's brother, my sister and I all worked together at Cal San."

Some Mexicanas, who had worked initially out of economic necessity, stayed in the canneries in order to buy the "extras"--a radio, a phonograph, jazz records, fashionable clothes. These consumers often had middle-class aspirations, and at times, entire families labored to achieve material advancement (and in some cases, assimilation), while in others, only the wives or daughters expressed interest in acquiring an American lifestyle. One woman defied her husband by working outside the home. Justifying her action, she asserted that she wanted to move to a "better" neighborhood because she didn't want her children growing up with "Italians and Mexicans."

Some teenagers had no specific, goal-oriented rationale for laboring in the food processing industry. They simply "drifted" into cannery life; they wanted to join their friends at work or were bored at home. Like the first women factory workers in the United States, the New England mill hands of the 1830's, Mexican women entered the labor force for every conceivable reason and for no reason at all. Work added variety and opened new avenues of choices.

In one sense, cannery labor for the unmarried daughter represented a break from the traditional family. While most young Mexicanas maintained their cultural identity, many yearned for more independence, particularly after noticing the more liberal lifestyles of self-supporting Anglo co-workers. Sometimes young Mexican women would meet at work, become friends, and decide to room together. Although their families lived in the Los Angeles area and disapproved of their daughters living away from home, these women defied parental authority by renting an apartment.

Kin networks, however, remained an integral part of cannery life. These extended family structures fostered the development of a "cannery culture." A collective identity among food processing workers emerged as a result of family ties, job segregation by gender, and working conditions. Although women comprised seventy-five percent of the labor force in California canneries and packing houses, they were clustered into specific departments--washing, grading, cutting, canning, and packing--and their earnings varied with production levels. They engaged in piece work while male employees conversely, as warehousemen and cooks, received hourly wages.

Mexicana family and work networks resembled those found by historian Thomas Dublin in the Lowell, Massachusetts, mills in the ante-bellum era. California canneries and New England cotton mills, though a century apart, contained similar intricate kin and friendship networks. Dublin's statement that women "recruited one another ... secured jobs for each other, and helped newcomers make the numerous adjustments called for in a very new and different setting" can be applied directly to the Mexican experience. Mexican women, too, not only assisted their relatives and friends in obtaining employment but also initiated neophytes into the rigor of cannery routines. For instance, in the sorting department of the California Sanitary Canning Company, seasoned workers taught new arrivals the techniques of grading peaches. "Fancies" went into one bin; those considered "choice" into another; those destined for fruit cocktail into a third box; and finally the tots had to be discarded. Since peach fuzz irritated bare skin, women shared their cold cream with the initiates, encouraging them to coat their hands and arms in order to relieve the itching and to protect their skin from further inflammation. Thus, as Dublin notes for the Lowell mills, one can find "clear evidence of the maintenance of traditional kinds of social relationships in a new setting and serving new purposes."

Standing in the same spot week after week, month after month, women workers often developed friendships crossing family and ethnic lines. While Mexicanas constituted tile largest number of workers, many Russian Jewish women also found employment in southern California food processing firms. Their day-to-day problems (slippery floors, peach fuzz, production speeds-ups, arbitrary supervisors, and even sexual harassment) cemented feelings of solidarity among these women, as well as nurturing an "us against them" mentality in relation to management. They also shared common concerns, such as seniority status, quotas, wages, and child care.

Child care was a key issue for married women who at times organized themselves to Secure suitable babysitting arrangements. In one cannery, the workers established an off-plant nursery, hired and paid an elderly Woman who found it "darn hard--- taking care of 25 to 30 little ones." During World War II, some Orange County cannery workers, stranded without any day care alternatives, resorted to locking their small children in their cars. These particular workers, as UCAPAWA members, fought for and won management-financed day care on the firm's premises, which lasted for the duration or World War II. Cooperation among women food processing workers was an expression of their collective identity within the plants.

At Cal San many Mexican and Jewish workers shared another bond--neighborhood. Both groups lived in Boyle Heights, an East Los Angeles working-class community. Although Mexican and Jewish women lived on different blocks, they congregated at street car stops during the early morning hours. Sometimes friendships developed across ethnic lines. These women, if not friends, were at least passing acquaintances. Later, as UCAPAWA members, they would become mutual allies.

Cannery workers employed a special jargon when conversing among themselves. Speaking in terms of when an event took place by referring to the fruit or vegetable being processed, workers knew immediately when the incident occurred, for different crops arrived on the premises during particular months. For instance, the phrase "We met in spinach, fell in love in peaches, and married in tomatoes" indicates that the couple met in March, fell in love in August, and married in October.

Historians Leslie Tentler and Susan Porter Benson, studying women workers on the east coast, have also documented the existence of female work cultures. However, unlike the women Tentler studied, Spanish-speaking cannery workers were not waiting for Prince Charming to marry them and take them away from factory labor. Mexican women realized that they probably would continue their seasonal labor after marriage. Also in contrast, Benson, delineating cooperative work patterns among department store clerks from 1890 to 1940, asserted that women experienced peer sanctions if they exceeded their "stint" or standard sales quota. Mexican cannery workers differed from eastern clerks in that they did not receive a set salary, but were paid according to their production level. Collaboration and unity among piece rate employees attested to the strength of the cannery culture. Although increasing managerial control at one level, gender-determined job segmentation did facilitate the development of a collective identity among women in varying occupations and of diverse ethnic backgrounds.

Of these work related networks, the cannery culture appeared unique in that it also included men, Comprising twenty-five percent of the labor force, men also felt a sense of identity as food processing workers. Familial and ethnic bonds served to integrate male employees into the cannery culture. Mexicans, particularly, were often related to women workers by birth or marriage. In fact, it was not unusual for young people to meet their future spouses inside the plants. Cannery romances and courtships provided fertile *chisme* which traveled from one kin or peer network to the next.

The cannery culture was a curious blend of Mexican extended families and a general women's work culture, nurtured by assembly line segregation and common interests. Networks within the plants cut across generation, gender, and ethnicity. A detailed examination of the California Sanitary Canning Company further illuminates the unique collective identity among food processing workers. Cal San, a one plant operation, handled a variety of crops--apricots and peaches in the summer, tomatoes and pimentoes in the fall, spinach in the winter and early spring. This diversity enabled the facility, which employed approximately four hundred people, to remain open at least seven months a year.

Female workers received relatively little for their labors due to the seasonal nature of their work and the piece rate scale. In the Cal San warehouse and kitchen departments, exclusively male areas, workers received an hourly wage ranging from fifty-eight to seventy cents an hour. On the other hand, in the washing, grading, cutting and canning divisions, exclusively female areas. employees earned according to their production level. In order to make a respectable wage, a woman had to secure a favorable position on the line, a spot near the chutes or gates where the produce first entered the department. Carmen Bernal Escobar, a former Cal San employee, recalled:

> There were two long tables with sinks that you find in old-fashioned houses and fruit would come down out of the chutes and we would wash them and put them out on a belt. I had the first place so I could work for as long as I wanted. Women in the middle hoarded fruit because the work wouldn't last forever and the women at the end really suffered. Sometimes they would stand there for hours before any fruit would come down for them to wash. They just got the leftovers. Those at the end of the line hardly made nothing.

Although an efficient employee positioned in a favorable spot on the line could earn as much as one dollar an hour, most women workers averaged thirty to thirty-five cents. Their male counterparts, however, earned from $5.25 to $6.25 per day.

Though wages were low, there was no dearth of owner paternalism. Cal San's owners, George and Joseph Shapiro, took personal interest in the firm's operations. Both brothers made daily tours of each department, inspecting machinery, opening cans, and chatting with personnel. Sometimes a favored employee--especially if young, female, and attractive--would receive a pat on the cheek or a friendly hug; or as one informant stated, "a good pinch on the butt."

While the Shapiros kept close watch on the activities within the cannery, the foremen and floor ladies exercised a great deal of autonomous authority over workers. They assigned them positions on the line, punched their time cards arid even determined where they could buy lunch. Of course, these supervisors could fire an employee at their discretion. One floor lady earned the unflattering sobriquet "San Quentin." Some workers, in order to make a livable wage, cultivated the friendship of their supervisors. One favored employee even had the luxury of taking an afternoon nap. Forepersons also hosted wedding and baby showers for "their girls." While the "pets" enjoyed preferential treatment, they also acquired the animosity of their co-workers.

The supervisors (all Anglo) neither spoke nor understood Spanish. The language barrier contributed to increasing tensions inside the plant, especially when management had the authority to discharge an employee for speaking Spanish. Foremen also took advantage of the situation by altering productions cards of workers who spoke only Spanish. One foreman, for example, was noted for routinely cheating his Mexicana mother-in-law out of her hard-earned wages. Some women sensed something was wrong but either could not express their suspicions or were afraid to do so. Bilingual employees, cognizant of management's indiscretions, were threatened with dismissal. In general, low wages, tyrannical forepersons, and the "pet" system prompted attempts at unionization. In 1937 a group of workers tried to establish an American Federation of Labor union but a stable local failed to develop. Two years later Cal San employees renewed their trade union efforts, this time under the banner of UCAPAWA-CIO.

The United Cannery, Agricultural, Packing and Allied Workers of America has long been an orphan of twentieth-century labor history even though it was the seventh largest do affiliate in its day. Probable reasons for this neglect include the union's relatively short life--1937-1950--and its eventual expulsion from the CIO on the grounds of alleged communist domination. UCAPAWA's leadership was left-oriented, although not directly connected to the Communist Party. Many of the executive officers and organizers identified themselves as Marxists, but others could be labeled New Deal liberals. As one UCAPAWA national vice-president, Luisa Moreno, stated, "UCAPAWA was a left union not a communist union." Union leaders shared a vision of a national, decentralized labor union, one in which power flowed from below. Local members controlled their own meetings and elected their own officers and business agents. National and state offices helped coordinate the individual needs and endeavors of each local.

Moreover, UCAPAWA's deliberate recruitment of Black, Mexican, and female labor organizers and subsequent unionizing campaigns aimed at minority workers reflected its leaders' commitment to those sectors of the working-class generally ignored by traditional craft unions.

This do affiliate, in its policies and practices, closely resembled the nineteenth-century Knights of Labor. Like the Knights, UCAPAWA leaders publicly boasted that their organization welcomed all persons regardless of race, nationality, creed, or gender. Both groups fostered grass roots participation as well as local leadership. Perhaps it was no coincidence that the official UCAPAWA motto "An Injury To One Is An Injury To All" paraphrased the Knights' "An Injury To One Is The Concern Of All."

In California UCAPAWA initially concentrated on organizing agricultural workers, but with limited success. The union, however, began to make inroads among food processing workers in the Northeast and in Texas. Because of its successes in organizing canneries and packing houses, as well as the inability of maintaining viable dues-paying unions among farm workers, union policy shifted. After 1939, union leaders emphasized the establishment of strong, solvent cannery and packing house locals, hoping to use them as bases of operations for future farm labor campaigns. One of the first plants to experience this new wave of activity was the California Sanitary Canning Company.

In July 1939, Dorothy Ray Healey, a national vice-president of UCAPAWA, began to recruit Cal San workers. Healey, a vivacious young woman of twenty-four, already had eight years of labor organizing experience, At the age of sixteen, she participated in the San Jose, California, cannery strike as a representative of the Cannery and Agricultural Workers Industrial Union (C&AWIU). Healey had assumed leadership positions in both the C&AWIU and the Young Communist League.

Dorothy Healey's primary task involved organizing as many employees as possible. She distributed leaflets and membership cards outside the cannery gates. Healey talked with workers before and after work, and visited their homes. She also encouraged new recruits who proselytized inside the plants during lunch time. As former Cal San employee Julia Luna Mount remembered, "Enthusiastic people like myself would take the literature and bring it into the plant. We would hand it to everybody, explain it, and encourage everybody to pay attention." Workers organizing other workers was a common trade union strategy, and within three weeks four hundred (out of 430) employees had joined UCAPAWA. This phenomenal membership drive indicates not only worker receptiveness and Healey's prowess as an activist but also the existence of a cannery culture. Membership cards traveled from one kin or peer network to the next. Meetings were held in workers' homes so that entire families could listen to Healey and her recruits.

The Shapiros refused to recognize the union or negotiate with its representatives. On August 31, 1939, at the height of the peach season, the vast majority of Cal San employees lent their stations and staged a dramatic walk-out. Only thirty workers stayed behind and sixteen of these stragglers joined the picket lines outside the plant the next day. Although the strike occurred at the peak of the company's most profitable season and elicited the support of most line personnel, management refused to bargain with the local. In fact, the owners issued press statements to the effect that the union did not represent a majority of the workers.

In anticipation of a protracted strike, Healey immediately organized workers into a number of committees. A negotiating committee, picket details, and food committees were formed. The strikers' demands included union recognition, a closed shop, elimination of the piece rate system, minimal wage increases, and the dismissal of nearly every supervisor. Healey persuaded the workers to assign top priority to the closed shop demand. The striking employees realized the risk they were taking, for only one UCAPAWA local had secured a closed shop contract.

The food committee persuaded East Los Angeles grocers to donate various staples such as flour, sugar, and baby food to the Cal San strikers. Many business people obviously considered their donations to be advertisements and gestures of goodwill toward their customers. Some undoubtedly acted out of a political consciousness since earlier in the year East Los Angeles merchants had financed El Congreso Dc Pueblos Que Hahian Espanol, the first national civil rights assembly among Latinos in the United States. Whatever the roots of its success, the food committee sparked new strategies among the rank and file.

Early in the strike, the unionists extended their activities beyond their twenty-four hour, seven days a week picket line outside the plant. They discovered a supplementary tactic--the secondary boycott. Encouraged by their success in obtaining food donations from local markets, workers took the initiative themselves and formed boycott teams. The team leaders approached the managers of various retail and wholesale groceries in the Los Angeles area urging them to refuse Cal San products and to remove current stocks from their shelves. If a manager was unsympathetic, a small band of women picketed the establishment during business hours. In addition, the International Brotherhood of Teamsters officially vowed to honor the strike. It proved to be only a verbal commitment, for many of its members crossed the picket lines in order to pick up and deliver Cal San goods. At one point Mexicana unions members became so incensed by the sight of several Teamsters unloading their trucks that they climbed onto the loading platform and quickly "depantsed" a group of surprised and embarrassed Teamsters. The secondary boycott was an effective tactic--forty retail and wholesale grocers abided by the strikers' request.

Action by National Labor Relations Board further raised the morale of the striking employees. The NLRB formally reprimanded the Shapiros for refusing to bargain with the UCAPAWA affiliate. However, the timing of the strike, the successful boycott, and favorable governmental decisions failed to bring management to the bargaining table. After a two and a half month stalemate, the workers initiated an innovative technique that became, as Healey recalled, "the straw that broke the Shapiros' back."

Both George and Joseph Shapiro lived in affluent sections of Los Angeles, and their wealthy neighbors were as surprised as the brothers to discover one morning a small group of children conducting orderly picket lines on the Shapiros' front lawns. These malnourished waifs carried signs with such slogans as "Shapiro is starving my Mama" and "I'm underfed because my Mama is underpaid." Many of the neighbors became so moved by the sight of these children conducting what became a twenty-four hour vigil that they offered their support usually by distributing food and beverages. And if this was not enough, the owners were reproached by several members of their synagogue. After several days of community pressures, the Shapiros finally agreed to meet with Local 75's negotiating team. The strike had ended.

A settlement was quickly reached. Although the workers failed to win the elimination of the piece rate system, they did receive a five cent wage increase, and many forepersons found themselves unemployed. More importantly, Local 75 had become the second UCAPAWA affiliate (and the first on the west coast) to negotiate successfully a closed shop contract.

The consolidation of the union became the most important task facing Cal San employees. At post-strike meetings, Dorothy Healey outlined election procedures and general operating by-laws. Male and female workers who had assumed leadership positions during the confrontation captured every major post. For example, Carmen Bernal Escobar, head of the secondary boycott committee, became "head shop steward of the women." Soon UCAPAWA organizers Luke Hinman and Ted Rasmussen replaced Dorothy Healey at Cal San. These two men, however, concentrated their organizing energies on a nearby walnut packing plant and, thus, devoted little time to Cal San workers. In late 1940, Luisa Moreno, an UCAPAWA representative, took charge of consolidating Local 75. Like Dorothy Henley, Moreno had a long history of labor activism prior to her tenure with UCAPAWA. As a professional organizer for the AF of L and later for the CIO, Moreno had unionized workers in cigar making plants in Florida and Pennsylvania.

Luisa Moreno helped insure the vitality of Local 75. She vigorously enforced government regulations and contract stipulations. She also encouraged members to air any grievances immediately. On a number of occasions, her fluency in Spanish and English allayed misunderstandings between Mexicana workers and Anglo supervisors. Participation in civic events, such as the annual Labor Day parade, fostered worker solidarity and anion pride. The employees also banded together to break certain hiring policies. With one very light-skinned exception, the brothers had refused to hire Blacks. With union pressure, however, in early 1942, the Shapiros relented and hired approximately thirty Blacks. By mid-1941, Local 75 had developed into a strong, united democratic trade union and its members soon embarked on a campaign to organize their counterparts in nearby packing plants.

In 1941, Luisa Moreno, recently elected-president of UCAPAWA, was placed in charge of organizing other food processing plants in southern California. She enlisted the aid of Cal San workers in consolidating Local 92 at the California Walnut Growers' Association plant, and Elmo Parra, president of Local 75, headed the Organizing Committee. Cal San workers also participated in the initial union drive at nearby Royal Packing, a plant which processed Ortega Chile products. Since ninety-five percent of Royal Packing employees were Mexican, the Spanish-speaking members of Local 75 played a crucial role in the UCAPAWA effort. They also organized workers at the Glaser Nut Company and Mission Pack. The result of this spate of union activism was the formation of Local 3. By 1942, this local had become the second largest UCAPAWA union.

Mexican women played instrumental roles in the operation of Local 3. In 1943, for example, they filled eight of the fifteen elected positions of the local. They served as major officers and as executive board members Local 3 effectively enforced contract stipulations and protective legislation, and its members proved able negotiators during annual contract renewals. In July, 1942, for example, *UCAPAWA News* proclaimed the newly-signed Cal San contract to be "the best in the state." Also, in 1943, workers at the Walnut plant successfully negotiated an incentive plan provision in their contract. The local also provided benefits that few industrial unions could match--free legal advice and a hospitalization plan.

Union members also played active roles in the war effort. At Cal San, a joint labor-management production committee worked to devise more efficient processing methods. As part of the "Food For Victory" campaign, Cal San employees increased their production or spinach to unprecedented levels. In 1942 and 1943, workers at the California Walnut plant donated one day's wages to the American Red Cross. Local 3 also sponsored a successful blood drive. Throughout this period, worker solidarity remained strong. When Cal San closed its doors in 1945, the union arranged jobs for the former employees at the California Walnut plant.

The success of UCAPAWA at the California Sanitary Canning Company can be explained by a number of factors. Prevailing work conditions heightened the union's attractiveness. Elements outside the plant also prompted receptivity among employees. These workers were undoubtedly influenced by the wave of do organizing drives being conducted in the Los Angeles area. One woman, for example, joined Local 75 primarily because her husband was a member of the CIO Furniture Workers Union. Along with the Wagner Act, passage of favorable legislation, such as the Fair Labor Standards Act, the Public Contracts Act, and the California minimum wage laws (which set wage and hour levels for cannery personnel), led to the rise of a strong UCAPAWA affiliate. Workers decided that the only way they could benefit from recent protective legislation was to form a union with enough clout to force management to honor these regulations.

World War II also contributed to the development of potent UCAPAWA food processing locals, not only in southern California, but nationwide. To feed U.S. troops at home and abroad, as well as the military and civilian population of America's allies, the federal government issued thousands of contracts to canneries and packing houses. Because of this increased demand for canned goods and related products, management required a plentiful supply of content, hard-working employees. Meanwhile the higher-paying defense industries began to compete for the labor of food processing personnel. Accordingly, canners and packers became more amenable to worker demands than at any other time in the history of food processing. Thus, during the early 1940s, cannery workers, usually at the bottom end of the socio-economic scale, had become "labor aristocrats" due to wartime exigencies.

They were in an atypical position to gain important concessions from their employers in terms of higher wages, better conditions, and greater benefits. As UCAPAWA members, women food processing workers utilized their temporary status to achieve an improved standard of living.

Of course, the dedication and organizing skills of UCAPAWA professionals Dorothy Ray Healey and Luisa Moreno must not be minimized. While Healey played a critical role in the local's initial successes, it was under Moreno's leadership that workers consolidated these gains and branched out to help organize employees in neighboring food processing facilities. The recruitment of minority workers by Healey and Moreno and their stress on local leadership reflect the feasibility and vitality of a democratic trade unionism.

Finally, the most significant ingredient accounting for Local 75's success was the phenomenal degree of worker involvement in the building and nurturing of the union. Deriving strength from their networks within the plant, Cal San workers built an effective local. The cannery culture had, in effect, become translated into unionization. Furthermore, UCAPAWA locals provided women cannery workers with the crucial "social space" necessary to assert their independence and display their talents. They were not rote employees numbed by repetition, but women with dreams, goals, tenacity, and intellect. Unionization became an opportunity to demonstrate their shrewdness and dedication to a common cause. Mexicanas not only followed the organizers' leads but also developed strategies of their own. A fierce loyalty developed as the result of rank and file participation and leadership. Forty years after the strike, Carmen Bernal Escobar emphatically declared, "UCAFAWA was the greatest thing that ever happened to the workers at Cal San. It changed everything and everybody."

This pattern of labor activism is not unique. Laurie Coyle, Gail Hershatter, and Emily Honig in their study of the Farah Strike documented the close bonds that developed among Mexican women garment workers in El Paso, Texas. Anthropologist Patricia Zavella has also explored similar networks among female electronics workers in Albuquerque, New Mexico, and food processing workers in San Jose. But while kin and friendship networks remain part of cannery life, UCAPAWA did not last beyond 1950. After World War II, red-baiting, the disintegration of the national union, Teamster sweetheart contracts and an indifferent NLRB spelled the defeat of democratic trade unionism among Mexican food processing workers. Those employees who refused to join the Teamsters were fired and blacklisted. The Immigration and Naturalization Service, moreover, deported several UCAPAWA activists, including Luisa Moreno. In the face of such concerted opposition, Local 3 could not survive. Yet, the UCAPAWA movement demonstrated that Mexican women, given sufficient opportunity and encouragement, could exercise control over their work lives, and their family ties and exchanges on the line became the channels for unionization.

The Development of Chicana Feminist Discourse, 1970-1980

Alma M.Garcia

Between 1970 and 1980, a Chicana feminist movement developed in the United States that addressed the specific issues that affected Chicanas as women of color. The growth of the Chicana feminist movement can be traced in the speeches, essays, letters, and articles published in Chicano and Chicana newspapers, journals, newsletters, and other printed materials.

During the sixties, American society witnessed the development of the Chicano movement, a social movement characterized by a politics of protest (Barrera 1974; Munoz 1974; Navarro 1974). The Chicano movement focused on a wide range of issues: social justice, equality, educational reforms, and political and economic self-determination for Chicano communities in the United States. Various struggles evolved within this movement: the United Farmworkers unionization efforts (Dunne 1967; Kushner 1975; Matthiesen 1969; Nelson 1966); the New Mexico Land Grant movement (Nabokov 1969); the Colorado-based Crusade for Justice (Castro 1974; Meier and Rivera 1972); the Chicano student movement (Garcia and de la Garza 1977); and the Raza Unida Party (Shockley 1974).

Chicanas participated actively in each of these struggles. By the end of the sixties, Chicanas began to assess the rewards and limits of their participation. The 1970's witnessed the development of Chicana feminists whose activities, organizations, and writings can be analyzed in terms of a feminist movement by women of color in American society. Chicana feminists outlined a cluster of ideas that crystallized into an emergent Chicana feminist debate. In the same way that Chicano males were reinterpreting the historical and contemporary experience of Chicanos in the United States, Chicanas began to investigate the forces shaping their own experiences as women of color.

The Chicana feminist movement emerged primarily as a result of the dynamics within the Chicano movement. In the 1960's and 1970's, the American political scene witnessed far-reaching social protest movements whose political courses often paralleled and at times exerted influence over each other (Freeman 1983; Piven and Cloward 1979). The development of feminist movements has been explained by the participation of women in larger social movements. Macias (1982), for example, links the early development of the Mexican feminist movement to the participation of women in the Mexican Revolution. Similarly, Freeman's (1984) analysis of the white feminist movement points out that many white feminists who were active in the early years of its development had previously been involved in the new left and civil rights movements. It was in these movements that white feminists experienced the constraints of male domination. Black feminists have similarly traced the development of a Black feminist movement during 1960's and 1970's to their experiences with sexism in the larger Black movement (Davis 1983; Dill 1983; Hooks, 1981,1984; Joseph and Lewis 1981; White 1984). In this way, then, the origins of Chicana feminism parallel those of other feminist movements.

Origins of Chicana Feminism

Rowbotham (1974) argues that women may develop a feminist consciousness as a result of their experiences with sexism in revolutionary struggles or mass social movements. To the extent that such movements are male dominated, women are likely to develop a feminist consciousness. Chicana feminists began the search for a "room of their own" by assessing their participation within the Chicano movement Their feminist consciousness emerged from a struggle for equality with Chicano men and from a reassessment of the role of the family as a means of resistance to oppressive societal conditions.

Historically, as well as during the 1960's and 1970's, the Chicano family represented a source of cultural and political resistance to the various types of discrimination experienced in American society (Zinn 1975a). At the cultural level, the Chicano movement emphasized the need to safeguard the value of family loyalty at the political level; the Chicano movement used the family as a strategic organizational tool for protest activities.

Dramatic changes in the structure of Chicano families occurred as they participated in the Chicano movement. Specifically, women began to question their traditional female roles (Zinn 1975a). Thus, a Chicana feminist movement originated from the nationalist Chicano struggle. Rowbotham (1974 p. 206) refers to such a feminist movement as "a colony within a colony." But as the Chicano movement developed during the 1970's, Chicana feminists began to draw their own political agenda and raised a series of questions to assess their role within the Chicano movement. They entered into a dialogue with each other that explicitly reflected their struggles to secure a room of their own within the Chicano movement.

Defining Feminism for Women of Color

A central question of feminist discourse is the definition of feminism. The lack of consensus reflects different political ideologies and divergent social-class bases. In the United States, Chicana feminists shared the task of defining their ideology and movement with white, Black, and Asian American feminists. Like Black and Asian American feminists, Chicana feminists struggled to gain social equality and end sexist and racist oppression. Like them, Chicana feminists recognized that the nature of social inequality for women of color was multidimensional (Cheng 1984; Chow 1987; Hooks 1981). Like Black and Asian American feminists, Chicana feminists struggled to gain equal status in the male-dominated nationalist movements and also in American society. To them, feminism represented a movement to end sexist oppression within a broader social protest movement. Again, like Black and Asian American feminists, Chicana feminists fought for social equality in the 1970's. They understood that their movement needed to go beyond women's rights and include the men of their group, who also faced racial subordination (Hooks 1981). Chicanas believed that feminism involved more than an analysis of gender because, as women of color, they were affected by both race and class in their everyday lives. Thus, Chicana feminism, as a social movement to improve the position of Chicanas in American society, represented a struggle that was both nationalist and feminist.

Chicana, Black, and Asian American feminists were all confronted with the issue of engaging in a feminist struggle to end sexist oppression within a broader nationalist struggle to end racist oppression. All experienced male domination in their own communities as well as in the large society. Ngan-Ling Chow (1987) identifies gender stereotypes of Asian American women and the patriarchal family structure as major sources of women's oppression. Cultural, political, and economic constraints have, according to Ngan-Ling Chow (1987), limited the full development of a feminist consciousness and movement among Asian American women. The cross-pressures resulting from the demands of a nationalist and a feminist struggle led some Asian American women to organize feminist organizations that, however, continued to address broader issues affecting the Asian American community.

Black women were also faced with addressing feminist issues within a nationalist movement. According to Thornton Dill (1983), Black women played a major historical role in Black resistance movements and, in addition, brought a feminist component to these movements (Davis 1983; Dill 1983). Black women have struggled with Black men in nationalist movements but have also recognized and fought against the sexism in such political movements in the Black community (Hooks 1984). Although they wrote and spoke as Black feminists, they did not organize separately from Black men.

Among the major ideological questions facing all three groups of feminists were the relationship between feminism and the ideology of cultural nationalism or racial pride, feminism and feminist-baiting within the larger movements, and the relationship between their feminist movements and the white feminist movement.

Chicana Feminism and Cultural Nationalism

Throughout the seventies and now, in the eighties, Chicana feminists have been forced to respond to the criticism that cultural nationalism and feminism are irreconcilable. In the first issue of the newspaper, *Hijas de Cuauhtemoc*, Anna Nieto Gomez (1971) stated that a major issue facing Chicanas active in the Chicano movement was the need to organize to improve their status as women within the larger social movement. Francisca Flores (1971b, p. i), another leading Chicana feminist, stated:

> [Chicanas] can no longer remain in a subservient role or as auxiliary forces in the [Chicano] movement. They must be included in the front line of communication, leadership and organizational responsibility... The issue of equality, freedom and self-determination of the Chicana--like the right of self-determination, equality, and liberation of the Mexican [Chicano] community--is not negotiable. Anyone opposing the right of women to organize into their own form of organization has no place in the leadership of the movement.

Supporting this position, Bernice Rincon (1971) argued that a Chicana feminist movement that sought equality and justice for Chicanas would strengthen the Chicano movement. Yet in the process, Chicana feminists challenged traditional gender roles because they limited their participation and acceptance within the Chicano movement.

Throughout the seventies, Chicana feminists viewed the struggle against sexism within the Chicano movement and the struggle against racism in the larger society as integral parts of Chicana feminism. As Nieto Gomez (1976, p. 10) said:

> Chicana feminism is in various stages of development. However, in general, Chicana Feminism
> is the recognition that women are oppressed as a group and are exploited as part of *La Raza*
> people. It is a direction to be responsible to identify and act upon the issues and needs of

Chicana women. Chicana feminists are involved in understanding the nature of women's oppression.

Cultural nationalism represented a major ideological component of the Chicano movement. It's emphasis on Chicano cultural pride and cultural survival within an Anglo-dominated society gave significant political direction to the Chicano movement. One source of ideological disagreement between Chicana feminism and this cultural nationalist ideology was cultural survival. Many Chicana feminists believed that a focus on cultural survival did not acknowledge the need to alter male-female relations within Chicano communities. For example, Chicana feminists criticized the notion of the "ideal Chicana" that glorified Chicanas as strong, long-suffering women who had endured and kept Chicano culture and the family intact. To Chicana feminists, this concept represented an obstacle to the redefinition of gender roles. Nieto (1975, p. 4) stated:

> Some Chicanas are praised as they emulate the sanctified example set by [the Virgin] Mary. The woman *par excellence* is mother and wife. She is to love and support her husband and to nurture and teach her children. Thus, may she gain fulfillment as a woman. For a Chicana bent upon fulfillment of her personhood, this restricted perspective of her role as a woman is not only inadequate but also crippling.

Chicana feminists were also skeptical about the cultural nationalist interpretation of machismo. Such an interpretation viewed machismo as an ideological tool used by the dominant Anglo society to justify the inequalities experienced by Chicanos. According to this interpretation, the relationship between Chicanos and the larger society was that of an internal colony dominated and exploited by the capitalist economy (Almaguer 1974; Barrera 1979). Machismo, like other cultural traits, was blamed by Anglos for blocking Chicanos from succeeding in American society. In reality, the economic structure and colony-like exploitation were to blame.

Some Chicana feminists agreed with this analysis of machismo, claiming that a mutually reinforcing relationship existed between internal colonialism and the development of the myth of machismo. According to Sosa Riddell (1974, p. 21), machismo was a myth "propagated by subjugators and colonizers, which created damaging stereotypes of Mexican/Chicano males." As a type of social control imposed by the dominant society on Chicanos, the myth of machismo distorted gender relations within Chicano communities, creating stereotypes of Chicanas as passive and docile women. At this level in the feminist discourse, machismo was seen as an Anglo myth that kept both Chicanos and Chicanas in a subordinate status. As Nieto (1975, p. 4) concluded:

> Although the term "machismo" is correctly denounced by all because it stereotypes the Latin man . . . it does a great disservice to both men and women. Chicano and Chicana alike must be free to seek their own individual fulfillment.

While some Chicana feminists criticized the myth of machismo used by the dominant society to legitimate racial inequality, others moved beyond this level of analysis to distinguish between the machismo that oppressed both men and women and the sexism in Chicano communities in general, and the Chicano movement in particular, that oppressed Chicana women (Chavez 1971; Cotera 1977; Del Castillo 1974; Marquez and Ramirez 1977; Riddell 1974; Zinn 1975b). According to Vidal (1971, p. 5), the origins of a Chicana feminist consciousness were prompted by the sexist attitudes and behavior of Chicano males, which constituted a "serious obstacle to women anxious to play a role in the struggle for Chicana liberation."

Furthermore, many Chicana feminists disagreed with the cultural nationalist view that machismo could be a positive value within a Chicano cultural value system. They challenged the view that machismo was a source of masculine pride for Chicanos and therefore a defense mechanism against the dominant society's racism. Although Chicana feminists recognized that Chicanos faced discrimination from the dominant society, they adamantly disagreed with those who believed that machismo was a form of cultural resistance to such discrimination. Chicana feminists called for changes in the ideologies responsible for distorting relations between women and men. One such change was to modify the cultural nationalist position that viewed machismo as a source of cultural pride.

Chicana feminists called for a focus on the universal aspects of sexism that shape gender relations in both Anglo and Chicano culture. While they acknowledge the economic exploitation of all Chicanos, Chicana feminists outlined the double exploitation experienced by Chicanas. Sosa Riddell (1974, p. 159) concluded. "It was when Chicanas began to seek work outside of the family groups that sexism became a key factor of oppression along with racism." Francisca Flores (1971a, p. 4) summarized some of the consequences of sexism:

> It is not surprising that more and more Chicanas are forced to go to work in order to supplement the family income. The children are farmed out to a relative to baby-sit with them, and since these women are employed in the lower income jobs, the extra pressures placed on them can become unbearable.

Thus, while the Chicano movement was addressing the issue of racial oppression facing all Chicanos, Chicana feminists argued that it lacked an analysis of sexism. Similarly, Black and Asian American women stressed the interconnectedness of race and gender oppression. Hooks (1984, p. 52) analyzes racism and sexism in terms of their "intersecting, complementary nature." She also emphasizes that one struggle should not take priority over the other. White (1984) criticizes Black men whose nationalism limited discussions of Black women's experiences with sexist oppression. The writings of other Black feminists criticized a Black cultural nationalist ideology that overlooked the consequences of sexist oppression (Beale, 1975; Cade 1970; Davis 1971; Joseph and Lewis 1981). Many Asian American women were also critical of the Asian American movement whose focus on racism ignored the impact of sexism on the daily lives of women. The participation of Asian American women in various community struggles increased their encounters with sexism (Chow 1987). As a result, some Asian American women developed a feminist consciousness and organized as women around feminist issues.

Chicana Feminism and Feminist-Baiting

The systematic analysis by Chicana feminists of the impact of racism and sexism on Chicanas in American society and, above all, within the Chicano movement was often misunderstood as a threat to the political unity of the Chicano movement. As Marta Cotera (1977, p. 9), a leading voice of Chicana feminism pointed out:

The aggregate cultural values we [Chicanas] share can also work to our benefit if we choose to scrutinize our cultural traditions, isolate the positive attributes and interpret them for the benefit of women. It's unreal that *Hispanas* have been browbeaten for so long about our so-called conservative (meaning reactionary) culture. It's also unreal that we have let men interpret culture only as those practices and attitudes that determine who does the dishes around the house. We as women also have the right to interpret and define the philosophical and religious traditions beneficial to us within our culture, and which we have inherited as our tradition. To do this, we must become both conversant with our history and philosophical evolution, and analytical about the institutional and behavioral manifestations of the same.

Such Chicana feminists were attacked for developing a "divisive ideology"--a feminist ideology that was frequently viewed as a threat to the Chicano movement as a whole. As Chicana feminists examined their roles as women activists within the Chicano movement, an ideological split developed. One group active in the Chicano movement saw themselves as "loyalists" who believed that the Chicano movement did not have to deal with sexual inequities since Chicano men as well as Chicana women experienced racial oppression. According to Nieto Gomez (1973, p. 35), who was not a loyalist, their view was that if men oppress women, it is not the men's fault but rather that of the system.

Even if such a problem existed, and they did not believe that it did, the loyalists maintained that such a matter would best be resolved internally within the Chicano movement. They denounced the formation of a separate Chicana feminist movement on the grounds that it was a politically dangerous strategy; perhaps Anglo inspired. Such a movement would undermine the unity of the Chicano movement by raising an issue that was not seen as a central one. Loyalists viewed racism as the most important issue within the Chicano movement. Nieto Gomez (1973, p. 35) quotes one such loyalist:

I am concerned with the direction that the Chicanas are taking in the movement. The words such as liberation, sexism, male chauvinism, etc., were prevalent. The terms mentioned above plus the theme of individualism is a concept of the Anglo society; terms prevalent in the Anglo women's movement. The *familia* has always been our strength in our culture. But it seems evident...that you [Chicana feminists] are not concerned with the *familia*, but are influenced by the Anglo woman's movement.

Chicana feminists were also accused of undermining the values associated with Chicano culture. Loyalists saw the Chicana feminist movement as an "anti-family, anti-cultural, anti-man and therefore an anti-Chicano movement" (Gomez 1973, p. 35). Feminism was, above all, believed to be an individualistic search for identity that detracted from the Chicano movement's "real" issues, such as racism. Nieto Gomez (1973, p. 35) quotes a loyalist as stating:

And since when does a Chicana need identity? If you are a real Chicana then no one regardless of the degrees needs to tell you about it. The only ones who need identity are the *vendidas*, the *falsas*, and the opportunists.

The ideological conflicts between Chicana feminists and loyalists persisted throughout the seventies. Disagreements between these two groups became exacerbated during various Chicana conferences. At times, such confrontations served to increase Chicana feminist activity that challenged the loyalists' attacks, yet these attacks also served to suppress feminist activities.

Chicana feminist lesbians experienced even stronger attacks from those who viewed feminism as a divisive ideology. In a political climate that already viewed feminist ideology with suspicion, lesbianism as a sexual life-style and political ideology came under even more attack. Clearly, a cultural nationalist ideology that perpetuated such stereotypical images of Chicanas as "good wives and good mothers" found it difficult to accept a Chicana feminist lesbian movement.

Cherrie Moraga's writings during the 1970's reflect the struggles of Chicana feminist lesbians who, together with other Chicana feminists, were finding the sexism evident within the Chicano movement intolerable. Just as Chicana feminists analyzed their life circumstances as members of an ethnic minority and as women, Chicana feminist lesbians addressed themselves to the oppression they experienced as lesbians. As Moraga (1981, p. 28) stated:

> My lesbianism is the avenue through which I have learned the most about silence and oppression...In this country, lesbianism is a poverty--as is being brown, as is being a woman, as is being just plain poor. The danger lies in ranking the oppression. The danger lies in failing to acknowledge the specificity of the oppression.

Chicana, Black, and Asian American feminists experienced similar cross-pressures of feminist-baiting and lesbian-baiting attacks. As they organized around feminist struggles, these women of color encountered criticism from both male and female cultural nationalists who often viewed feminism as little more than an "anti-male" ideology. Lesbianism was identified as an extreme derivation of feminism. A direct connection was frequently made that viewed feminism and lesbianism as synonymous. Feminists were labeled lesbians, and lesbians as feminists. Attacks against feminists--Chicanas, Blacks, and Asian Americans--derived from the existence of homophobia within each of these communities. As lesbian women of color published their writings, attacks against them increased (Moraga 1983).

Responses to such attacks varied within and between the feminist movements of women of color. Some groups tried one strategy and later adopted another. Some lesbians pursued a separatist strategy within their own racial and ethnic communities (Moraga and Anzaldua 1981; White 1984). Others attempted to form lesbian coalitions across racial and ethnic lines. Both strategies represented a response to the marginalization of lesbians produced by recurrent waves of homophobic sentiments in Chicano, Black, and Asian American communities (Moraga and Anzaldna 1981). A third response consisted of working within the broader nationalist movements in these communities and the feminist movements within them in order to challenge their heterosexual biases and resultant homophobia. As early as 1974, the "Black Feminist Statement" written by a Boston-based feminist group--the Combahee River Collective--stated (1981, p. 213): "We struggle together with Black men against racism, while we also struggle with Black men against sexism." Similarly, Moraga (1981) challenged the white feminist movement to examine its racist tendencies; the Chicano movement, its sexist tendencies; and both, their homophobic tendencies. In this way, Moraga (1981) argued that such movements to end oppression would begin to respect diversity within their own ranks.

Chicana feminists as well as Chicana feminist lesbians continued to be labeled *vendidas* or "sellouts." Chicana loyalists continued to view Chicana feminism as associated, not only with melting into white society, but more seriously, with dividing the Chicano movement. Similarly, many Chicano males were convinced that Chicana feminism was a divisive ideology incompatible with Chicano cultural nationalism. Nieto Gomez (1976, p. 10) said that "[with] respect to [the] Chicana feminist, their credibility is reduced when they are associated with [feminism] and white women." She added that, as a result, Chicana feminists often faced harassment and ostracism within the Chicano movement. Similarly, Cotera (1973, p. 30) stated that Chicanas "are suspected of assimilating into the feminist ideology of an alien [white] culture that actively seeks our cultural domination."

Chicana feminists responded quickly and often vehemently to such charges. Flores (1971a, p. 1) answered these antifeminist attacks in an editorial in which she argued that birth control, abortion, and sex education were not merely "white issues." In response to the accusation that feminists were responsible for the "betrayal of [Chicano] culture and heritage," Flores said, "Our culture hell"--a phrase that became a dramatic slogan of the Chicana feminist movement.

Chicana feminists' defense throughout the 1970's against those claiming that a feminist movement was divisive for the Chicano movement was to reassess their roles within the Chicano movement and to call for an end to male domination. Their challenges of traditional gender roles represented a means to achieve equality (Longeaux y Vasquez 1969a, 1969b). In order to increase the participation of and opportunities for women in the Chicano movement, feminists agreed that both Chicanos and Chicanas had to address the issue of gender inequality (Chapa 1973; Chavez 1971; Del Castillo 1974; Cotera 1977; Moreno 1979). Furthermore, Chicana feminists argued that the resistance that they encountered reflected the existence of sexism on the part of Chicano males and the antifeminist attitudes of the Chicana loyalists. Nieto Gomez (1973, p. 31), reviewing the experiences of Chicana feminists in the Chicano movement, concluded that Chicanas "involved in discussing and applying the women's question have been ostracized, isolated and ignored." She argued that "in organizations where cultural nationalism is extremely strong, Chicana feminists experience intense harassment and ostracism" (1973, p. 38).

Black and Asian American women also faced severe criticism as they pursued feminist issues in their own communities. Indeed, as their participation in collective efforts to end racial oppression increased, so did their confrontations with sexism (Chow 1987; Hooks 1984; White 1984). Ngan-Ling Chow (1987, p. 288) describes the various sources of such criticism directed at Asian American women:

Asian American women are criticized for the possible consequences of their protests: weakening the male ego, dilution of effort and resources in Asian American communities, destruction of working relationships between Asian men and women, setbacks for the Asian American cause, co-optation into the larger society and eventual loss of ethnic identity for Asian Americans as a whole. In short, affiliation with the feminist movement is perceived as a threat to solidarity within their own community.

Similar criticism was experienced by Black feminists (Hooks 1984; White 1984).

Chicana Feminist and White Feminists

It is difficult to determine the extent to which Chicana feminists sympathized with the white feminist movement. A 1976 study at the University of San Diego that examined the attitudes of Chicanas regarding the white feminist movement found that the majority of Chicanas surveyed believed that the movement had affected their lives. In addition, they identified with such key issues as the fight to legal abortions on demand and access to low-cost birth control. Nevertheless, the survey found that "even though the majority of Chicanas...could relate to certain issues of the women's movement, for the most part they saw it as being an elitist movement comprised of white middle-class women who [saw] the oppressor as the males of this country" (Orozco 1976, p. 12).

Nevertheless, some Chicana feminists considered the possibility of forming coalitions with white feminists as their attempts to work within the Chicano movement were suppressed. Since white feminists were themselves struggling against sexism, building coalitions with them was seen as an alternative strategy for Chicana feminists (Rincon 1971). Almost immediately, however, Chicana feminists recognized the problems involved in adopting this political strategy. As Longeaux y Vasquez (1971, p. 11) acknowledged, "Some of our own Chicanas may be attracted to the white women's liberation movement, but we really don't feel comfortable there. We want to be a Chicana *primero* [first]." For other Chicanas, the demands of white women were "irrelevant to the Chicana movement" (Hernandez 1971, p. 9).

Several issues made such coalition building difficult. First, Chicana feminists criticized what they considered to be a cornerstone of white feminist thought, an emphasis on gender oppression to explain the life circumstances of women. Chicana feminists believed that the white feminist movement overlooked the effects of racial oppression experienced by Chicanas and other women of color. Thus, Del Castillo (1974, p. 8) maintained that the Chicana feminist movement was "different primarily because we are [racially] oppressed people." In addition, Chicana feminists criticized white feminists who believed that a general women's movement would be able to overcome racial differences among women. Chicanas interpreted this as a failure by the white feminist movement to deal with the issue of racism. Without the incorporation of an analysis of racial oppression to explain the experiences of Chicanas as well as of other women of color, Chicana feminist believed that a coalition with white feminists would be highly unlikely (Chapa 1973; Cotera 1977; Gomez 1973; Longeaux y Vasquez 1971). As Longeaux y Vasquez (1971, p. 11) concluded: "We must have a clearer vision of our plight and certainly we cannot blame our men for the oppression of the women."

In the 1970's, Chicana feminists reconciled their demands for an end to sexism within the Chicano movement and their rejection of the saliency of gender oppression by separating the two issues. They clearly identified the struggle against sexism in the Chicano movement as a major issue, arguing that sexism prevented their full participation (Fallis 1974; Gomez 1976). They also argued that sexist behavior and ideology on the part of both Chicano males and Anglos represented the key to understanding women's oppression. However, they remained critical of an analysis of women's experiences that focused exclusively on gender oppression.

Chicana feminists adopted an analysis that began with race as a critical variable in interpreting the experiences of Chicano communities in the United States. They expanded this analysis by identifying gender as a variable interconnected with race in analyzing the specific daily life circumstances of Chicanas as women in Chicano communities. Chicana feminists did not view women's struggles as secondary to the nationalist movement but argued instead for an analysis of race and gender as multiple sources of oppression (Cotera 1977). Thus, Chicana feminism went beyond the limits of an exclusively racial theory of oppression that tended to overlook gender and also went beyond the limits of a theory of oppression based exclusively on gender that tended to overlook race.

A second factor preventing an alliance between Chicana feminists and white feminists was the middle-class orientation of white feminists. While some Chicana feminists recognized the legitimacy of the demands made by white feminists and even admitted sharing some of these demands, they argued that "it is not our business as Chicanas to identify with the white women's liberation movement as a home base for working for our people" (Longeaux y Vasqnez 1971, p. 11).

Throughout the 1970's, Chicana feminists viewed the white feminist movement as a middle-class movement (Chapa 1973; Cotera 1980; Longeaux y Vasquet 1970; Martinez 1972; Nieto 1974; Orozco 1976). In contrast, Chicana feminists analyzed the Chicano movement in general as a working-class movement. They repeatedly made reference to such differences, and many Chicana feminists began their writings with a section that disassociated themselves from the "women's liberation movement." Chicana feminists as activists in the broader Chicano movement identified as major struggles the farmworkers movement, welfare rights, undocumented workers, and prison rights. Such issues were seen as far removed from the demands of the white feminist movement, and Chicana feminists could not get white feminist organizations to deal with them (Cotera 1980).

Similar concerns regarding the white feminist movement were raised by Black and Asian American feminists. Black feminists have documented the historical and contemporary schisms between Black feminists and white feminists, emphasizing the socioeconomic and political differences (Davis 1971, 1983; Dill 1983; LaRue 1970). More specifically, Black feminists have been critical of the white feminists who advocate a female solidarity that cuts across racial, ethnic, and social class lines. As Thornton Dill (1893, p. 131) states:

> They cry "Sisterhood is powerful!" has engaged only a few segments of the female population in the United States. Black, Hispanic, Native American, and Asian American women of all classes as well as many working-class women, have not readily identified themselves as sisters of the white middle-class women who have been in the forefront of the movement.

Like Black feminists, Asian American feminists have also had strong reservations regarding the white feminist movement. For many Asian Americans, white feminism has primarily focused on gender as an analytical category and has thus lacked a systematic analysis of race and class (Chow 1987; Fong 1978; Wong 1980; Woo 1971).

White feminist organizations were also accused of being exclusionary, patronizing, or racist in their dealings with Chicanas and other women of color. Cotera (1980, p. 227) states:

> Minority women could fill volumes with examples of put-down, put-ons, and out-and-out racism shown to them by the leadership in the [white feminist] movement. There are three major problem areas in the minority-majority relationship in the movement: (1) paternalism or maternalism, (2) extremely limited opportunities for minority women..., (3) outright discrimination against minority women in the movement.

Although Chicana feminists continued to be critical of building coalitions with white feminists toward the end of the seventies, they acknowledged the diversity of ideologies within the white feminist movement. Chicana feminists sympathetic to radical socialist feminism because of its anti-capitalist framework wrote of working-class oppression that cut across racial and ethnic lines. Their later writings discussed the possibility of joining with white working-class women but strategies for forming such political coalitions were not made explicit (Cotera 1977; Marquez and Ramirez 1977).

Instead, Del Castillo and other Chicana feminists favored coalitions between Chicanas and other women of color while keeping their respective autonomous organizations. Such coalitions would recognize the inherent racial oppression of capitalism rather than universal gender oppression. When Longeaux y Vasqnez (1971) stated that she was "Chicana *prirnero*," she was stressing the saliency of race over gender in explaining the oppression experienced by Chicanas. The word *Chicana* however, simultaneously expressed a woman's race and gender. Not until later--in the 1980's-would Chicana feminist ideology call for an analysis that stressed the interrelationship of race, class, and gender in explaining the conditions of Chicanas in American society (Cordova et al. 1986; Zinn 1982), just as Black and Asian American feminists have done.

Chicana feminists continued to stress the importance of developing autonomous feminist organizations that would address the struggles of Chicanas as members of an ethnic minority and as women. Rather than attempt to overcome the obstacles to coalition building between Chicana feminists and white feminists, Chicanas called for autonomous feminist organizations for all women of color (Cotera 1972; Gonzalez 1980; Nieto 1975). Chicana feminists believed that sisterhood was indeed powerful but only to the extent that racial and class differences were understood and, above all, respected. As Nieto (1974, p. 4) concludes:

> The Chicana must demand that dignity and respect within the women's rights movement which allows her to practice feminism within the context of her own culture...Her approaches to feminism must be drawn from her own world.

Chicana Feminism: An Evolving Future

Chicana feminists, like Black, Asian American, and Native American feminists, experience specific life conditions that are distinct from those of white feminists. Such socioeconomic and cultural differences in Chicano communities directly shaped the development of Chicana feminism and the relationship between Chicana feminists and feminists of other racial and ethnic groups, including white feminists. Future dialogue among all feminists will require a mutual understanding of the existing differences as well as the similarities. Like other women of color, Chicana feminists must address issues that specifically affect them as women of color. In addition, Chicana feminists must address those issues that have particular impact on Chicano communities, such as poverty, limited opportunities for higher education, high school dropouts, health care, higher education, immigration reform, prison reform, welfare, and most recently, United States policies in Central America.

At the academic level, an increasing number of Chicana feminists continue to join in a collective effort to carry on the feminist legacy inherited from the 1970's. In June 1982, a group of Chicana academics organized a national feminist organization called Mujeres Activas en Letras y Cambio Social (MALCS) in order to build a support network for Chicana professors, undergraduates, and graduate students. The organization's major goal is to fight against race, class, and gender oppression facing Chicanas in institutions of higher education. In addition, MALCS aims to bridge the gap between academic work and the Chicano community. MALCS has organized three Chicana/Latina summer research institutes at the University of California at Davis and publishes a working paper series.

During the 1982 conference of the National Association for Chicano Studies, a panel organized by Mujeres en Marcha, a feminist group from the University of California at Berkeley, discussed three major issues facing Chicana feminists in higher education in particular and the

Chicano movement in general. Panelists outlined the issues as follows (Mujeres en Marcha 1983, pp. 1-2).

1. For a number of years, Chicanas have heard claims that a concern with issues specifically affecting Chicanas is merely a distraction/diversion from the liberation of Chicano people as a whole. What are the issues that arise when women are asked to separate their exploitation as women from the other forms of oppression that we experience?
2. Chicanas are confronted daily by the limitations of being a woman in this patriarchal society; the attempts to assert these issues around sexism are often met with resistance and scorn. What are some of the major difficulties in relations amongst ourselves? How are the relationships between women and men affected? How are the relationships of women to women and men to men affected? How do we overcome the constraints of sexism?
3. It is not uncommon that our interests as feminists are challenged on the basis that we are simply falling prey to the interests of white middle-class women. We challenge the notion that there is no room for a Chicana movement within our own community. We, as women of color, have a unique set of concerns that are separate from white women and from men of color.

While these issues could not be resolved at the conference, the panel succeeded in generating an ongoing discussion within the National Association for Chicano Studies (NACS). Two years later, in 1984, the national conference of NACS, held in Austin, Texas, adopted the theme "Voces de la Mujer" in response to demands from the Chicana Caucus. As a result, for the first time since its founding in 1972, the NACS national conference addressed the issue of women. Compared with past conferences, a large number of Chicanas participated by presenting their research and chairing and moderating panels. A plenary session addressed the problems of gender inequality in higher education and within NACS. At the national business meeting, the issue of sexism within NACS was again seriously debated as it continues to be one of the "unsettled issues" of concern to Chicana feminists. A significant outcome of this conference was the publication of the NACS 1984 conference proceedings, which marked the first time that the association's anthology was devoted completely to Chicanas and Mexicanas (Cordova et al. 1986).

The decade of the 1980's has witnessed a rephrasing of the critical question concerning the nature of the oppression experienced by Chicanas and other women of color. Chicana feminists, like Black feminists, are asking what are the consequences of the intersection of race, class, and gender in the daily lives of women in American society, emphasizing the simultaneity of these critical variables for women of color (Garcia 1986; Hooks 1984). In their labor-force participation, wages, education, and poverty levels, Chicanas have made few gains in comparison to white men and women and Chicano men (Segura 1986). To analyze these problems, Chicana feminists have investigated the structures of racism, capitalism, and patriarchy, especially as they are experienced by the majority of Chicanas (Ruiz 1987; Segura 1986; Zavelia 1987). Clearly, such issues will need to be explicitly addressed by an evolving Chicana feminist movement, analytically and politically.

Note

AUTHOR'S NOTE: Research for this article was supported by Rev. Thomas Terry, S.J., university research grant awarded by Santa Clara University. Two substantively different versions of this article were presented at the 1985 Annual Conference of the National Association of Chicano Studies, Sacramento, CA, and the 1986 International Congress of the Latin American Studies Association, Boston, MA. I would like to thank Maxine Baca Zinn, Ada Sosa Riddell, Vicki L. Ruiz, Janet Flammang, Judith Lorber, and the referees for their constructive criticism. I am grateful to Francisco Jimenez for his thoughtful editorial suggestions and for his moral support and encouragement during this entire project.

1. For bibliographies on Chicanas see Balderama (1981); Candelaria (1980); Loeb (1980); Portillo, Rios, and Rodriguez (1976); and Baca Zinn (1982, 1984).

Woman of the Year
For a lifetime of labor championing the rights of farmworkers
Dolores Huerta

by Julie Felner

"Why is it that farmworkers feed the nation but they can't get food stamps?" Dolores Huerta, co-founder and secretary-treasurer of the United Farm Workers (UFW), asks an adoring crowd. Huerta has a gift for crafting sound bites of substance, and tonight, like most nights, she is reeling them off, this time before a group celebrating the 20th anniversary of the Chicana/Latina Foundation, a San Francisco-based leadership organization. As Huerta segues from topic to topic--from promoting women's studies to preventing domestic violence to preserving affirmative action--the women feed off her enthusiasm. What started out as a stately affair has become relaxed and interactive, with the well-heeled guests chiming in throughout Huerta's speech. When she says, "I have a T-shirt that says, 'Behind every successful woman is herself,'" California assemblywoman Liz Figueroa, the first Latina in northern California elected by a non-Latino district, shouts out, "Or other Latina women!"

The evening's theme is "Las Generaciones: Our Past, Present, and Future," and perhaps no one embodies the spirit of that theme better than Huerta, the link between the past, present, and future of both the UFW and the Chicano civil rights movement. Thirty-five years ago, Huerta and Cesar Chavez brought the union to life, and quickly transformed it from a hand-to-mouth organization with a staff of five to a powerhouse boasting more than 400 staffers and 70,000 members. Throughout the union's heyday in the late 1960's and 1970's, Huerta was on the front lines and in the back rooms. She wrote up the UFW's first contract and became its foremost and fiercest negotiator. She directed the grape boycott of 1968-70, one of the largest and most successful boycotts in U.S. history, which resulted in the first collective bargaining agreements for California farmworkers. She stayed with the union through a slump in the 1980's when membership fell to about 20,000 and the UFW faced long and expensive legal battles to enforce its contracts. And now, four years after Chavez's death, Huerta is helping to bring the UFW into the 21st century as it mounts its most ambitious campaign in years--organizing the 20,000 workers in California's strawberry industry, many of whom tack the basic rights that Huerta and Chavez first fought for--a living wage, clean drinking water and toilets in the fields, decent housing, health benefits, and the freedom to work without sexual harassment and assault.

As Huerta's speech comes to a close, she leads the crowd in a rousing round of *vivas* (long live...) and *abajos* (down with...). "*Viva la* Latina/Chicana Foundation! *Viva* the UFW! *Abajo* Sexism! Racism! Homophobia! *Abajo* Newt and Wilson!" And then with hands clapping, voices chanting, energy racing, the crowd breaks into a chorus of *Si, se puede*, the UFW's enduring motto: Yes, it can be done. *Si-se-pue-de*.

This isn't the first time Dolores Huerta has turned a posh affair into a political rally. For Huerta, every moment is an organizing opportunity, every person a potential activist, every minute a chance to change the world. And her schedule reflects this single-minded devotion to social change. During any given week, you'll find the peripatetic 67-year-old flying from

138

Washington state to Washington, D.C., with three or four stops along the way, attending union conferences or political rallies, giving lectures on college campuses or testimony before Senate subcommittees.

Huerta never slows down, never really stops moving. "She's indefatigable," says Eleanor Smeal, president of the Feminist Majority Foundation, where Huerta has served as a board member for ten years. "I don't know of any other leader who has the schedule she has...she'll fly in from South America on the red-eye for a board meeting and she'll stay and participate the whole time. If you say, 'Can you stay another day?' she will." Huerta spends most of her "downtime" up in the air, reading newspapers and a book or two as she flies to her next destination. "She's like a character on *Star Trek*. She doesn't really need sleep or food," says her daughter Juanita Chavez, the eighth of Huerta's 11 children.

Huerta's almost superhuman stamina is legendary. This is, after all, a woman who gave birth to her first child at age 20 and her eleventh at 46. And who, ten years Later, in 1988, survived a brutal beating at a San Francisco rally, when a six-foot-seven police officer clubbed the five-foot-one Huerta in the back, sending her to the hospital, where she had emergency surgery to remove a ruptured spleen and repair three broken ribs. Huerta, who had been demonstrating against then-presidential candidate George Bush over his position on pesticides, lost so much blood she should have died. Instead she recovered fully and successfully sued the city's police department to change its crowd-control procedures during protests.

"I imagine that if I had known Emma Goldman, she would have been something like Dolores," says Gloria Steinem, who has known Huerta for three decades. "She's not a person whose life is divided into public and private, work and play--it's all of a piece." Huerta's approach to mothering was equally undivided. Rather than choose between being with her children and going to work, she brought her children to work (and, as they became adults, put them to work). In the early days of the union, Huerta, then a twice-divorced single mother raising seven children, would nurse the youngest between meetings, pack them all in the car at night and on weekends as she drove around the state visiting migrant labor camps, move them from Chicago to New York to Los Angeles as she led the grape boycotts in those cities. Her children grew up on the picket lines, and they have inherited Huerta's sense of civic duty (among them are a doctor, a lawyer, a massage therapist, a teacher, a budding public health specialist, an aspiring filmmaker, a poet).

But both Huerta and her children admit that there were a lot of sacrifices along the way. There were her long absences when the children would stay with family members or union supporters, countless missed birthdays and school events. Huerta was earning between $5 and $35 a week, whatever money the union had left after paying all the bills, and the family often lived on donated food and clothing. "Like most working women, you have these guilt complexes, especially in my case because we lived in poverty and my kids didn't have the proper care they needed," she says. "But when people ask, 'How could you do it?' Well, you do it without thinking about it, because if you think about it, you can't do it."

The union always came first, says Huerta's 43-year-old daughter Lori de Leon--before the children and before her long-distance companion of more than 25 years, Richard Chavez, Cesar's brother and the father of Huerta's four youngest children. "I remember, as a child, one time talking to her about my sadness that she wasn't going to be with me on my birthday," recalls Lori. "And she said that the sacrifices we as her children make would help hundreds of other children in the future. How can you argue with something like that?"

But Lori also emphasizes that her mother has always managed to let her children know how important they are to her: "It never fails to amaze me that each time I was in the hospital having a baby...and I was there lying on the table and my mom's supposed to be 2,000 or 3,000 miles away, she shows up at the foot of the bed saying, 'O.K., push.'"

Twenty-six year-old Juanita says that her mother is without question her hero. "But what I love about my hero is that she doesn't try to be perfect. She will be the first to admit her faults." Indeed, Huerta readily fesses up that the woman responsible for winning some of the labor movement's most decisive battles is equally good at losing things--wallets, papers, keys, clothing, a computer. Once she even managed to misplace a piano. Lori affectionately calls her mother "the disorganized organizer." Friends and family members note that Huerta often shows up at the airport without ID, without luggage, without a plane ticket even, but she always manages to get where she needs to be.

Huerta's assistant has taken to buying replacement reading glasses by the cartonful. Thankfully, Huerta, who manages to go through two pairs of glasses a week, has never lost her true vision. It is a vision of social change she's had since she was a teenager growing up in Stockton, a port town at the tip of the San Joaquin Valley, California's agricultural center.

Huerta was born in 1930 in Dawson, New Mexico. Her parents divorced when she was five, and her mother, Alicia, moved Dolores and her siblings to Stockton, where Alicia worked as a waitress and cook and eventually opened a hotel in a neighborhood of Latino, black, Italian, Japanese, and Native American families. Dolores inherited a passion for justice (and a commitment to farmworkers' rights) from her mother, who would often let indigent farmworkers stay for free at the hotel. "She absolutely got her feminism from our mother," says Alicia Arong, Dolores' younger sister. "Mom was a women's libber before her time. She felt very strongly that women should get out and work and participate in the community."

So it is no surprise that in 1955, when a young Anglo organizer named Fred Ross wanted to form a Stockton chapter of the Community Service Organization, a Mexican American rights group he had started a few years earlier in the barrios of L.A., both mother and daughter signed on. Huerta was working as an elementary school teacher at the time, but something clicked when she met Ross. "When I saw all these things they were able to do--bring in health clinics, fight the police--it was like a revelation," she says. Soon Huerta was working as a full-time activist, leading voter registration drives and storming the welfare department to demand public assistance for farmworkers.

She had an innate political savvy, and politicians began to take notice. One was Phil Burton, then an unabashedly liberal state assemblyman, who encouraged Huerta to begin lobbying for farmworkers' rights in Sacramento, the state capital. From 1960 to 1962, Huerta successfully lobbied for 15 bills, including landmark legislation that allowed farmworkers to receive public assistance, retirement benefits, and disability and unemployment insurance, regardless of whether they were U.S. citizens.

It was through the CSO that Huerta first met another of Ross' star recruits, Cesar Chavez. Though the shy and unassuming Chavez didn't make much of an impression on her at first, they were both drawn to the plight of the farmworkers and began to work closely together. Huerta and Chavez became like brother and sister--throughout their lives, they would fight bitterly over strategy but always remained fiercely loyal to one another.

Farmworkers have historically been excluded from federal labor laws that guarantee the right to picket and form unions. Back then, a combination of racism and apathy had led the largely white leadership of mainstream unions to dismiss the idea of organizing farmworkers--a migrant workforce mostly made up of Filipinos and Latinos, many of whom were undocumented. In 1962, Chavez said to Huerta, "You know, there's never going to be a £armworkers' union unless we start it."

And so they formed the National Farm Workers Association, the precursor to the UFW, with Chavez as president and Huerta as second in command. The first few years were frustrating; Huerta was daunted by the slow and arduous task of building a membership. But things picked up in 1965, when the NFWA joined up with the Agricultural Workers Organizing Committee, a small group of striking Filipino grape workers. Years before, Huerta had also helped start the AWOC; now the two groups came together to organize the Delano Grape Strike, an event that catapulted them into the national spotlight. After their victory in Delano, the NFWA and AWOC merged to become the United Farm Workers Organizing Committee, which later became the United Farm Workers of America, AFL-CIO.

And the rest is history. Or at least it should be. Perhaps the greatest irony of Huerta's career is that you're more likely to find a detailed report of her activities in FBI files and police records (she's been arrested more than 20 times) than in the pages of history books. At the height of the Delano strike, an FBI report called Huerta "the driving force on the picket lines of Delano and Tulare County," but in John Gregory Dunne's popular chronicle of the events, *Delano: The Story of the California Grape Strike*, Huerta gets merely one passing mention. While volumes have been devoted to Chavez's life, a search through the library for articles about Huerta yields little more than a smattering in progressive magazines.

Much of why Huerta was never given her proper due is pure and simple sexism. She went up against growers who had never before dealt directly with a Chicano, much less a Chicana. Though some refused at first to work with her, growers eventually came to begrudgingly respect this forthright woman who, in one grower's words, "had balls". But Huerta also had to confront sexism within the union's own ranks. Though the UFW had always made a point of aiming for gender equity and supporting women's rights, the culture inside the union was still rife with sexism. "For a long time I was the only woman on the executive board," she remembers. "And the men would come out and say their stupid little jokes about women. So I started keeping a record. At the end of the meeting, I'd say, 'During the course of this meeting you men have made 58 sexist remarks.' Pretty soon I got them down to 25, then ten, and then five."

Huerta acknowledges that when the union first started, she wasn't really thinking about the rights of women. "In the sixties and seventies, many of us were working hard to get justice for *Ia raza*, not for women. We should have been doing more for women at the same time. We've had to do a lot of catching up," she says.

These days Huerta is making up for lost time. She has made sexual harassment a centerpiece of the strawberry workers' campaign. She has fought vigorously against state and federal legislation that takes away women's rights--from the Welfare Reform Act to California's anti-affirmative action Proposition 209. And she has pushed to get women into leadership positions inside and outside the union. From 1991 until Chavez's death in 1993, Huerta took a leave from the UFW to work on the Feminist Majority's Feminization of Power campaign, traveling around the U.S. encouraging Latinas to run for office. Friends and family believe that one of her dreams for the future is to create a grassroots Latina leadership organization.

As the Chicana/Latina Foundation banquet winds to a close, a small group is out on the dance floor. It is midnight, and in a few hours' time Huerta will arrive at her daughter Camila's place in Oakland, catch some sleep, and leave at the crack of dawn (without her wallet) to join

Jesse Jackson for an anti-209 rally in Sacramento. But right now all Huerta wants to do is dance. She has always loved dancing--everything from ballroom to the Macarena. As Huerta joins friends on the dance floor, the band starts to play an unintentional, though fitting tribute: Gloria Gaynor's classic feminist anthem "I will Survive."

Asian American Women

In this section I have attempted to include stories that deal with the diverse groups that comprise this category. "Voices From the Past" is the story of Filipina womens' experiences in the United States. "Okaasan" is an excerpt recounting the story of the author's grandmother who came to the United States as a "picture bride" from Japan. Judy Yung has researched the stories of Chinese immigrant women in "Unbound Feet: A Social History of Chinese Women in San Francisco." The Vietnamese are a group that has immigrated to the United States in large numbers, yet their history is relatively unknown. "To Become an American Women: Education and Sex Role Socialization of the Vietnamese Immigrant Woman" gives an interesting perspective.

Voices from the Past: Why They Came

Dorothy Cordova

Their numbers are rapidly dwindling--those hardy, adventurous, pioneering Filipino women who came to America from the early 1900's to the 1930's. They came as part of the "Second Wave" of Filipino immigration to this country. Though the largest group of Filipino immigrants during this period was comprised of young single men, a very small minority were married; and a few of the more fortunate ones brought their families with them to the new land. In addition to the few women who accompanied their spouses, other women arrived to seek educational opportunities, employment, and cultural and social freedom. Several women shared their experiences in a series of interviews.

Mercedes Balco came to study. She arrived here in 1930 as a *pensionada* her living and school expenses paid for by the government or school.

> I came by boat in one of those Empress of Russia boats. And then by train through Canada ... to Toronto and [then] to Washington, D.C. I stayed at the boarding house of the...School of Social Work of Catholic University where I had a scholarship for two years...There were several *pensionadas* before I came. They were all women. They all did go to the School of Social Work.

Second Wave Filipinas constituted the first group of professionals who immigrated here in large numbers. In California they became the first teachers of Filipino descent; in New York, the first nurses of Filipino descent; in Washington, the first pharmacist of Filipino descent; they were the first Filipino Americans to enter office work and other employment previously denied to Filipino men, who had been primarily working jobs in the culinary and custodial industries.

Maria Abastilla Beltran was one of the Filipina professionals who came to the United States. After working in the Philippines she emigrated to obtain further professional education and training.

> Those days, you know, you can go to nursing without completing high school. But when I came over here, I've got to take graduate work. I have to finish my high school [education] through correspondence because otherwise I cannot get my credits. [In the Philippines] my first job was industrial--in the mining company. Then I was a school nurse, and then I became a Red Cross nurse for four years.... I went all over the north and then in the central Philippines, you know, Manila. I...wanted to come and finish my B.A. in nursing here [in America], public health nursing, so I could go back again and work for the Red Cross.

Not all those who emigrated from the archipelago nation left with such clear goals in mind, however. A few women came in an attempt to escape the restricted life that they faced in their homeland-- lives of family--determined marriages, of poverty and hardship.

Alberta Asia was only ten years old when she arrived in Hawaii with her widowed mother, her brothers, and her sisters. She recalls her family's difficult times in the Philippines and her mother's search for a better life for herself and her children.

I was born in Cebu---Carcar--in 1900...My parents is poor. We have our own land, I think about five acre for sugar cane and two acre for corn. Then one acre my dad plant vegetable. Then [came] that pestilence in 1904. The crop is dry; even the water is dry! We got no water, so my dad suffered too much to look around...for food for us---his children. So it happen in 1910 my dad passed away June the thirteenth. My dad left the five acres of land to us, but we cannot do the land, you know, plant something, because we are small...Uncle Lucity only twelve years old, and I am ten. We are seven sister and and brother...

So it happen my mother said, "You stay here in Carcar, because I go down to Cebu to look for job." So my grandma said, "No, don't leave your children alone because I am too old, too. We cannot take care of the children." So my mother bring us to Cebu. And it happen we reach Cebu. For one week...we stay in Cebu. My mother found a job for babysitting. Just only one peso--one peso and cincuenta a week. Can you imagine that? She support us on one peso and cincuenta a week!

Asis's family soon met an elderly woman whose job it was to recruit people to go to Hawaii as laborers.

She is agent of immigration...She go around the block looking for even women. "Son," one day my mama said, "I thinks...we go to Hawaii." So my brother Ceto said, "What you going to do in Hawaii?" "You should be, got to know, you got lots of work in there," the old woman said, the agent woman...We call our grandmother, you know, to let [her] know that we go to Hawaii. And then my grandmother goes to Cebu to bid us all goodbye...When we leave Cebu, goes to Manila...for one week; then they ship us to Hong Kong...Then they put us in the Japanese ship...name is *Shumaru*. We arrive in Hawaii, December 25, 1910.

The plantation boss, they give us a house and we are fifty-seven people, include the children...The big boss on the plantation, Mr. Renton, said [we] live near to his house because mother got no husband. And then my mama said, "[When] we are in the Philippines...we got no nothing...Babysitting for one peso and fifty centavos...not enough for my children, not enough for me...come...I thought Hawaii is good." Then Mr. Renton [told] my mother, "Okay, I give you work in the plantation store...Just sweep the floor...Twenty-five cents an hour."

In 1924 Ambrosa Marquez left her home in Ilocos Norte and came to the United States--also to escape. What she fled, however, was not poverty, it was an unwanted marriage.

Our neighbors, they like me marry, but I don't like. That's why I like to run away from my house...Not my parents, but the boy's grandpa, [he's] the one who like [me] to marry to the grandson...My mother no like, because the mother of that boy sometimes she fight my mother. I no like, too, because he got a sweetheart in our [town]...My agent come to my house...[recruiting] two men and two women...[He] tell, "The workmen need laundry ladies, and you can wash their clothes, because they have no more wife. And [if] you like it, you can take it." My mother said, "You go to Hawaii. If you don't like that man, you go Hawaii."

Marquez left the Philippines with her brother, a girl friend, and another man from the province. She eventually settled on the island of Kauai in Hawaii, the only single Filipina in the entire labor camp.

From 1920 to 1929, 65,618 Filipino men were brought by the Hawaiian Sugar Plantation Association to work on the Hawaii sugar plantations. During that same period, only 5,286 women with their 3,091 children settled there. According to the 1930 census, there were 42,328 males and 2,940 females--less than seven Pinays (Filipino women) for every one hundred men. On the mainland the disparity in the female to male ratio was even greater.

Many Filipino women saw the treacherous voyage across the Pacific as a necessary step to see husbands, fathers or fiances. They came to rejoin loved ones who had come earlier to seek their fortune in the promised land of milk and honey--the United States. Leonora Mangiben, like Alberta Asis who had arrived one decade earlier, was also just a little girl when she came to America in the late 1920's. And like many others, her mother had immigrated with the children to rejoin her husband.

Mother ran a little grocery store underneath the house...Then mother got mad because dad wouldn't send us any money for support. So she sold all the land we had, and we came here.

When Mangiben's family finally arrived in San Francisco, she was given the responsibility of seeking out her long-absent father.

I had to find my father, and at two-and-a-half you can't remember what your father looked like. I used to look at his pictures. Mother let me out because she had to be checked out [by immigration]. She said, "You go out and see if you can find your father." So I went out and looked at all those Filipinos just standing there, and I went directly to my dad and threw my arms on him. He was shaking like a leaf. That's how I found dad. It was my father.

Though outnumbered by Filipino men, Filipinas still made their presence known and usually were the focal points of the extended family. Regardless of their age or appearance, the few women received special treatment, often finding themselves escorted to special events by a whole group of single Filipino men who were content just to be near a Pinay.

The journeys across the ocean were long and sometimes very rough. Mangiben recalls her trip with vivid memory.

I remember coming over here...It was not first class. All Filipinos never came first class. We took third class because of the women. We had cabins...maybe six or eight in a cabin. We shared a bathroom. When the ship was in motion...most of the women were seasick. I was the youngest one. I used to go in the top of the deck and look at the ocean. I used to get...sick [for land]; come down and tell my mother there's no land at all. Used to cry 'cause it was about twenty-eight days coming here. Can you imagine, twenty-eight days on the ship?
     The first port of call was China, Hong Kong. We couldn't go down 'cause there was always some wars in China...The next stop was Tokyo. We were able to go down there...Oh, yes, we went on shore. We went out to dinner. Mother was fine then. Soon as the ship stopped she was fine. That was the only time she ate. Then from Tokyo we went to Hawaii. We stayed there overnight. Then we came here--straight to San Francisco.

Nurse Maria Beltran also describes her trip to the United States in detail.

There were no planes those days. So I came with three hundred Filipinos in the boat...There were many meningitis cases in the boat. I offered my services there, you know, in the boat. And so when we arrived in Seattle, they quarantined everybody [for meningitis], and the women, they took us to Firland [Sanitarium]. There were about three Japanese and me and...two Russians. I roomed with the two Russian women, and the Japanese were in the other room.

Despite the confinement of the new arrivals to a health facility, Beltran remembers that her stay at Firland helped her decide to stay in this new country, a decision which paralled that of many Filipinas.

The immigration people took us there [to Firland], and we were quarantined for ten days. And the head nurse at Firland, when she found out I was a nurse, you know, she told me that [one] school was giving special work for public health nurses. That's the only school in the whole world that was giving that, and I want to do it. I played safe so I went to apply after I was released. I met Miss DeCano [another Filipino nurse]. So we both went to apply and we were both admitted.

Pensionada Mercedes Balco had planned to return to her homeland, but her plans were diverted.

I didn't quite make it back to the Philippines...I met my husband at the time when I was supposed to go back to the Philippines, and so we decided to get married...A daughter was born to us, and we stayed in Washington, D.C., from then on. [My husband] was a secretary to Senator Claro M. Recto, who was with the Mission of Independence at the time...When the Mission of Independence was finished, my husband stayed in Washington and got a job in the U.S. government...assigned to the War Department.

Though the mission on which Balco's husband worked resulted in the end of U.S. colonial rule over the Philippines, it ironically left the Filipino people in a less favorable immigration status. The Tydings-McDuffie Act, which was enacted by Congress on March 24, 1934, granted independence to the Philippines in ten years. At the same time, though, it limited entry of Filipinos to the United States to only fifty per year.

Prior to the new law, Filipinos were considered U.S. nationals and were free to come to America as long as they had the money to buy a boat ticket; now they were aliens and subject to the immigration quota. During the financial boom of the 1920's, Filipino workers were welcome; with the trauma and hardships of the Depression, however, these same workers came to be viewed as a "growing economic and social threat."

Consequently the already small but steady trickle of Filipino women to America dwindled to almost nothing. Over the next seven years, until just before World War II, the only women coming from the Philippines aside from students were those joining husbands or fiance's already settled in the United States. The growth that Filipino communities experienced prior to the mid-1930's virtually ceased until the end of the war.

Filipinas had settled throughout the country--in Hawaii, California, Washington, Oregon, Alaska, Illinois, New York, Louisiana, and Washington, D.C. However, because their numbers were so small, the feeling of loneliness sometimes became unbearable. While the following sentiments of nurse Beltran were expressed before the enactment of the immigration quotas, such feelings of isolation could not help but become much worse.

> I went to Chicago; I work in Chicago; and I didn't like it. I went to Cleveland and I work in Cleveland and I was not happy. I was all alone; there were no Filipinos. They didn't even know what I was in those places, especially in Cleveland. In Philadelphia, they just give me a look. I didn't like it over there, so I go back to Chicago.

Happily, in many areas the loneliness did not last, because after the end of World War II many more Filipinas immigrated to America; they were part of the "Third Wave." Some came as children and grandchildren of Spanish-American War veterans who had chosen to remain in the Philippines at the end of that war. Others came as war brides and children of Filipino soldiers who became American citizens by virtue of having fought in the U.S. armed forces; as American citizens and military dependents, they did not fall under the immigration quota limits.

Filipino immigration to the United States reached its zenith in the "Fourth Wave." This influx occurred after the enactment of the 1965 amendment to the Immigration Nationality Act, which abolished the exclusionary regulations of previous immigration laws. The amendment established an annual ceiling of twenty thousand immigrants from each country, including the Philippines.

The arrival and settlement of new groups of Filipinas, coupled with the birth of second- and third-generation Filipino Americans, caused their ethnic communities to become more and more established. As guardians of Filipino culture in America, the women played an important role. They sought to preserve the language, traditions such as folk dance and music, and a sense of family and community.

The women came as war brides, students, plantation workers, teachers, housekeepers, seamstresses, wives, kitchen helpers, labor camp cooks, entertainers, and nurses. Some were small business entrepreneurs who ran pool halls, restaurants, grocery stores, beauty parlors, and gambling concessions. Regardless, they were welcome arrivals to the Filipino men who had immigrated earlier.

> American life was stark for lonely brown men. The women who had joined them in this faraway, hostile society serve as symbols of the mothers, sisters and wives those men had left behind in the Philippines...
>
> The heart and soul of development of the Filipino American experience were personified in Pinays...[They] have been the yeast that set their men and children rising and the leaven that got their communities producing.

Publisher's Note: Grace Shibata had not laid eyes on the manuscript of this book when she wrote this moving portrait of her mother. But as if to flesh out the text of the foregoing segment, "Okaasan" (mother) gives us a real life story of an Issei woman, which, in its broad outlines, parallels exactly the historical account that author Mei Nakano has set down. When Nakano read "Okaasan," she wondered aloud if it could somehow be included in her work, knowing full well that such an inclusion would defy conventional publishing practices. We found a way. With Shibata's permission we placed her writing here, an appropriate transition, we thought, between the "Issei" and "Nisei" segments. Grace Shibata's deeply felt portrayal of her Issei mother adds richness and texture to our understanding of the Issei woman.

Okaasan

"Tadaima, kaeri mashita," (I'm home) I would call as loudly as I could, as I rushed into the house. Lying my books on the dining table, I would listen for Mother's soft and reassuring voice, which soon came: *"Okaeri na sai."* (Welcome home.) Mother always spoke to me in Japanese. Satisfied, I would bound up the stairs to my bedroom to change my starched school clothes to jeans, shirt and scruffy shoes.

Through the open window came the sound of splashing water, and I knew Mother must be in the garden watering plants. Outside, I walked quickly over the gravel path which was bordered with quarter-inch board and lined with chicken and hen cactus, to find her. She heard my footsteps, looked up and smiled, still holding the long, black hose. "Kyo wa do deshita ka?" (How was your day?) She was always interested in what I did.

At age forty-three, Mother is slightly under one hundred pounds, energetic and fit. The soft-spoken Issei woman stands five feet tall, looking relaxed in her print cotton dress, which falls loosely to her ankles. Under her wide-brimmed straw hat, her straight, black hair is pulled softly back to a bun. Her eyebrows are just two light puffs. Her skin, void or any makeup, is smooth and soft as a young girl's. Her small eyes dance as she smiles easily. She is enjoying one of her favorite pastimes, gardening. Early mornings and late afternoons, she tends her snapdragons, sweet peas, dahlias and myriad other flowers which bloom in their season. At the far end of the garden are several golden sunflowers, full of dark seeds, towering perhaps eight feet tall. A chubby yellow and black bumblebee searches for nectar on a dahlia, and two small white butterflies flutter silently, dipping left and then right. The serenity of the garden befits Mother's character.

This scene of Mother in the early 1930's seems placid enough, but it veils the hardships endured by a woman who had pioneered the frontier days in San Luis Obispo County with her husband Tameji Eto. Resourceful and patient in time of need, she stoically endured unbelievable odds to make a home and living for her family as a pioneer woman in the new world.

Born in 1889 In Okunaga village, Chida city, Kumamoto-ken, Japan, the third child in a family or six, Mother had a relatively easygoing happy childhood. Her parents, prosperous farmers, gave their children a warm and cheerful environment and encouraged them to play as well as study.

After *Jo-gakko* (high school), attending nursing school was Mother's dream, but as nursing was considered demeaning in those days, she could not get her parents' consent. Instead, she went to a weaving school and became an adept seamstress. Little did she know how useful this training would be when she raised eight children in America.

I often wondered why Mother came to America. All four of her brothers in Japan were university graduates and professionals: the eldest, a city councilman; the second, a dentist; the third, captain of a freighter; and the fourth, a mining engineer. Did she feel she had to accomplish more to keep up with them?

For his part, Father had landed in San Francisco in 1904 and after doing odd jobs, growing fava beans, sugar beets, potatoes and onions, he become foreman for the Pacific Coast Railroad Company. He then started a modest farm and soon after asked for Mother's hand by letter to his family in Japan. Father had been a classmate of Mother's eldest brother and used to see her playing at school, an image that had apparently stayed with him. The brother encouraged the parents to accept the proposal and after much thought, they agreed.

In those days in Japan, a young girl married without question whomever her parents chose for her, but Mother must have considered this marriage something of an adventure as well as a challenge. Although shy, she could be spirited and plucky. She was an avid *karuta* (card game played on New Year's Day) player. For example, and could easily trounce her brothers. She was also a strong swimmer and a fast and lithesome runner. She enjoyed competition and liked to win.

Clutching a photo of this man she did not know, Mother and her father boarded the train to Yokohama where a ship waited to take her to the United States. She was nineteen, leaving her family for the first time to wed a man who was a stranger. Too, she was destined for an alien country to be confronted with a completely foreign culture and language. For her future, she had relied solely on the judgment of her parents and eldest brother in whom she had absolute trust.

On the train, passing rice fields reminded her of home in Okunaga. It made her suddenly sad.

The *Minnesota* took about thirteen days to reach Seattle. Aboard she met a dozen or so other picture brides, and the kimono-clad young women compared photos of their future husbands, discussing their anxieties, sometimes joking uneasily about their future. The journey was pleasant enough, but Mother was soon struck by the cultural differences she faced. For example, in the dining room she was bewildered by the array of silverware before her and waited, shy and uncomfortable, until a kind waiter inconspicuously pointed out the correct one to use. One evening she lost her appetite at the sight of the main entree, meat with bones attached to it. In Japan, only thinly sliced meat was served. Another time a beautifully rolled yellow globular object had been placed on a small dish. Thinking it an egg yolk, she put the whole thing into her mouth, only to experience a horrid taste in her mouth. Too shy to spit it out, she swallowed it, an egg-yolk sized blob of butter. Many more cultural shocks would follow.

Upon reaching their destination, all her new acquaintances joined their spouses or spouses-to-be. But Mother's excited hopes of seeing the United States and meeting her future husband were dashed when immigration officers detained her because of a possible eye infection. The young couple had to be content to communicate by letter for ten days of quarantine. When Father at last saw Mother, he was surprised to see a plump young woman instead of the slight and sprightly girl he had remembered. "*Sumo* tori ga *kita to omotta*," (I thought a sumo wrestler had arrived) he would tease her later. But she was not to keep her extra pounds very long.

Mother, on the other hand, was pleased to see Father standing straight and tall with lots of hair. The picture that she brought with her had not deceived her. In fact he was quite handsome. And he seemed kind.

The couple was married at the U.S. Immigration Office by the assistant minister from the Seattle Buddhist church, Rev. E. Fujiyeda, on May 21, 1908.

When Father took Mother to a Seattle department store to purchase western clothes for the trip to California, she bought a dress with puff shoulders, long sleeves and a tight-wasted, long skirt, a wide-brimmed hat with a feather, and high laced shoes. She looked lovely but felt constrained by such apparel.

After another boat trip from Seattle to San Francisco, the newlyweds boarded a train to San Luis Obispo. By horse and buggy they traveled to Arroyo Grande where Father's brother, friends and neighbors gave them a wedding reception at the Parrish ranch. Wash tubs were used as drums to hail the new couple, and the event was published in the *Arroyo Grande Recorder*. Mother was touched by the kindness of these rural people.

Arroyo Grande was a frontier town set in a valley of sloping hills, scrub oaks and green grass. Deer, coyotes, raccoons, jack rabbits and opossums roamed the area, and neighbors lived miles away.

From the very first day, Mother plunged into a mental and physical endurance test of frontier life, meeting the challenge head-on. Her husband's brother taught her cooking and house chores, which included starting a fire by gathering dry kindling, chopping wood, drawing well water by bucket and pulley and carrying the filled container to the house.

She learned how to stoke the fire in the wood stove, and to "read" the oven temperature by placing her hand for an instant inside like big black oven. She learned how to make yeast and bake bread, biscuits and pancakes, to kill, dress and cook a chicken. She learned to wash, rubbing the yellowish-brown soap into the clothes over a washboard. She learned to heat the heavy black iron on the hot stove, making sure the fire did not go out. Water had to be kept hot for washing and rinsing dishes. These were all back-breaking chores, but she labored, uncomplaining, patient. For a woman who had lived a relatively tranquil, easy life back in Japan, pioneering was a jolting change. Fortunately she was healthy and strong.

Mother kept the rustic house clean and tidy, and she soon learned the necessity of keeping a watchful eye on the pantry inventory. Once, she forgot to pat "rice" on the grocery list. That resulted in one of the few times Father gave her a stern lecture: It required a full day's walk with a horse to Oceano from Arroyo Grande to purchase the rice, which meant the loss of a day's work. A year later Father made enough profit on his farm to buy a buggy. This made shopping much easier.

The hired men enjoyed Mother's cooking and even on Sundays hung close during meal times. To this day, some of them recall nostalgically the sweet delicious taste of her *dango-jiru*, a red bean soupy dessert with sweet flour dumplings. But even Sunday was not a day off for Mother. This was the day for laundering and ironing in addition to cooking three full meals. Her chores usually ended at midnight. She would be up again at four in the morning to start the fire for breakfast.

"It was not easy," she used to say later, "but it was my future as well as his, and I wanted to be a part of it. Father never demanded I work so hard. I did it because it was necessary and I wanted to." This attitude and support freed Father from daily problems to concentrate on his farm full time.

I should add that with his loud voice Father seemed gruff, but he was in fact a kind and humane man who treated mother with respect and kindness.

In 1909, a year after arriving at Arroyo Grande, Mother gave birth to my oldest sister, Kofuji, when she was twenty years old.

The following year, the family moved to Oso Flaco where Father worked for the Waller Seed Company and later contracted growing seeds for them. Mother, now with baby Kofuji on her back and another on the way, helped pick nasturtium seeds. To harvest these flower seeds, the nasturtium bushes were pulled by hand, stacked in piles, then pitched on to a horse-drawn wagon. The bushes were then dumped on a large canvas and beaten with pitchforks to separate the seeds from the plants. However, many of the seeds, the size of green peas, fell to the ground while harvesting and Mother and the other women gathered them up. "It was like picking up money," she said. "Nothing went to waste."

In 1910, a second child Toshiko was born during a particularly cold and rainy season in December. Not only was the cold weather difficult, Mother had a terrible time trying to dry the diapers. Four years later, in the summer of 1914, Alice, another daughter, came into the world. Mother was now caring for three children, at the same time doing the house chores and helping on the farm. Her workload had become ever more demanding.

But in spite or her arduous schedule, Mother always made time to plant vegetables. She loved to see the plants grow. She was also a practical, resourceful woman, and knew the garden would supply her with instant groceries when she needed them: eggplants, carrots, cucumbers, and a host of other common vegetables, not to mention the more esoteric Japanese vegetables, like Japanese pumpkins.

During the winter months when farm production was low, Father would go surf fishing in Pismo for perch and bullheads. There he observed that it was not bitter cold during mid-winter when Oso Flaco was frigid and white with frost. Why not grow English bush peas which would command high winter prices in the market when the item was scarce? he thought. Soon after, he leased some land in Pismo and moved his family near the Pacific Ocean. Having made this fortuitous decision on a hunch, he succeeded handsomely as a pioneer in bush peas. This earned him the name "Pea King."

Since there were no wells for irrigation, Father had to dry farm. This required planting a crop after the first rain, usually in December. To preserve moisture and to draw it from the bottom, he would repeatedly cultivate the soil to create a mulch. Father and Mother referred to this work as *kana beta* (cultivating). For years, we children used to say "kana beta-ing", as if it were a regular English word. Japanese English became a part of our daily conversation.

At the height of the pea season, Mother would go out to the fields. Squatting between two rows of bush peas, her hands moved rapidly as she picked the peas, careful not to ruin the vines for future crops. She was undoubtedly the fastest pea picker, for the men would grudgingly but good naturedly say, *"Eto no obasan ni wa kanawanai na!"* (We're no match for Mrs. Eto!)

With three children under five years of age and another on the way, our parents became concerned about the youngster's education. Afraid the children might lose their heritage or the Japanese culture and language, they anguished about what to do, but finally decided to send the two older daughters to their grandparents in Japan. Many years later, when one sister asked why they had been sent away, Mother replied that their parting had been like a knife piercing her own flesh and that the pain in her bosom remained for months. But at the time, she explained, Father

153

and she both thought they were doing what was best for the children. Although the pain of separation had been severe for both children and parents, the sacrifice enabled the two daughters to learn the Japanese language and be exposed to its culture. Father and Mother felt that was important.

In 1916, Father's two brothers sent for their picture brides in Japan. Though nine months pregnant, Mother prepared a huge wedding party when they arrived. The very next day she gave birth to her only son, Masaji. After three daughters, this ten-pound baby caused quite a stir. Now Father had a son to continue his farm.

In the midst of all these demands on her, Mother managed to find diversions. To expand his production, Father and his brothers purchased 125 acres of Morro Bay farm land to grow flower seeds and later, artichokes. Consequently, he had less and less time at home. He taught Mother how to hitch a horse and buggy so she could go to town for shopping. She would dress up the two younger children and go to Guadalupe for Japanese groceries or to San Luis Obispo for mail and other farm necessities. (At this time, Pismo consisted of only a few tent houses and one hotel.) As Mother gained confidence in her new-found independence, she began to visit her friend Mrs. Oishi, the wife of a labor contractor, on the way home from shopping. Her "shopping day" became longer each time, and Father teased what a mistake it had been to teach her to drive the horse and buggy.

Mother always took advantage of what nature had to offer. Pismo clams were plentiful back then, and waves scattered them over the long stretch of sand. There were so many that Mother used them as chicken feed as well as for food for us. She often drove the horse and buggy on the wet beach sand while her two sisters-in-law stooped to pick up the clams. In later years, one of them lamented laughingly, "Take-san would just sit there bolding the reins while we had to do the hard work!" Mother would break into a smile and claim, "But I was the only one who could handle the horses."

Daughter Mary's arrival in 1918 was an especially joyous occasion, as she was born on March 3, Girl's Day. Since Mother cherished tradition and festivities, this event could not have pleased her more.

Although petite, Mother was courageous and stout-hearted in many ways. Many evenings she was left alone in the house with her three young children when Father went to San Luis Obispo to bank and to take his products to the train station for shipping. Other times he would go as far as Morro Bay. The house was located close to Highway 101, and many hobos used to come knocking at her door. One late evening, there was a banging that would not stop. Mother lay quietly in bed, hoping the children would not waken. She could hear footsteps circling the house and ultimately stopping under her window. When she asked what be wanted, the stranger replied that he needed a place to sleep. She asked if he smoked, and when he said no, she gave him permission to use the barn. Next morning, while preparing breakfast, she was startled to see a huge, burly, disheveled hobo standing silently by the door peering down at her. Heart pounding but outwardly calm, Mother offered him coffee and then added some toast. She found the hoboes generally honest and harmless, and they often offered to do chores in exchange for this kind of favor. But she always declined, happy to see them go.

Strong though she was, there were times when sadness and nostalgia overwhelmed Mother, like the time she discovered a large red abalone on a rocky promontory on the beaches of Pismo. Anticipating that she would return to Japan in the not-too-distant future, she polished the beautiful rainbow-colored shell until it shone, carefully wrapped it and stored it in her steamer trunk. There were no shells so lovely in Japan, and she wanted to share it with her family. Many years later, after having borne more children, and having moved once again, Mother's hope of seeing her homeland had dissolved into a dream. Reluctantly, she gave away the treasured shell. Then there were those quiet evenings, her chores done, the children asleep, when she would stand outdoors and face East toward her homeland, and tears would well in her eyes.

Mother was a skillful doctor and nurse at home. She adeptly bandaged our cuts and bruises and performed whatever other remedies necessary to keep us in good health. We never went to the doctor except when we had tonsillitis. In addition, all of us were born at home.

As a child I used to wonder why other Issei commented on how amazing it was that all eight of us grew up healthy. Much later, I realized it was because fatalities among young children was not uncommon in those days for at least one member in the family, as grave markers in Japanese cemeteries attest. No doubt we were spared the same fate because of the infinite care Mother had given us.

After five years in Pismo, Father wanted his own farm to grow products that brought year round income. He left the Pismo farm to his older brother and the Morro Bay Farm to his younger brother and then struck out on his own, purchasing 150 acres in Los Osos Valley. Here the Eto family settled permanently. It was the place would call home.

The Alien Land Law, which prohibited Asian non-citizens from owning land, forced Father to buy his farm under the name of a Caucasian friend. He formed a corporation of three officers: 'Osca-san,' a Japanese accountant, and himself. Then he brought his family of five to this new farm in the bulky horse-drawn seed wagon loaded with household goods.

This was in December in the year 1919. Mother was again heavy with child, her sixth. The next weeks would severely test her fortitude and patience, for the former owner refused to vacate the house, and the family had to live in a tent and endure the bitter cold with their three children, aged six, four and two. This was the coldest part of the valley in winter; it was not unusual for the temperature to plummet to 26 degrees F. But the family was finally able to move into the three-bedroom, 1200 square foot, wooden farm house. Shortly thereafter, on January 14, 1920, number six child, Susie, was born.

Mother was always supportive of Father, however bad things seemed, and worked right by his side. She was a vital moral and spiritual strength to him. Father started his newly acquired farm by growing sweet peas and English bush peas. Production was high, but no matter how well the farm did, 'Osca-san' constantly drained the profits. Father could not seem to get ahead: one way or another, 'Osca-san' continued to deplete his assets until Father was slowly becoming immersed in debt.

Mother had never seen Father, an optimistic man by nature, so depressed. This must have been one of their darkest moments. Out in the dusk, as Father worked late, Mother quietly reassured him: "Even if we have to eat as little as one grain of rice a day, we'll somehow survive. Let's free ourselves of 'Osca-san' and try it alone."

Father eventually dissolved the corporation, established a new one in his children's names, and started all over again. Gradually, Father's and Mother's diligence and determination began to pay off, and the family farm began to take hold and grow.

Another daughter Nancy arrived on Girl's Day, March 3, 1923. In spite of her growing family, Mother's amazing stamina and fortitude enabled her to care for them as well as cook for a crew, now forty to fifty men, working on the farm.

The kitchen and the dining area where the employees ate were in a separate building There were huge black woks, or "kama" in a row. She would start the fires inside the three tunnel-like openings below the cement structure that held the woks. The first wok contained rice, the second hot water for tea, and the third a concoction of meat and vegetables, or sometimes chicken or seafood. For breakfast, she always served "Mother's Oats." In addition to the regular crew, during the height of a season, neighbors came to help as was the custom in those days, and Mother would set extra places at the table.

Finally, the farm became established to a point where Father and Mother, along with their youngest daughter, were able to take the long-awaited trip to Japan for a whole month. It had been fifteen long years that Mother had been away from family and friends. What a joyful reunion that must have been!

By this time, Father and Mother had long considered the United States their home, feeling their roots grow deeper in American soil. The children were citizens by birth, spoke English, attended American schools, and had many friends. They too were becoming more integrated into the Caucasian community as well as the Japanese community.

My father helped establish The Guadalupe Children's Home, a very important event for my mother, for then she was able to recall her two older daughters from Japan. This home was a dormitory school where children were taught the Buddhist religion and the Japanese language, after attending American school. Now Mother had all her children nearby.

Father, with Mother's help, was constantly expanding and improving Los Osos Farm, and its operations became extensive. He introduced the first truck farming in San Luis Obispo County by growing lettuce, celery and later, tomatoes and asparagus. He started shipping produce to San Francisco and Los Angeles through the Post Office and later built a packing house in San Luis Obispo to ship produce to the East by refrigerated freight trains.

Father finally hired a cook for the working crew, which gave Mother more time for herself. She used these extra hours to design clothes for her children, stitching them up on her treadle sewing machine. Mother had an artistic bent as well as being adept with her hands. She often did exquisite embroidery work in the evenings. The piece I remember best is a black silk cushion with a peacock's brilliantly colored tail spread out like a fan.

She also made butter from the cow she milked. She even had an ice box, but as it was a twelve-mile trip to town to purchase ice, she usually had an ice-box with no ice.

Mother sometimes showed her spunk in unexpected ways. Father had bought a black Dodge, which she had not learned to drive. One evening, when Father had had one too many at a Guadalupe party and had fallen asleep, Mother put the car in low gear and slowly drove thirty miles to Los Osos Valley. In those days, the road was windy, narrow and sometimes hilly. It was a very long drive in low gear, but Mother negotiated all the curves and made it home safely.

In 1925, I was horn in mid-December, the last of the Eto children.

Father negotiated for the first electricity and telephone service to be brought to Los Osos Valley. He also led the Japanese Association drive to import 200 cherry trees from Japan to donate to the local Senior High School. The lovely trees lined both sides of a wide avenue, beautifying the entrance to the school. This was a source of great pride to mother, not only because of the beauty the trees provided, but because she felt a part of Japan was here.

During prohibition days, Mother made *sake* for Father who liked to have a drink with dinner. She mixed *koji* (fermented rice) with cooked rice and water in a ten-gallon crock and stirred it periodically for several weeks while it fermented. It was tightly covered and, as the days passed, it started to bubble and foam. She poured this concoction into a clean linen sack which had been placed in a square wooden box, v-shaped at the bottom. With a weight on the sack, there came the drip, drip, drip of *sake* into the jug below. Father happily drank his sake with dinner.

The 1930 depression years were difficult. Peas sold for three to five cents a pound, from which the freight cost to the market had to be subtracted. A three-layer box of tomatoes sold for thirty cents. Wages were about ten cents an hour, but at times Father could not even pay that. Piano lessons were often paid for with eggs, fruits or vegetables. Mrs. Riley from Baywood came to barter for fresh vegetables with her clams.

These were harsh times, but Mother never complained. Instead, she taught us not to waste anything and to take good care or our possessions. She carefully rolled up string from packaged goods and used it to tie pole beans or sweet peas. She saved newspapers for starting fires, and even cut the blank column on the side to use for scratch paper. Vegetables and fruit peelings were buried to fertilize the soil. No matter how tired and late it was, she would tidy up the washing machine and cover it carefully when the laundry was done, never overloading it when in use. "A machine is like your body," she would say. "If you want it to last, do not abuse it." I learned the value of not being wasteful from her.

Mother was also creative in her frugality. She originated a simple but delicious dish she named "hamburger pea." It was inexpensive and easy to prepare, consisting of hamburger, sliced onions and fresh green peas, flavored only with salt. To this day, I have not seen or heard of anyone else making it, but it remains a favorite dish in our family.

Father was away a lot, organizing the Southern Central Japanese Agricultural Assn. to help support the price of produce. He created the San Luis Obispo Packing House Exchange and helped strawberry growers and many others who needed advice. Therefore, Mother's responsibility overseeing the farm while Father was away became extensive. She helped by supervising the planting and harvesting and by generally keeping the men busy. In addition, she had enough energy and patience to raise five hundred egg-laying chickens. Ever resourceful, she bought newborn chicks and kept them warm with a kerosene heater under a brooder. When they became stronger, they were let out to the larger chicken compound. With the help of my brother, Mother built a large chicken coop facing southeast to catch the morning sun.

Mother was a gracious and able hostess. The Los Osos Farm was midway between Los Angeles and San Francisco and many friends made their stop at the ranch home. Mother and Father shared their food, drinks and sometimes lodging. When unexpected guests arrived, Mother never seemed harassed. Quietly she would go out to the backyard, catch one of her chickens and proceed to prepare dinner. With the vegetable garden providing the greens, she somehow always managed to prepare a respectable meal. Because she was extremely well-organized, she performed her work inconspicuously and efficiently. I never realized, until much later, the enormity or her task.

Mother also showed unlimited patience with us children. None of us can recall her ever being angry or raising her voice, unbelievable though this may be.

In 1932, she received the honor of being named Mother of the Year from *Shin Nichi Bei* of Los Angeles. It must have come as a great surprise to her, for she sought no honor and believed what she did was nothing unusual.

In spite of her huge responsibilities, she encouraged us to have fun. She said she had wonderful memories of her childhood and wanted us to have the same. "There is enough work and commitment after you grow up and get married," she used to say. Work for my sisters and me extended to helping with the housework, doing the washing and ironing and occasionally assisting in the packing shed. At the same time, we planned picnics, played tennis, climbed mountains, or went walking to the beach with our red wagon packed with *onigiri* (rice balls), linked wieners, marshmallows and cold water. We stripped willow branches to roast our hot dogs and marshmallows. We always remember those fun activities linked with warm memories of Mother who encouraged them.

When sister Mary was studying Shakespeare, we improvised plays and dragged all the empty lettuce crates, which had been stacked neatly by the barn, to make castles, moats and drawbridges. We performed *Hamlet* and *Romeo and Juliet* and asked our neighbors to attend our production. Once, we asked Mother if we could charge a penny for our performance, but she said no.

Mother loved the outdoors and the sea and made the most or it whenever she could spare time from the farm. She watched the tide by the position of the moon. Whenever it was close to full moon, the tide low, she would urge Father to drive us out to Pismo Beach for clams, or more often, to Pecho for abalone hunting. Mother took four or five sacks and tire wrenches to pry the mollusks from the rocks. With our trousers rolled up, we scrambled down the craggy hillside to the rocky beach below. Carefully stepping from one slippery, seaweed-covered rock to another, we'd peer under a large boulder to find abalone, always with one eye to the oncoming wave. Mother was always quickest to find her limit of five abalone. Then she would come to help us find ours, we meanwhile having been more interested in playing than looking for abalone. We also found among the tide pools, crabs, mussels, small black sea snails and sea urchins. Mother would boil these in a huge pot as soon as we returned home. Eating these delicious morsels capped our day.

Masaji, our brother, used to hunt for rabbit, duck and quail at the farm, which contained a five-acre lake, surrounded by lush pampas grass. Some of the best lunches Mother packed for us included roast quail with *onigiri* (rice balls). When Masaji had luck hunting, he brought down mallard ducks or sea brant geese and occasionally, a Canadian goose. Mother saved the soft down to make pillows and cushions. While dressing the wild game or fish, she would explain the anatomy of the carcass to us.

Mother loved to go mushroom hunting. She found small mushrooms, firm and white, in the willow forest, or *kashi naba* (oak tree mushroom) under large oak trees, surrounded by peat moss about a foot deep. She also picked mushrooms from pastures, miraculously never poisonous ones. How she knew the difference remains a mystery to me. I used to watch her put a dime into whatever pot the mushroom was cooking to see if it would turn black, but in later years, I learned that this was not an accurate test of toxicity.

Once a week, we went shopping, usually on Saturdays when Father was available to drive. This was a big day, going into "town," and we all had something on the list. Grocery shopping came last so the food would not spoil in the car. The best part was in the end, when Father would say: "Orai, (all right) everybody finish?" And Mother would say, "Hai, Papa. Ice cream wa doh?" That was music to my ears, for I knew Father would say with a grin, "Orai, orai." Our heads poking out the window, we eagerly watched Father come out of the ice cream parlor with six vanilla cones stuck firmly in a cardboard container. They dripped a little on the side softening the white paper napkins wrapped around them. Mother beamed as she looked at our happy faces.

Mother was philosophical and the Buddhist religion meant a great deal to her. Our parents worked on Sundays (crops had to be readied for the Monday market), but they sent the children to the San Luis Obispo Buddhist Sunday School. Father was one of the founders of this church and was largely responsible for acquiring the original ten acres on which the church sat. Mother always wanted to know what we learned in class and the songs we sang. She impressed on us the importance of remembering what we had learned.

When Alice was attending Mills College and Masaji going to California Polytechnic School, the four younger sisters, Mary, Susie, Nancy and I spent a lot of time together. During Hana Matsuri (April 8, the birthday of Lord Buddha), we would go out to our neighbor's pasture early in the morning (with their permission), duck under the barbed wire fence and pick baskets and baskets of buttercups an lavender lupine. We would return to the car, the lower parts of our skirts dripping wet from the dew, our shoes muddy. Shivering, but invigorated by the early morning adventure, we would drive to church where we joined other members to decorate the *Hana Mido* (altar for the Lord Buddha), using the yellow and lavender blooms. Usually it was the girls who performed this service, since the boys were helping on the farm.

On December 7, 1941, I was setting the table for lunch, as music flowed from the radio in the living room. Suddenly, the program was interrupted again and again by the newscaster announcing that Pearl Harbor was being bombed by Japan. Was it really true? Mother could not really understand the broadcast, but was concerned. When Father came home and heard the news, there was total disbelief and bewilderment on his face. *"Sonna koto wa nai hazu da!"* (That cannot be!) But as the news continued, reality sunk in, and we became somber. Mother turned pale.

Early the next morning when I came downstairs, I found Mother sitting silently by the unlit wood stove (the stove was now used as a heater), one light still on. She looked up, but did not give her usual smile. She appeared not to have slept. Her clothes were the same as the ones she had worn the day before, and her hair had not been combed. And she wasn't bustling. Mother was always bustling in the morning

"What happened Mama?" I asked, puzzled.

"Around eleven last night, after we all went to bed, the police came and took Father away," she explained, her voice grave. "They were very apologetic and polite, saying it was FBI orders and that they were instructed to take him in for questioning. He complied without hesitation, for he knows these men, and there was no reason to be afraid. But it's 4:30, and he still has not returned. I'm afraid something serious has happened."

"Why didn't you wake us?" I pressed.

In typical fashion, she said, "You had school, and there was no reason you should lose sleep over this. I thought he might be home by this time."

Unknown to us, the FBI had picked up numerous community leaders, Buddhist priests, Japanese school teachers and other "dangerous aliens."

Immediately, my brother went to the police station, but was unable to see Father or get any information about his whereabouts. In the meantime, there was a call for sister Mary from the police station. Father told her he was well and would be sent south. He was allowed to speak only in English, and that was the end of the conversation.

The very next day, the *S.L.O. Telegram Tribune* ran an article about Father's arrest. Rumors in the Japanese community were rampant as to where the Issei were being detained. Several weeks passed before Mother received a letter from Mrs. Matsuura of the Guadalupe Buddhist Church, informing her that Father was in the Santa Barbara jail and was anxiously waiting to see his family.

Masaji, Toshiko and Mother hurriedly drove to see him. Nancy and I stayed at home because

Mother did not want us to see Father in custody.

At the jail, the visitors were allowed three minutes each. The usually robust Father appeared drawn. My sister asked how he was. "I'm fine," he said, "but I miss the outside, the fresh air." Masaji wanted to know what he could get for him, and Father asked for some clothes and cigarettes. Mother told Father, "Don't worry, Papa. Everything is being taken care of. Just take good care of yourself."

My sister and brother were informed the detainees would be transferred again, so gathering articles Father had asked for, they rushed back to Santa Barbara. By this time, aliens were restricted from traveling, and Mother could not go to see Father. When Toshiko and Masaji got there, Father was already gone. If the wardens knew where he was, they feigned not to. My sister and brother were sent to the Los Angeles FBI office for information and, after a lot of running about, they were finally able to locate his whereabouts: the CCC Camp in Tujunga.

Toshiko and Masaji stayed overnight in Los Angeles and left early the next morning for Tujunga. It was a long, lonely ride, but they were overjoyed when they were permitted to visit Father.

With guards hovering nearby, Father came out to the open-fenced compound. He looked much better than when they had last seen him. They were allowed five minutes. Father asked about Mother and the family and then discussed with my brother what should be done about the farm. "Drive carefully," were his parting words, as he stood and waved until the car turned the corner and they could see him no more.

At home, my brother conferred with Mother daily on how to take care of the farm. Amidst rumors of an evacuation, the farm still had to be operated. Mother's judgment was vital, now that Father was gone. In the event of evacuation, the ranch had to be leased, or goods packed, the equipment and trucks sold. Then there was the furniture, the chickens, the cars. The Buddhist Church property had to be tended to, besides. We depended on kind and helpful friends like Mr. Ernest Vollmer, Mr. Pete Bachino and Dr. George Dunklee during these uneasy times.

We received word one day that Father was to be transferred to someplace very cold and would need warm clothes, also that his train would be passing the San Luis Obispo station that evening. It was Christmas Eve, and all the stores had already closed. My sister Kofuji called Mr. Sinsheimer, the owner of a department store and the city mayor for twenty years, to explain our problem. Mr. Sinsheimer knew Father well, for he had entertained many of his guests from Japan. He kindly opened his store, and my sister came out with a bundle or warm clothes.

We waited at the train station for several hours, to no avail. Masaji found out when the next train was due, and we waited for that one too, but Father was not on it. We waited past midnight, and when told there would be no other trains that night, we went home despondent and worried. We were to learn much later that Father's train had been rerouted through Barstow, the southern route. Mother had had such high hopes of seeing Father and had been so eager and bright at the station. Now she looked sad, but did not let down for an instant.

Meanwhile, our phone lines had been tapped, and the road to our farm was under surveillance. We knew this because the FBI came often to the house and questioned us about those who lad called or visited us. Sometimes while Mother spoke on the phone, a voice would say, "Speak English." She was cut off from all other Issei and must have felt very much alone, though she never complained. However, Rev. Todoroki, a fearless Buddhist priest from the S.L.O. Buddhist church, visited her often to offer encouragement and strength. He himself was eventually picked up by the FBI.

About thirty miles north of our farm, a mini-Japanese submarine attacked an American oil tanker near the coast. A local paper accused Father of plowing his farm so that the furrows pointed to the ports where the ships had been anchored. The newspaper also charged that it was known to the authorities that Father had secret meetings with Japanese spies. Mother gasped at the accusations and grimly shook her head. My older sisters, however, incensed, wrote a letter to the newspaper, repudiating the false allegations. It was more than a welcome comment, then, that came from my English teacher, Miss Katherine Sharpsteen, the next morning: "Good, for the Eto sisters!" she announced to the class. "These are trying times, and we must remain calm."

The evacuation orders which first came, divided California in three zones vertically. Zone one covered west of Highway 1 near the coast where we lived, and we were required to move by March. Zone two was west of Highway 99, and we were told we would probably be able to stay there permanently. Not wanting to be too far away from home, we joined our sister Kofuji and her husband, who had rented a farm in Ducor, near Delano. We left Los Osos in March 1942 and slept under the stars in the open field at Ducor.

Even as we unpacked and began constructing makeshift living quarters, Mother put vegetable seeds in the ground so we would have fresh vegetables and *tsukemono* (pickles). She remained calm throughout these hectic times, trying to maintain some sort or normalcy. My brother-in-law planted tomatoes as soon as possible, but about four months later, Ducor was declared a restricted zone, and he was forced to leave his plants. We would have to move again.

Discouraged by this latest government order, we lost the will to fight and decided to enter a government relocation camp instead of trying to relocate ourselves elsewhere. So, we boarded a train in the hot July heat for Manzanar, a camp in the California desert. My sister Toshiko, a nurse, had volunteered to work at the Manzanar hospital on the condition that our family could stay together.

Having grown up in the open spaces, we found Manzanar life oppressive and stifling. Not only were the living conditions inadequate, being thrown in with ten thousand other strangers in one square mile of desert was utterly depressing. We felt like cattle in a corral. People from our home town had gone to Arizona, and we were virtually strangers here. Mother tried to keep our spirits up by telling us how great it was that we didn't have to cook three times a day. She reminded us we should be grateful we were together as one family.

As usual, Mother adapted to the new situation gracefully and kept herself busy knitting dresses for us or creating garments, like the lovely cape, lined in red, which she made from a black pea coat. Not surprisingly, she was thinking of others despite worries of her own: Father had been interned in a high-security concentration camp, and she was having trouble with her dentures. Just before we left for Manzanar, the dentist had to pull out all her teeth. The swelling of her gums had not subsided when the dentures were fitted, so they were painful to wear. She was grateful for the kind cooks at Block 34 mess hall, who were aware of her problem and tried to give her soft pieces of food.

Mother received letters from Father periodically, but a large portion of the letters were cut out or blanked out in ink, censored. She was, however, grateful that Father appeared to be in good health.

We were anxxious to leave Manzanar. It was an abnormal way to live without a family life, as we had known it. Also I was still in high school and wanted a legitimate diploma to continue my education.

Seven months after our internment, we left for Payette, Idaho, where sister Alice and her husband had leased a farm. They gave us housing and work for the duration of the war. Mother cared for her son's first daughter, Lois, and also helped on the farm. She was grateful to her daughter and son-in-law for taking care of her family and wanted to do her part. Only fifty-four years old, she had already experienced more than a lifetime of events.

In the meantime, Father was being shifted with other internees to concentration camps in Montana, Oklahoma, Louisiana, Texas and New Mexico. We were never sure why all this movement was taking place, except that people were continually being taken into these camps, as for example, persons or Japanese ancestry from South American countries. We wondered if the camps were getting overcrowded.

When Father was in Louisiana, Mother learned that sister Susie from an Arkansas camp was able to visit Father with her husband, who had already been inducted in the 442nd Combat Team. My sister recalls how impressed she was at Father's understanding and compassion.

"This is your country," he had said, "and I am proud my son-in-law is serving. You do your best to fight for your country. My internment should make no difference." The son-in-law was to give up his life on an Italian battlefield.

One day, Mother received a odd letter from Father, asking her opinion about the family repatriating to Japan. We thought his morale must have been very low to even ask such a question. Mother's answer was a resolute no. "The United States is our home," she said, "Our family is here, and I do not wish to leave this country."

Mother was overjoyed when Father was finally released from the New Mexico internment camp in the fall of 1944 to join his family in Payette, Idaho. The FBI was not able to charge Father with any wrongdoing. Since he was passing Boise, Idaho, where Nancy and I were going to school, we went to meet him at the train station. With a guard beside him, Father got off the train briefly to see us. I was appalled at his ashen face. Although he stood straight and tall, his clothes hung loosely on his thin body. I admired my sister, so strong and controlled, greeting father and talking with him. I could only hold onto his sleeve and cry, happiness and sadness filling meat once.

In October of 1945, Mother returned with the family to Los Osos to find their yard and home in total disarray. Weeds were so high, they could hardly see their home. The door was partly off the hinge and would not close. To make the deteriorated house somewhat livable, required at least two weeks of repair and cleaning. What had been locked upstairs in a room, had been stolen or thrown out of the window. Mother found the remnants of the beautiful *O Hina Sama* dolls she used to display each year on Girl's Day broken and strewn on the ground.

Nothing could be planted in the fields because the tomato crops were being harvested by the tenants, and they did not want to give this up. Mother, Father and my brother and his family had to make a new beginning.

At age fifty-six, Mother was again helping on the farm as it slowly became reestablished, bunching broccoli, asparagus, or packing tomatoes. It was not easy, but she was determined to get the family back on its feet. "We have been through worse times," she said. This is nothing."

The city of San Luis Obispo had honored Father before the war by naming one of its streets Eto Street. During the war, it was renamed Brook Street. The message was loud and clear. The Eto's were dishonored simply because they were Japanese. This greatly pained my parents, for they had always tried to live uprightly and had contributed to the community as though they were bona fide citizens.

In the summer of 1953, I had to give Mother the bad news that Father must undergo a cancer operation. The doctor later claimed the surgery a success and told us if the cancer did not return in five years, he should be all right. Mother stayed by his side throughout his ordeal and nursed him back to health.

In December of that same year, my parents' lifelong wish was realized, when they proudly became citizens of the U.S. Mother did not speak English fluently, but understood it enough to receive her citizenship. Now America had become their country, and their roots had become firm in the country of their choice.

Father's commitment to public service became even stronger during the post-war period. He wanted the relationship between Japan and the U.S. to improve and thus became involved in an agricultural exchange student program. The students from Japan learned about America as well as agriculture, an important feature of the program to Father and Mother. Even before the war, he used to tell me how crucial people-to-people relationships were between countries. He felt wars were created by heads of governments and that private citizens should get more involved to influence the leaders.

When the Oyama case was brought to court, challenging the Alien Land Law, Father had joined in with many others to support the case.

My parents' public efforts did not go unnoticed. In 1954, they were honored as "Mr. & Mrs. Issei of the Year" at the annual Los Angeles Nisei Festival. Other events followed, but one that I Can remember well was when Lord and Lady Abbot Otani from the Nishi Hongwanji of Kyoto visited their home for lunch. Mother prepared her meal, using many ingredients from her garden. The guests were especially thrilled with the abalone and the clam *sashimi* served in their own shells. "Everything in America is so large," they commented, "even the abalone and the clams."

In 1956, Father received the Fourth Order of the Rising Sun from the Emperor of Japan for his service in bettering relationships between Japan and the U.S. He was privileged to receive it at the Emperor's Palace in Tokyo. Mother was very proud and could not help but reminisce about her many years with him since coming to America.

Perhaps the proudest moment in Mother's life came in January of 1959. A statue of Father was built in his honor at Chida City, Kyushu, Japan for his continuing aid to the Kumamoto citizens who had sought help in the United States as well as his support to the orphanage and schools there. Mother accompanied him for this cherished moment inasmuch as this was also her home town. Little did she dream when she left for America some fifty years earlier that fate would bring them to this happy end.

That very summer, Mother and Father celebrated their 50th wedding anniversary. Father, however, was starting to lose weight. The cancer that had invaded his body five years ago, had reappeared, this time in his liver. He had won many battles in the past, but this was one he could not win.

Mother cared for him and was constantly by his side. When the end was near, Father said goodbye to his family. Then Mother cradled his hand in hers and said, "Please go peacefully. You must not worry about anything, the family or the business. I wish you rest in peace."

Father had always called her his best nurse, his "number one nurse." When he died at 75, Mother was 69 years old. They had lived a full life together. Mother grieved silently and sorely missed him, but she said she had no regrets "I did everything in my power for him while he lived, and he knew that. That is all that matters."

Life had not been easy many times, but Mother and Father had managed to send seven children to college. Now she had time for her own pursuits. At age seventy, Mother began to study *ikebana*, the art of flower arranging. She continued to grow her own flowers and took pride in taking them to her class and sharing them with her friends. She actively participated in arranging flowers at her local Buddhist Church at *Obon* Festivals (memorial festivals of the dead) or during special occasions such as weddings and community functions. My eldest sister Kofuji took her to lessons in Arroyo Grande regularly twice a month. She was happy to see Mother so interested in her classes.

At home, until the age of ninety, Mother made *sushi*, prepared *sashimi*, and even took active part in the *mochi tsuki* by rolling the mass of hot *mochi* with her bare hands while it was being pounded. She also had her vegetable garden, and she took pleasure in the visits from family members.

She asked for so little and gave so much, it was a great pleasure for my sisters, brother, and me to give her a ticket to the Hawaiian Islands to celebrate her 88th birthday. My husband and I accompanied her. She was still very lively and curious, thrilled to see the proteas, anthuriums, the pineapples and the sugar plantations, and eagerly climbed a volcanic mountain. Her eyes shone like a young girl's. Before leaving the Islands, she carefully hand-carried the beautiful flowers given her and wrapped the stems in wet, paper towels to bring them all the way home to Los Osos Valley. Next to her family, plants and nature had been her lift.

Mother had many friends. Many came from neighboring towns to see her in her later days. They kindly brought her flowers and vegetables from their own gardens, or fresh fish from the sea. Since she went out very little during these days, she appreciated their company.

She was walking more slowly now but took daily walks and enjoyed feeding Buster, Masaji's dog. Her favorite pastime was watering her plants and gazing at them as she rested.

Mother lived to be ninety-six years old. In the end, this diminutive woman struggled against all odds, but could not overcome the stroke that befell her. She died three months later.

One of her favorite Buddhist songs was "*Kohoro Hare Bare*," sung at her funeral in October, 1985. Part of the translation reads: "There will certainly be rainy and stormy days. But whether sunny or cloudy, my days are embraced by an emancipating path, the *nembutsu* (Buddhist invocation) of a bright, clear *kokoro* (heart; spirit)."

In every sense, Mother was the embodiment of the words, "*en no shita no chika mochi*," a pillar to her family. She loved us all with boundless patience. Her strength and understanding sustained us, embraced us with comfort and security. Her name, Take, or bamboo, befitted her: she knew how to bend with the wind; she grew straight and strong and had put firm roots in the ground.

Mother's memory evokes happiness, sadness and warmth all at the same time. Her life is an inspiration to me. I cannot adequately express the gratitude I feel for what she has given me, what she was, and what she accomplished in her lifetime. This story, then, is but a token tribute to that end.

Journey to Gold Mountain

At the time of Sieh King King's speech, China was still suffering under the stranglehold of Western imperialism and the inept rule of the Manchus. China's defeat in the Sino-Japanese War (1894-95) and the Boxer Rebellion (1900) resulted in further concessions of extraterritorial rights and war indemnities to the imperialist powers, including Japan, Germany, Russia, France, England, and the United States. China's subjugation, by adding to the humiliation and economic burden of an overtaxed Chinese population, only strengthened the resolve of nationalists to modernize their country and rid China of both foreign domination and Manchu rule. But even after Sun Yat-sen's Tongmenghui (United Covenant League) succeeded in overthrowing the Qing dynasty in 1911, the problems of foreign control, internal dissension, and economic deterioration persisted. Political and social upheavals continued unabated as warlords, and then Nationalists, Communists, and Japanese, fought for control of China. Life for the ordinary Chinese remained disrupted; survival was precarious. Oppressed by the competition of imported foreign commodities, inflation, heavy taxes, increased rents, and rampant banditry, peasants could not hope to make enough money to meet their expenses. A common saying at the time was "The poor man who faces two swords--heavy farm rent and high interest--has three roads before him: to run away at night, hang himself, or go to jail." Consequently, many able-bodied peasants in Southeast China continued to emigrate overseas where kinfolk had already settled. Despite the Chinese Exclusion Acts and anti-Chinese hostilities, a good number went to America, the Gold Mountain, by posing as members of the exempt classes or by smuggling themselves across the borders.

Chinese immigration declined drastically during the Exclusion period (1883-1943). Since many Chinese in the United States were also returning to China (90,299 between 1908 and 1943), the Chinese population in the United States dropped significantly, from 105,465 in 1880 to 61,439 in 1920. By 1900 the industrial revolution was over, the American West had been conquered, and Chinese labor was no longer being recruited. Many Chinese continued to disperse eastward to cities, where they could find work and where their presence was better tolerated. By 1910, 40.5 percent of the Chinese in the United States were concentrated in cities with populations above 25,000; by 1920, the percentage had increased to 44 percent. Most worked in ethnic enterprises in Chinatowns, as domestic servants for European American families, or opened small laundries, grocery stores, and restaurants in out-of-the-way places. Others found seasonal employment in agriculture or in canneries. Those who had the economic means got married and started families or sent for their wives and children from China.

Although there was a precipitous drop in the immigration of Chinese women to the United States following the passage of the Chinese Exclusion Act, their numbers began increasing steadily after 1900. A number of reasons explain this increase despite the effort to keep Chinese and their families out of the country. Conditions at home were worsening and becoming unsafe for family members left behind by overseas Chinese. These deteriorating conditions, combined with the lowering of cultural restrictions against women traveling abroad, encouraged increasing numbers of Chinese women to emigrate overseas to join their husbands or to pursue educational and employment opportunities on their own. Unlike in he nineteenth century, when there were no gainful jobs for them in America, they now had an economic role to play in the urban economy or in their husbands' small businesses. Only immigration legislation continued to limit the numbers of women as well as dictate who could come at all.

Most Chinese women entered the country as merchant wives, the class most favored by immigration legislation throughout the Exclusion period. Until 1924, wives of U.S citizens were also admissible but the passage of the Immigration Act of 1924, which was aimed primarily at curbing immigration from eastern, southern, and central Europe, dealt Asian immigration a deadly blow when it included a clause that barred any "alien ineligible to citizenship" admittance. By law, this group included the Chinese, Japanese, Koreans, and Asian Indians. On May 25, 1925, the U.S. Supreme Court ruled that Chinese merchant wives were still admissible because of treaty obligations: the Chinese wives of U.S. citizens, however, being themselves ineligible for citizenship, were not. Alarmed by what this interpretation would mean for their future in America, American-born Chinese fought back through the organized efforts of the Chinese American Citizens Alliance. Arguing persuasively that every male American citizen had the right to have his wife with him, that it was inhumane to keep husbands and wives separated, and that aliens (merchants) should not be entitled to more rights under the immigration laws than U.S. citizens, they moved Congress to amend the 1924 act in 1930 to permit the entry of Chinese alien wives of U.S. citizens--but only those who were married prior to May 26, 1924. Another way for Chinese men to come to the United States was as daughters of U.S. citizens. In this case, however, they were allowed entry only if they claimed derivative citizenship through the father (not the mother), and they had to be unmarried. A few women also came as students, one of the classes exempted from exclusion. But Chinese female students amounted to only about thirty annually in the 1910's and several dozens annually in the 1920's.

Even those with the legal right to immigrate sometimes failed to pass the difficult interrogations and physical examinations required only of Chinese immigrants. Aware of intimidating entry procedures, many were discouraged from even trying to immigrate. Many Chinese Americans shared the sentiments of Pany Lowe, an American-born Chinese man who was interviewed in 1924:

> Sure I go back to China two times. Stay ten or fifteen months each time. I do not want to bring my wife to this country. Very hard get her in. I know how immigration inspector treat me first time when I come back eighteen years old...My father have to go to court. They keep me on boat for two or three days. Finally he got witness and affidavit prove me to be citizen. They let me go, so I think if they make trouble for me they make trouble for my wife...I think most Chinese in this country like have their son go China get married. Under this new law [Immigration Act of 1924], can't do this. No allowed marry white girl. Not enough American-born Chinese to go around, China only place to get wife. Not allowed to bring them back. For Chinaman, very unjust. Not human. Very uncivilized.

American immigration laws and the process of chain migration also determined that most Chinese women would continue to come from the rural villages of Guangdong Province, where traditional gender roles still prevailed. Wong Ah So and Law Shee Low, both of whom immigrated in 1922, serve as examples of Guangdong village women who came as obedient daughters or wives to escape poverty and for the sake of their families. Jane Kwong Lee, who also came to the United States in 1922, was among the small number of urbanized "new women" who emigrated on their own for improved opportunities and adventure. Together, these three women's stories provide insights into the gender roles and immigration experiences of Chinese women in the early twentieth century.

"I was born in Canton [Guangdong] Province," begins Wong Ah So's story, "my father was sometimes a sailor and sometimes he worked on the docks, for we were very poor." Patriarchal cultural values often put the daughter at risk when poverty strikes: from among the five children (two boys and three girls) in the family, her mother chose to betroth her, the eldest daughter, to a Gold Mountain man in exchange for a price of 450 Mexican dollars.

> I was 19 when this man came to my mother and said that in America there was a great deal of gold. Even if I just peeled potatoes there, he told my mother I would earn seven or eight dollars a day, and if I was willing to do any work at all I would earn lots of money. He was a laundryman, but said he earned plenty of money. He was very nice to me, and my mother liked him, so my mother was glad to have me go with him as his wife.

Out of filial duty and economic necessity, Ah So agreed to sail to the United States with this laundryman, Huey Yow, in 1922: "I was told by my mother that I was to come to the United States to earn money with which to support my parents and my family in Hongkong." Sharing the same happy thoughts about going to America as many other immigrants before her, she said, "I thought that I was his wife, and was very grateful that he was taking me to such a grand, free county, where every one was rich and happy."

Huey Yow had a marriage certificate prepared and told her to claim him as her husband to the immigration officials in San Francisco, although there had been no marriage ceremony. "In accordance to my mother's demands I became a party to this arrangement," Ah So admitted later. "On my arrival at the port of San Francisco, I claimed to be the wife of Huey Yow, but in truth had not at any time lived with him as his wife."

Law Shee Low (Law Yuk Tao was her given name before marriage), who was a year younger than Wong Ah So, was born in the village of Kai Gok in Chungshan District, Guangdong Province. Economic and political turmoil in the country hit her family hard. Once well-to-do, they were reduced to poverty in repeated raids by roving bandits. As Law recalled, conditions became so bad that the family had to sell their land and give up their three servants; all four daughters had to quit school and help at home.

> My grandmother, mother, and an aunt all had bound feet and it was so painful for them to get around. When they got up in the morning, I had to go fetch the water for them to wash up and carry the night soil buckets out. Every morning, we had to draw water from the well for cooking, for tea, and for washing. I would help grandmother with the cooking, and until I became older, I was the one who went to the village marketplace every day to shop.

Along with one other sister, Law was also responsible for sweeping the floor, washing dishes, chopping wood, tending the garden, and scrubbing the brick floor after each rainfall. In accordance with traditional gender roles, none of her brothers had to help. "They went to school. It was work for girls to do," she said matter-of-factly.

As in the case of Wong Ah So, cultural values and economic necessity led her parents to arrange a marriage for Law with a Gold Mountain man. Although aware of the sad plight of other women in her village who were married to Gold Mountain men--her own sister-in-law had gone insane when her husband in America did not return or send money home to support her--Law still felt fortunate: she would be going to America with her husband.

> I had no choice; we were so poor. If we had the money, I'm sure my mother would have kept me at home...We had no food to go with rice, not even soy sauce or black bean paste. Some of our neighbors even had to go begging or sell their daughters, times were so bad...So my parents thought I would have a better future in Gold Mountain.

Her fiance said he was a clothing salesman in San Francisco and a Christian. He had a minister from Canton preside over the first "modern" wedding in his village. Law was eighteen and her husband, thirty-four. Nine months after the wedding, they sailed for America.

Jane Kwong Lee was born in the same region of China (Op Lee Jeu village, Toishan District, Guangdong Province) at about the same time (1902). But in contrast to Law Shee Low and Wong Ah So, she came from a higher-class background and emigrated under different circumstances. Her life story, as told in her unpublished autobiography, shows how social and political conditions in China made "new women" out of some like herself. Like Law and Ah So, Jane grew up subjected to the sexist practices of a patriarchal society. Although her family was not poor, her birth was not welcomed.

I was the second daughter, and two girls in a row were too many, according to my grandparents. Girls were not equal to boys, they maintained. Girls, after they married, belonged to other families; they could not inherit the family name; they could not help the family financially no matter how good they were at housework. In this atmosphere of emotional depression I was an unwanted child, and to add to the family sadness the weather seemed to be against me too. There was a drought, the worst drought in many years, and all the wells dried up except one. Water had to he rationed. My long (youngest) uncle went out to get the family's share daily. The day after I was born, the man at the well gave him the usual allotment, but my uncle insisted on obtaining one more scoop. The man asked why and the answer was, "We have one more mouth." Then, and only then, the villagers became aware that there had been a baby born in their midst. My grandparents were ashamed of having two granddaughters consecutively and were reluctant to have their neighbors know they had one more person in their family. They wanted grandsons and hoped for grandsons in the future. That is why they named me "Lin Hi," meaning "Link Young Brother." They believed in good omens and I did not disappoint them. My brother was born a year and a half later.

Compared to Law's hard-working childhood, Jane lived a carefree life, playing hide-and-seek in the bamboo groves, catching sparrows and crabs, listening to ghost stories, and helping the family's *mui tsai* tend the vegetable garden. It was a life punctuated by holiday observances and celebrations of new births and marriages as well as the turmoil of family illnesses and deaths, droughts and floods, political uprisings and banditry.

Like Law, Jane came from a farming background. Her grandfather was successful in accumulating land, which he leased out to provide for the family. Her uncle and father were businessmen in Australia; their remittances made the difference in helping the family weather natural disasters and banditry and provided the means by which Jane was able to acquire an education at True Light Seminary in Canton. Social reforms and progressive views on women's equality at the time also helped to make her education possible:

Revolution was imminent. Progress was coming. Education for girls was widely advocated. Liberal parents began sending their daughters to school. My long [youngest] aunt, sixth aunt-in-law, godsister Jade and cousin Silver went to attend the True Light Seminary in Canton. Women's liberation had begun. It was the year 1911--the year the Ching [Qing] Dynasty was overthrown and the Republic of China was born.

Her parents were among the liberal ones who believed that daughters should be educated if family means allowed it. Her father had become a Christian during his long sojourn in Australia, and her mother was the first in their village to unbind her own feet. From the age of nine, Jane attended True Light, a boarding school for girls and women sponsored by the Presbyterian

Missionary Board in the United States. She completed her last year of middle school at the coeducational Canton Christian College. It was during this time that she adopted the Western name Jane. By then, "the Western wind was slowly penetrating the East and old customs were changing," she wrote.

The curriculum stressed English and the three R's--reading, writing, and arithmetic--but also included classical Chinese literature. In addition, students had the opportunity to work on the school journal, learn Western music appreciation, and participate in sports--volleyball, baseball, and horseback riding. The faculty, all trained in the United Sates, exposed students to Western ideas of democracy and women's emancipation. During her last year in school, Jane, along with her classmates, was swept up by the May Fourth Movement, in which students agitated for political and cultural reforms in response to continuing foreign domination at the end of World War I:

> The 21 demands from Japan stirred up strong resentment from the students as well as the whole Chinese population. We boycotted Japanese goods and bought only native-manufactured fabrics. We participated in demonstration parades in the streets of Canton. Student delegates were elected to attend student association discussion meetings in Canton; once I was appointed as one of two delegates from our school. Our two-fold duty was to take part in the discussions and decisions and then to convince our schoolmates to take active parts in whatever action was decided. It was a year of turmoil for all the students and of exhaustion for me.

By the time she graduated from middle school, Jane had decided she wanted to become a medical doctor, believing "it would give me not only financial independence, but also social prestige." Her only other choices at the time were factory work or marriage. But further education seemed out of the question because her father's remittances from Australia could no longer support the education of both Jane and her younger brother. Arguing that graduates trained in American colleges and universities were drawing higher salaries in China than local graduates, Jane convinced her mother to sell some of their land in order to pay her passage to the United States. Her mother also had hopes that she would find work teaching at Chinese schools in America and be able to send some of her income home. In1922, Jane obtained a student visa and sailed for the United States, planning to earn a doctorate and return home to a prestigious academic post. Her class background, education, and early exposure to Western ideas would lead her to a different life experience in America than Law Shee Low and Wong Ah So, who came as obedient wives from sheltered and impoverished families.

Detainment at Angel Island

Like thousands of immigrants before them, Law Shee Low, Wong Ah So, and Jane Kwong Lee had to pass immigration inspection upon their arrival in America. In contrast to the frightening but relatively brief stay of European immigrants at Ellis Island in New York Harbor, most Chinese immigrant women experienced humiliation and despair during their extended detainment at the Port of San Francisco owing to the strict implementation of the Chinese Exclusion laws. Prior to the building of the Angel Island Immigration Station in1910, Chinese immigrants were housed in a dilapidated wooden shed at the Pacific Mail Steamship Company wharf. The testimony of Mai Zhouyi, a missionary from Canton and wife of a Chinese merchant,

169

describes the ordeal of detainment suffered by Chinese immigrant women. Locked in the shed for over forty days pending investigation of her right to land, she spoke out against the inhumane treatment she received there at a public gathering in Chinatown following her release:

> All day long I faced the walls and did nothing except eat and sleep like a caged animal. Others--Europeans, Japanese Koreans--were allowed to disembark almost immediately. Even blacks were greeted by relatives and allowed to go ashore. Only we Chinese were not allowed to see or talk to our loved ones and were escorted by armed guards to the wooden house. Frustrated, we could only sigh and groan. Even the cargo was picked up from the docks and delivered to its destination after custom duties were paid. Only we Chinese were denied that right. How can it be that they look upon us as animals? As less than cargo? Do they think we Chinese are not made of flesh and blood? That we don't have souls? Human beings are supposed to be the superior among all creatures. Should we allow ourselves to be treated like cargo and dumb animals?

Her sentiments echo those of European immigrants who experienced Ellis Island as the "Island of Tears," of bars, cages, and callous brutality on the part of immigration officials. As Fannie Kligerman, who had fled the pogroms in Russia, recalled:

> It was like a prison. They threw us around. You know that children don't know anything. They would say, "Stay here. Stay there." And you live through it, you just don't fight back. And when it came to food we never had fresh bread, the bread was always stale. Where they got it, we don't know...Everybody was sad there. There was not a smile on anybody's face. Here they thought maybe they wouldn't go through. There they thought maybe my child won't go through. There was such a sadness, no smile any place...Just so much sadness there that you have to cry.

Whereas most European immigrants remember the confusion of being quickly processed through the cursory physical, mental, and legal examinations, and the brief moment of fear at possibly being refused entry for reasons of health, morals, or finances, Chinese immigrants who passed through Angel Island have more haunting memories of being locked up in the "wooden building" for weeks and months, the fearful interrogation sessions where they were asked hundreds of questions regarding their past, and the frustration and humiliation of being treated as criminals for nothing more than the simple desire to enter the promised land. Ellis Island was an island not just of tears but also of hope for most European immigrants; for Chinese immigrants, however, Angel Island (nicknamed the "Ellis Island of the West" by immigration authorities) was a prison to men and women alike.

Jane Kwong Lee's status as a student spared her the agony of Angel Island. Along with other first-class passengers who were members of the exempt classes, she had her papers inspected aboard ship and was allowed to land immediately. In contrast, after their ship docked in San Francisco Bay, Law Shee Low and Wong Ah So were separated from their husbands and taken to Angel Island for physical examination and interrogation.

Like hundreds of other Chinese before her, Law had an unfavorable first impression of America via Angel Island. Unaccustomed to disrobing before male doctors and presenting stool samples in a test for parasitic diseases, Chinese women suffered personal humiliation during the physical examination. "Those with bookworms had to go to the hospital," said Law. "Liver fluke was incurable, but hookworm was. There was a new bride who had liver fluke and was deported."

After the physical examination, Law remembers being locked up indefinitely in the women's barracks with a dozen other Chinese women to await interrogation.

It was like being in prison. They let us out for meals and then locked us up again when we came back. They brought us knitting things but we didn't know how. They were willing to teach us but we weren't in the mood. We just sat there all day and looked out the windows…We didn't even care to go out to eat, the food was so bad…The bean sprouts was cooked so badly you wanted to throw up when you saw it. There was rice but it was cold, I just took a few spoonfuls and left. Same food all the time. We began craving for salted fish and chicken. We wanted preserved bean paste. Their food was steamed to death; smelled bad and tasted bad. The vegetables were old and the beef was of poor quality and fatty. They must have thought we were pigs.

Fortunately for Law, her husband sent her some *dim sum* (Chinese savory pastries), fresh fruit, and Chinese sausages, which she gladly shared with other women in the barracks. "The Western woman we called Ma [Deaconess Katharine Maurer, appointed by the Women's Home Missionary Society of the Methodist Episcopal Church to tend to the needs of Chinese women at Angel Island] delivered it. Called our names. Searched it first for fear of coaching notes [to help her during her interrogation]," Law explained.

Finally, after ten days of waiting, Law was called to appear before the Board of Special Inquiry. Following the advice of the other women, she drank a few mouthfuls of cold water to control the fear within her.

One woman who was in her fifties was questioned all day and then later deported, which scared all of us. She said they asked her about [life in China:] the chickens and the neighbors, and the direction the house faced. How would I know all that? I was scared. Fortunately, they didn't ask me all that. Just when I got married. When the interpreter asked me whether I visited my husband's ancestral home during the wedding, I said no because I was afraid he was going to ask me which direction the house faced like the woman told me and I wouldn't know. Evidently their father [her husband] had said yes. So when they asked me again and I said no, their father, who was being interrogated at the same time the second time around, said, "*Choy*! You went back; why don't you say so?" The Westerner [immigration officer] hit the table with his hand [in objection] and scared me to death. So when he slapped the table, I quickly said, "Oh, I forgot. I did pass by [in the wedding sedan chair] but I didn't go in." So they let me land. But when they led me back to the barracks, I thought I would be deported so I cried. Later at 4 P.M., they called me to get on the boat to go to San Francisco and the others happily helped me gather my things together to leave.

Compared to others, Law's interrogation was unusual in that her husband was allowed to sit in and the process was concluded in one day. "It could have been because this church lady helped us," she suggested. It was generally known that a supporting letter from Donaldina Cameron of the Presbyterian Mission Home often helped get cases landed.

For many other Chinese immigrants, the ordeal at Angel Island was much more agonizing and prolonged. Because affidavits and records had to be reviewed and the testimonies given by immigrants and their witnesses corroborated, even the most expeditious case generally took at least a week. According to one study of procedures at Angel Island, "Each applicant is asked from two or three hundred questions to over a thousand. The records of the hearing generally runs in length from twenty to eighty typewritten pages, depending on the nature of the case." In contrast, European immigrants at Ellis Island were asked a total of twenty-nine questions. In all the Chinese cases, the burden of proof rested on the detainee to show that he or she was not an inadmissible alien. For those who failed the interrogation--usually because of discrepancies in their answers to detailed questions relating to their family history or village life in China--appeals to the Commissioner of Immigration in Washington, D.C., led to additional expenses and extended stays at Angel Island of another six months to a year. According to the testimony of an immigration inspector who was assigned to the Angel Island Immigration Station from 1929 to 1940, "More than 75 percent passed the interrogation at Angel Island. Of those that were denied here, there was always an appeal to Washington and probably only 5 percent of those denied were ever really deported." These statistics were similar in the experience of European immigrants at Ellis Island, where in general only 2 percent of them were deemed "undesirable aliens" and deported. But statistics do not reveal the different process that only Chinese immigrants were subjected to, a process different not only in degree but also in kind.

The disparate responses of Chinese men and women confronted by this harsh treatment reveal their respective gender roles as defined by their home culture and then adapted to their new environment at Angel Island. While the men passed the time actively--reading Chinese newspapers, playing sports outdoors in a fenced-in area, listening to Chinese phonograph records, and gambling or debating among themselves--the women sat around and waited quietly, some occupying their time with needlework. A few took advantage of the weekly walks outside under the watchful eyes of a guard. Whereas the men organized a Self-Governing Association for mutual assistance and to protest conditions at Angel Island, the women did not organize and seemed unable to voice objections to their harsh treatment. Their one defender and friend was Methodist Deaconess Katharine Maurer, known as the "Angel of Angel Island." Assigned to work among the Chinese detainees beginning in 1912, she shopped for the women, provided them with needlework materials, taught them the Bible and English, wrote letters, organized holiday programs for them, and administered to their various needs. Men were able to vent their anger and frustrations by carving poems into the barrack walls, many of which are still visible today. Women, deprived of education, were less literate, and although some remember seeing lines of poetry on the barrack walls, most could not express themselves in writing. One Chinese woman who was illiterate resorted to memorizing the coaching information on her family back-ground by putting it into song.

As women waited for the ordeal to pass, many shared the sentiments of a Mrs. Jew, who was detained on Angel Island the same year as Law Shee Low and Wang Ah So:

There wasn't anything special about it. Day in, day out, the same thing. Every person had to be patient and tell herself, "I'm just being delayed, it doesn't matter." I never even bathed. I kept thinking each day that I would be ready to leave and as each day went by, I just waited. I didn't eat much, nor move around much, so I never perspired. I had no clothes to wash. I kept thinking, "Had I known it was like this, I never would have wanted to come!"

Confined in the barracks together for indefinite sentences, women maintained a pragmatic attitude and bonded in an effort to cope with the situation. They chatted with one another, shared whatever food they had, dressed one another's hair, consoled those who had failed the in-terrogation, and accompanied one another to the bathroom after hearing stories of women who had hung themselves there. When asked who comforted the women when they became depressed, Law replied:

Who was depressed? There were two women who had been there for three months. They didn't cry; didn't seem to care. They even sang sometimes and joked with the man who came in to do the cleaning. Whenever this foreign woman offered to take us out for walks, usually on Fridays, just the two would go. They were two friends and very happy and carefree. They had little going for them, but they managed to struggle on.

Although sobbing was often heard in the women's barracks and there were known cases of suicide, this cultural attribute of "making do" helped many Chinese women through detainment at Angel Island. When finally granted permission to land, immigrant women like Law Shee Low and Wong Ah So tried to put Angel Island behind them as they began their new lives in America.

"New Women" in the
Modern Era of Chinatown

The San Francisco Chinatown that Law Shee Low, Wong Ah So, and Jane Kwong Lee came to call home was different from the slum of "filth and depravity" of bygone days. After the 1906 earthquake and fire destroyed Chinatown, Chinese community leaders seized the opportunity to create a new "Oriental City" on the original site. The new Chinatown, in stark contrast to the old, was by appearance cleaner, healthier, and more modern with its wider paved streets, brick buildings, glass-plated storefronts, and pseudo-Chinese architecture. Dupont Street (now Grant Avenue), lined with bazaars, clothing stores, restaurants, newspaper establishments, grocery stores, drugstores, bookstores, and meat and fish markets, became the main business thoroughfare for local residents and a major tourist attraction by the time of the Panama Pacific International Exposition in 1915. But behind the facade of the "Oriental City," hastily built with tourism and business in mind, was a ghetto plagued by overcrowding, substandard housing, and poor sanitation. Dwelling units for bachelors were constructed above, below, and behind shops in crowded quarters and often with poor lighting and ventilation. There were so few Chinese families then that little thought was given to their housing needs.

Aside from the change in physical appearance, Chinatown was also socially transformed by life under Exclusion. Internal economic and political strife mounted as the Chinese community-- kept out of the professions and trades, and isolated within a fifteen-block area of the city-- developed its own economic infrastructure, political parties, and social institutions. Merchant associations, trade guilds, and tongs fought over control of the distribution and commercial use of Chinatown's limited space and economic resources, often engaging in bloody warfare in the period from the 1880's to the 1920's. At the same time, strife developed among political factions that disagreed on the best strategy to save China. The Zhigongtang (the American counterpart of the Triad Society in China) favored restoring the Ming emperor; the Baohuanghui advocated a constitutional monarchy; and the Tongmenghui (forerunner of the Guomindang) saw a democratic republic as the answer to China's future. In an effort to establish order in the community, nurture business and protect the growing numbers of families, the merchant elite and middle-class bourgeoisie established new institutions: Chinese schools, churches, a hospital, newspapers, and a flurry of organizations such as the Chinese Chamber of Commerce, Chinese American Citizens Alliance, Chinatown YMCA and YWCA, Christian Union, and Peace Society. Many of these new social groups also formed alliances with outside law enforcement agents and moral reformers to eliminate gambling, prostitution and drugs in an effort to clean up Chinatown's image. Their work was met with strong resistance from the tongs that profited by these vice industries, but the progressive forces eventually won out. As reported in the community's leading newspaper, *Chung Sai Yat Po (CSYP)*, soon after the 1911 Revolution in China, queues and footbinding were eliminated, tong wars and prostitution reduced, and more of Chinatown's residents were dressing in Western clothing and adopting democratic ideas. Arriving in San Francisco Chinatown at this juncture in time gave immigrant women such as Wang Ah So, Law Shee Low, and Jane Kwong Lee unprecedented opportunities to become "new women" in the modern era of Chinatown.

Decline in Prostitution

Fortunately for Wong Ah So, prostitution was already on the decline by the time she arrived in San Francisco, thanks to the efforts of Chinese nationalists, Protestant missionaries, and those who supported the social purity movement. As her case demonstrates, Chinese women brought to the United States as prostitutes at this time continued to suffer undue hardships but benefited from the social historical forces intent on eliminating prostitution in the city. Moreover, it reveals the inner workings of the Chinese prostitution trade, the complicit role of Chinese madams in the illegal business, and the coping mechanisms Chinese prostitutes devised to deal with their enslavement.

Upon landing, Ah So's dreams of wealth and happiness vanished when she found out that her husband, Huey Yow, had in fact been paid $500 by Sing Yow, a madam, to procure her as a slave.

> When we first landed in San Francisco we lived in a hotel in Chinatown, a nice place, but one day, after I had been there for about two weeks, a woman came to see me. She was young, very pretty, and all dressed in silk. She told me that I was not really Huey Yow's wife, but that she had asked him to buy her a slave, that I belonged to her, and must go with her, but she would treat me well, and I could buy back my freedom, if I was willing to please, and be agreeable, and she would let me off in two years, instead of four if I did not make a fuss.

For the next year, Ah So worked as a prostitute for Sing Yow in various small towns. She was also forced to borrow $1,000 to pay off Huey Yow, who was harassing her and threatening her life. Then, seeking higher profits, Sing Yow betrayed her promise and sold Ah So to another madam in Fresno for $2,500. "When I came to America," Ah So's story continues, "I did not know that I was going to live a life of slavery, but understood from women with whom I talked in Hongkong that I was to serve at Chinese banquets and serve as an entertainer for the guests. I was very miserable and unhappy. My owners knew this and kept very close watch over me, fearing that I might try to escape."

Meanwhile, her family in China continued to write her asking for money. Even as her debts piled up and she became ill, she fulfilled her filial obligation by sending $300 home to her mother, enclosed with a letter that read in part:

> Every day I have to be treated by the doctor. My private parts pain me so that I cannot have intercourse with men. It is very hard…Next year I certainly will be able to pay off all the debts. Your daughter is even more anxious than her mother to do this. As long as your daughter's life lasts she will pay up all the debts. Your daughter will do her part so that the world will not look down upon us.

In another letter to her mother, aside from reconfirming her commitment to fulfill the responsibilities of a filial daughter, Ah So also expressed the desire to "expiate my sin" by becoming a Buddhist nun--the correct move by traditional moral standards. She had indeed internalized the social expectations of virtuous Chinese women, putting these values to good use in helping herself cope with her present, desperate situation.

But before Ah So could realize her wish, help arrived. One evening at a tong banquet where she was working, she was recognized by a friend of her father's, who sought help from the Presbyterian Mission Home on her behalf. Ten days later, Ah So was rescued and placed in the care of Donaldina Cameron. As she wrote, "I don't know just how it happened because it was all very sudden. I just know that it happened. I am learning English and to weave, and I am going to send money to my mother when I can. I can't help but cry, but it is going to be better. I will do what Miss Cameron says." A year later, after learning how to read Chinese and speak English and after becoming a Christian, Ah So agreed to marry Louie Kwong, a merchant in Boise, Idaho.

Her connections to Cameron and the Presbyterian Mission Home did not end there, though. A few years later, Ah So wrote to complain about her husband and to ask Cameron for advice. Louie Kwong had joined the Hop Sing Tong, refused to educate his own daughters (by a previous marriage), had struck her and refused to pay her old boarding fees in the Mission Home, and, worst of all, threatened to send for a concubine from China because she had not borne him a son. This complaint to Cameron about her husband shows that she had evidently changed her attitude regarding traditional gender roles. In support, Cameron promptly sent a Chinese missionary worker to investigate the matter. It must have helped because five years later, in another letter to Cameron dated December 28, 1933, Ah So wrote about being happily married and "busy, very busy" raising her husband's three daughters, their own two sons and a daughter, plus an adopted daughter and a brother-in-law's ten-year-old son. Ah So had made it back to China only to find that her mother had died and entrusted her with the lives of her two younger brothers and two younger sisters. "I am very grateful and thankful to God that my husband is willing to care for these smaller brothers and [unmarried] sister and help them," she wrote. With the closing assurance that "the girls and I are getting along fine," she enclosed a photograph of herself with her husband and enlarged family.

Wong Ah So's story harks back to the plight of the many Chinese women who were brought to the United States as prostitutes to fill a specific need in the Chinese bachelor society. By the 1920's, however, the traffic had gone underground and was on the decline. In 1870, the peak year of prostitution, 1,426 or 71 percent of Chinese women in San Francisco were listed as prostitutes. By 1900 the number had dropped to 339 or 16 percent; and by 1910, 92 or 7 percent. No prostitutes could be found in the 1920 census, although English- and Chinese-language newspaper accounts and the records of the Presbyterian Mission Home indicate that the organized prostitution of Chinese women in San Francisco continued through the 1920's. The last trial of a prostitution ring occurred in 1935, in which damaging testimony by two courageous Chinese prostitute--Leung Kwai Ying and Wong So--led to the conviction of Wong See Duck, a hardware merchant and longtime dealer in prostitution, and his three accomplices. The Exclusion Acts and other anti-prostitution legislation passed in the late nineteenth century had succeeded in stemming the traffic, but not eradicating it. Even the earthquake and fire of 1906, which destroyed Chinatown, did not wipe out prostitution, for brothels were reopened in the new buildings. As law enforcers stepped in to curb the trade, prices escalated and ingenious methods were devised to circumvent the law. After the earthquake, prostitutes sold for $3,000, and the services of lawyers hired to keep them in the possession of their owners averaged $700 a case.

By the 1920's, the price of a young Chinese woman in her teens had risen to as much as $6,000 to $10,000 in gold.

To bypass immigration restrictions, women were coached to enter the country disguised as U.S. citizens or wives of U.S. citizens. One newspaper account reported that they came with "red certificates," a document issued to American-born Chinese females who had departed for China between 1880 and 1884. Although immigration inspectors suspected that these certificates--which were never marked "Canceled"-- were being reused by women assuming bogus identities, they could not prove it, especially when an abundance of Chinese witnesses was on hand to vouch for the women's identities. Still another newspaper account stated that American-born Chinese men were being paid to bring in "wives" when they returned from visits to China. Other women reportedly came in disguised as theatrical performers, gained entry by bribing immigration officials, or were smuggled in as stowaways or across the Canadian or Mexican border. As the importation of women became more difficult, local sources were tapped, and the kidnapping of young women and the sales of *mui tsai* into prostitution increased.

Public opposition to prostitution and other social vices, spurred by female moral reformers and Chinese nationalist leaders, was on the rise in the early 1900's and contributed greatly to the demise of the trade. In 1900, Donaldina Cameron took over as superintendent of the Presbyterian Mission Home. The youngest daughter of Scottish sheep ranchers, Cameron was born in 1867, two years before her parents moved from New Zealand to California. At the age of twenty-five, after breaking off an engagement, she found her calling at the Presbyterian Mission Home, assisting matron Margaret Culbertson in her rescue work. Deeply religious, maternal, and committed to Victorian moral values, Cameron seemed the perfect choice for the job. Called *lo mo* (mother) by her young charges and *fan gwai* (foreign devil) by her critics in the Chinese community, she became well known for her rescue work. Numerous accounts describe in vivid detail the dangerous raids led by Cameron, who was credited with rescuing hundreds of Chinese slave girls during her forty years of service at the Mission Home. Following the tradition established by Culbertson, Cameron provided a home for the rescued women, educated them, trained them in job skills, and inculcated them with Victorian moral values. The goal was to regroom them to enter society as Christian women. While some women chose to return to China under Christian escort, others opted to enter companionate marriages, pursue higher education, or become missionary workers. Indeed, the Mission Home's goal was best expressed in a drama devised and presented by Cameron and her staff at a national jubilee held at the home in 1920:

> "The Pictured Years" showed the Chinese work under that militant Saint, Miss Culbertson, and also under Miss Cameron and Miss Higgins. Realistic scenes of rescue work in the cellars and on the roofs of the Chinese quarter were thrillingly presented; ...the days of the exodus, after the earthquake and during the great fire of 1906; a prune-picking scene, prettily staged, showing the latest experience of our Chinese girls; and the climax--a tableau of a Christian Chinese family (the wife and mother a former ward of the Board), with the daughter in University cap and gown.

Such was the ideal transformation that Cameron as the benevolent white mother wanted for her Chinese "harvest of waifs gathered from among an alien and heathen people," as she herself described them. Yet she was also known for defending Chinese women against stereotyping, sensationalization, and ideas of racial determinism. Although some historians have criticized Cameron for her patronizing attitude and the regimented way in which she ran the Mission Home, those who knew and worked with her have only a high regard for her work among the Chinese.

While Cameron and the Presbyterian Mission took the leadership role and credit for rescuing Chinese prostitutes, they did not work alone. They sought and received the cooperation of immigration and juvenile authorities, law enforcement agents, lawyers, the judicial system, and both the English- and Chinese-language presses, as well as civic-minded groups and individuals. Dramatic newspaper accounts of rescue raids helped to keep the anti-prostitution campaign alive while at the same time promoting the Protestant women's crusade for moral reform. The celebrated case of Kum Quey was one such well-publicized story that shows not only Cameron's uncanny skills at rescue work, but also the extent of public support that was needed to free one Chinese girl from slavery.

According to popular accounts, Kum Quey was first rescued by Cameron from a brothel in Baker Alley and was living in the Mission Home when her owner and a constable from San Jose came to arrest her on trumped-up charges of grand larceny. Suspecting foul play, Cameron accompanied Kum Quey to Palo Alto and insisted on staying with her in jail while she awaited trial. Early that morning, three men broke into the jail cell, overpowered Cameron, and abducted Kum Quey. The men got a judge to hold an impromptu trial on a country road in their favor, and then forced Kum Quey into marrying one of them. Meanwhile, with the help of a Palo Alto druggist, a network of informants, and the cooperation of a policeman, Cameron caught up with the party in San Francisco and had one of the abductors arrested. Her retelling of the abduction, well covered in the local newspapers, incensed private citizens as well as Stanford University students. They condemned the affair and the complicity of local officials at a town hall meeting, raised funds for Kum Quey's cause, and stormed the local jail in protest.

Through her Chinese contacts, Cameron found out that Kum Quey had come to the United States two years before as one of seventy "Oriental maidens" for the Omaha Exposition but instead was put to work in a Chinatown brothel. With this new information in hand, Cameron solicited the help of immigration authorities. During the trial Kum Quey defied her owner's instructions, admitting instead that she had entered the United States illegally and been forced into prostitution. Not giving up, the abetting constable slipped out of the courtroom and attempted to run off with Kum Quey, but was successfully pursued and apprehended by an immigration officer and a private citizen. The court gave Kum Quey into Cameron's guardianship, and a San Jose grand jury later indicted the judge, constable, and abductors involved in the crime. And so happily ended the story of Kum Quey.

The developments in the Kum Quey case were followed closely in *CSYP*. Edited by the Presbyterian minister Ng Poon Chew, the newspaper was influential in molding public opinion against Chinese prostitution in the context of its overall advocacy of the modernization of China and social reform in Chinatown. Numerous editorials in *CSYP* argued that *mui tsai* and prostitutes were signs of Chinese decadence in the eyes of Westerners and should be eradicated. Those involved in the prostitution trade were told to search their consciences and mend their ways. With the establishment of shelters for prostitutes rescued by missionaries and through the efforts of both the American and Chinese governments to suppress prostitution, "your Profits will suffer and your reputation [will be] ruined," admonished one editorial. Attempts were also made by middle-class institutions such as the Chinese consulate, Chinese Six Companies, Chinese Society of English Education, Chinese Students Alliance, Chinese American Citizens Alliance, and Chinese Cadet Corps to discourage if not stop the prostitution trade in Chinatown. All opponents had to put their lives at risk in the face of the overwhelming power of tongs in Chinatown, specifically the secret societies that had most to lose from the demise of prostitution.

By the early 1900's, however, the nation's purity crusade had reached the West Coast. After the 1906 earthquake, Catholic, Protestant, and Jewish moral reformers joined efforts to mount an all-out attack against prostitution and commercialized vice in San Francisco. The American Purity Federation even threatened to seek a national boycott of the upcoming Panama-Pacific International Exposition if the city failed to clean up its image. In the atmosphere of progressivism that had gripped the entire nation, there rose a public outcry against venereal diseases and the international trafficking of white slavery-"the procuring, selling, or buying of women with the intention of holding or forcing them into a life of prostitution." Melodramatic stories of innocent white women who had been tricked and forced into a brutal life of prostitution--not unlike the situation of Chinese prostitutes--drew the passionate ire of humanitarians and purity reformers committed to correcting sexual mores in the nation. Their efforts culminated in the 1910 passage of the White Slave Traffic Act (also known as the Mann Act after its author, Congressman James R. Mann), which in effect outlawed the interstate and international trafficking in women.

As there were few convictions, and as the act did not address voluntary prostitution, individual states next stepped in with the enactment of "red-light" abatement laws, which sought to prosecute the brothel owners. Prostitution was finally curtailed in San Francisco after the California legislature passed the Red-Light Abatement Act in 1913. The first raid and test case under this act was a Chinese brothel at Dupont and Bartlett Alley owned by Woo Sam. The prosecution was upheld by both the U.S. District Court and the California Supreme Court in 1917, and after that, local police closed almost all brothels in the city, including those in Chinatown. With the advent of World War I, further legislation was passed to wipe out the remaining traces of prostitution that had gone underground, this time in the interest of protecting the health of American soldiers. Public Law No. 12, signed into law by President Woodrow Wilson in 1917, authorized the secretary of war to arrest any prostitutes operating within five miles of a military camp. So many women were arrested as a result that prison and health facilities in San Francisco became seriously overcrowded. The anti-prostitution measure continued to be enforced after the war, effectively shutting down the red-light district in San Francisco, including Chinatown, for good. Any other traces of Chinese prostitution were left in the hands of Donaldina Cameron and Jack Manion, the police sergeant assigned to head the Chinatown detail in 1921, to finish off.

By 1920, the ratio of Chinese males to females in San Francisco had dropped from 6.8 to 1 in 1910 to 3.5 to 1, and there were visible signs of family life. The Methodist Mission records showed fewer rescues and more attention being paid to abused wives, daughters, and orphans. By 1930, the sex ratio had declined further, to 2.8 to 1, and the Presbyterian Mission redirected its program to the growing numbers of neglected children. Wong Ah So—a direct beneficiary of the community's reform climate and the efforts of Protestant missionary women-was among the last to be rescued, Christianized, and married to a Chinese Christian. As the presence of wives and families increased and commercialized vices associated with a bachelor society declined, Chinese immigrant men shed their sojourner identities, and Chinatown assumed a new image as an upstanding community and major tourist attraction.

To Become an American Woman: Education and Sex Role Socialization of the Vietnamese Immigrant Woman

Gail Paradise Kelly

In late April 1975, 129,000 Vietnamese immigrated to the United States. Before being allowed to settle in this country, they were held in four camps in the U.S., Camp Pendleton in California, Fort Chaffee in Arkansas, Eglin Air Force Base in Florida and Fort Indian Town Gap in Pennsylvania. At the camps, the immigrants received medical examinations and applied for and awaited entry visas. American authorities, aware that many of the refugees had little exposure to American life, took this waiting time, which for many was about six months, to "introduce" Vietnamese to the country, and teach them, behavior deemed minimal for living in an American social setting. Within each refugee camp were scores of programs to do precisely this. They consisted of formal and informal programs, some designed to teach the English language, others offering advice on child raising and medical care, and still others counseling Vietnamese on how to keep houses clean, buy clothes, and so on. These programs are the focus of this paper. I shall analyze how the camps' formal and informal education programs attempted to mold Vietnamese women into roles thought consonant with American culture, but at variance with ones these women had assumed within the Vietnamese family and society.

Women's Roles in Vietnam

Vietnamese women, immigrant and nonimmigrant alike, worked for a living. (Only fourteen percent of women refugees reported their occupations as "housewife.") Vietnamese women, as a whole, worked--they worked out of economic necessity. This was just as true of urban, middle-class women as of peasant women or the urban poor; it has, however, not always been the case in Vietnam. Peasant women worked with the land with their families for survival; they also brought in cash income from petty trading. During the 1920's and 1930's rural markets were filled with women selling prepared food, dogs, handicrafts, and the like--unusually to other Vietnamese. In villages depending on fishing, women earned a living either in fishing, marketing fish, producing other foodstuffs on household plots, or in handicrafts. Poverty obliterated sex role divisions that occurred in richer Vietnamese families. Within upper-class families, however, except among urbanized, Westernized groups, women tended not to be part of economic life. They were sheltered within the household, and their sole function was to produce male heirs for the continuity of the corporate family.

The distinction between women's roles among classes changed domestically over the past twenty years of warfare and inflation in Vietnam. Peasant women continued, as before, to work as farmers, traders, or craftspeople to sustain the family. Petty trade items changed, as many began to sell Coca-Colas and other Western manufactured items siphoned from American stores. The war, especially after 1964, forced urbanization. Strategic hamlets, the establishment of free-fire zones, defoliation programs, search and destroy missions, and programs like Phoenix, which assassinated countless villagers thought to be Vietcong, made the countryside uninhabitable. Cities like Saigon, Hue, and Da Nang swelled. Saigon alone tripled its population between 1962 and 1975. Changes in locale brought changes in peasant women occupations and intensified the pressures of subsistence. Peasant women became bar girls, prostitutes, laundresses, and maids as well as continued in petty trade in Coca-Cola, cigarettes, liquor and beer, and drugs with urban Vietnamese and the military, both American and Vietnamese. Further, as the toll in death and mutilation of men, mostly of the lower classes who could not afford to buy their way out of military service, increased, women became more often than not the sole support of their families, either as heads of households or as the only persons capable of earning a living. Women emerged from partnership in the struggle for survival of the family to the sole person responsible for that survival.

The war also appreciably altered the roles of the middle-class woman, because the war brought incredible inflation to urban areas, obliterating the buying power of the men supporting the family. The American press has talked much about how this inflation led to widespread corruption that included bribery and theft from American military warehouses. Corruption was one outgrowth of the inflation; another result was extensive moonlighting. Men like Mr. D., whom I interviewed at length, a professor of English at Saigon University, worked three other jobs trying to live in the style to which he and his family was accustomed. Additionally, in his family--and, he claimed, in others of his class in Saigon--five men working full time at several jobs did not produce adequate income. Thus his mother, who, he said, had before 1964 tended solely to the household, began working. She opened a "knitting factory" in the house during the days, employing his sisters, sisters-in-law, and aunts. She had to do this despite the fact that her husband was a highly placed government official, one of her sons was a colonel in the Vietnamese army, another a businessman, and yet another a customs official. Other urban families underwent such experiences. And that experience undermined traditional sex roles of that class within the family and the economy. The war, in short, had changed women's roles in all classes. Women became an integral part of the Vietnamese economy, working often as the sole support of the family.

While women's roles within the family changed dramatically through the war, families themselves survived. Vietnamese immigrated to the U.S. as families. Few refugees came alone, male or female. Of the 5,849 women who were processed at Fort Indian Town Gap, only fifty-three immigrated without relations. Further, those families which came usually spanned three generations, and included brothers and sisters and their children, as well as grandparents. Several of these families had over a hundred members. Motivations for leaving Vietnam also reflected the persistence of the family as the basic unit in Vietnamese life. Many refugees whom I interviewed said they immigrated because they feared the new Vietnamese government would harm them because either a sister, an aunt, a cousin, a second cousin had worked for the Americans.

Vietnamese refugee women, then, were connected to families. Their roles, in reality or by self-definition, were not that of housewife, nor were they those roles arising from Confucian notions of womanhood which camp officials and, many Americans working with refugees believed. Occupationally, most did not fit into American job categories. For the most part, as I will show in this article, it was assumed that in America they would take on the role of housewife and mother consistant with American conceptions of sex role behavior. This was not only assumed, but enforced; educational efforts in the camps, almost without exception, were directed at resocializing these women to American stereotypic roles in English-language classes, in vocational courses, in cultural orientation meetings, and in printed materials circulated in the camps.

Adult Education: New Language, New Roles

Within the refugee camps there were two types of organized classroom instruction for adults: English classes and vocational training, both run by professional educators under contract from the U.S. Department of Health, Education, and Welfare (HEW). The "school" had but one purpose--to make Vietnamese more "sponsorable." Under the Indochina Refugee Act, Vietnamese could officially enter the United States only if they either had a cash reserve of four thousand dollars per person, or if an American family, group, or organization was willing to assume moral and financial responsibility for the immigrant, either as an individual or as a family, for three years. The responsibilities were such that most Americans were reluctant to assume them unless it was clear that those they sponsored would be self-supporting in a relatively short time. The key to being self-supporting was not only that refugees have skills marketable in the United States, but that the refugees be able to speak English, to enable them to get jobs working with and for Americans. About fifty percent of the refugees could speak some English; of these, only about half could carry on a conversation in English.

Camp authorities therefore placed great emphasis, when the refugee camps opened, on language classes for the refugees. Through HEW funds, they contracted local agencies (in the case of Fort Indian Town Gap, the Pennsylvania State Department of Education; at Fort Chaffee, Fort Smith Community College; at Camp Pendleton, the San Diego County School system) to set up formal instruction, using volunteers wherever possible rather than paid professionals as teachers. Instruction was centered on "survival" English; that is, on teaching only that English considered minimally necessary for functioning in the United States. It was directed only to *heads* of households. The decision to teach only heads of households in practice meant that women and children were excluded from class, for camp authorities, school administrators, and teachers believed that men would support their families and women would care for the family at home. The classes, twenty-six in all, were initially flooded with Vietnamese of both sexes and all ages--and were too large to allow adequate individual work on English pronunciation. Thus, women and children were told to leave.

This led to a large controversy at Indian Town Gap between the Pennsylvania Commission for Women, which assumed the role of immigrant women advocate, and school and camp personnel. The latter justified their policies on several grounds: first, they argued that men, not women, would be breadwinners and therefore had priority; second, that permitting women in class would disrupt the Vietnamese family. Women, they said, might learn the language faster than men, the men would lose "face" because of this, which would, in turn, lead to marital conflicts and divorce. Further, they argued that there were other types of classes for women that would suitably adjust them to American life: classes in birth control, child care, sewing, and cooking, as well as, after September, the Pennsylvania Commission for Women's sessions called "Women in America." In short, American sex role stereotypes were imposed by determining who could go to English class. This broke down several months later as more refugees left the camps and space became available to women.

English classes taught more than language. They were designed to teach immigrants how to live in America and this involved teaching sex role behavior. This was clear in the curricular materials used in class, the conduct of class, and in teacher attitudes. It was explicit in interviews I had with school personnel.

Two types of curricular materials were used in teaching English at Fort Indian Town Gap: The

HEW-developed "Survival" English course, and, as a supplement, the MacMillan 900 English language texts. The Survival English course, taught at three levels, had sixteen lessons that covered topics (in the order presented) that included meeting strangers, finding a place to live, occupations, renting apartments, shopping, John's interest, and applying for jobs. The first lesson began with greetings and sex identifications. Students were drilled on phrases such as "Hello," "Good Afternoon," "My name is, ..." "I'm a man," "I'm a woman." "I'm a boy," "I'm a girl," "Do you speak English?" Subsequently vocabulary taught locations of lavatories, days of the week, numbers, food, time, parts of the body, and job titles. Once vocabulary was introduced as words in isolation, lessons centered on pattern sentences and conversations. In all but two of the sixteen lessons the conversations took place between a "Mr. Brown" and a "Mr. Jones" with Mr. Brown responding to Mr. Jones' questions. For example, Mr. Jones (no doubt the refugee) inquired, in the lesson on numbers, how he might go about buying a house. In the lesson on occupations, Mr. Jones asked what kind of job he might get to support his wife and two children. Mr. Jones said he could work as a room clerk, salesman, cashier, laborer, plumber, bricklayer, cook, cleaning person, secretary, typist, seamstress, nurses' aide. Women appeared in the dialogues only in two instances: in a lesson on budgeting and shopping, and in a lesson called "Conversation." Both are explicit in delineating male/female roles. In the conversation Miss Jones becomes part of the drill in two places--with the partner sentence, "Miss Jones missed the bus to the Miss Universe competition," and "She is an attractive girl." In the shopping sequences, all levels of English classes made it clear that women could shop only for small items. In the basic classes teaching persons who knew no English, Mrs. Brown shopped for dresses, shoes, food, aspirins, baby needs, and cosmetics; Mr. Brown on the other hand shopped for shirts, houses, cars, and furniture. In the advanced classes this division of labor between the sexes was expanded. "Marie" (no doubt the advanced classes' equivalent of Mrs. Brown) compared prices on food and other commodities, thereby saving her husband *his* hard-earned money. She was wise and would buy nothing but food without consulting her husband, Tim. In the lesson she found out where the cheapest sofa and sewing machine in town could be bought, but took her husband to the stores to decide for them where they should make their purchases.

The MacMillan English Language 900 Series, used as a supplement to Survival English course, was not written specifically for Vietnamese refugees. It is a series of texts designed for non-English speakers, be they Italian, Arab, Chinese, German, or French. These texts, interestingly enough, are quite different from the materials devised specifically for Vietnamese. Women are not absent in the text, nor so inactive. They travel, they work, go to the doctor; shop, ask questions. Despite this, the roles portrayed for women are quite limited. In lesson one, Book Three, for intermediate students, for example, Judy talks with John about buying a new sofa, not because it is needed, but because it's pretty and a bargain. In Unit 2, Barbara and Ella talk about baking a cake for Harry while Frank and Tom discuss hammers and nails; in Unit 4, marriage is discussed, as are bridal dresses; in Unit 5, Mr. James buys a house, and Mabel has coffee klatches with her new neighbors; in Unit 8, on health and sickness, Dr. Smith and his female nurse give Mrs. Adams advice on her children's health and Mr. Lewis advice on his own heath; in Unit 9, mother puts kids to bed and wakes them up while father goes off to work. Designed primarily to teach English, the readers tended to focus less on sex role depictions than on teaching first-and second-person patterns of speech. "I-You" is more apparent in the text than "He-She."

English-language classes, in short, transmitted, as do many American texts used in schools, stereotypical roles--women were noticeably absent in class materials. When they appeared, their qualities were reduced to beauty and interest in it, and their role was that of wife and mother, particularly shopper. It is interesting to note that in the Survival English course, designed specifically for Vietnamese refugees, occupations reserved for American women (typists, seamstresses, nurses' aides) were presented as jobs for Vietnamese men. The programs were not only allocating Vietnamese men into lower-class and female occupations; they also presented immigrant men with roles traditionally reserved for U.S. women. It is Mr. Jones, in the Survival English course, who finds out where stores are, gets a doctor, selects a church, locates the children's school, and so on. In the Survival English materials, women ventured out of the house only to shop.

While the sex bias evident in the MacMillan 900 series may be unconscious--publishers of children's books and school texts in the U.S. have explained their past practices in this way--this was not the case in camp-prepared materials. Many camp officials and school personnel were gravely concerned about the stability of the immigrant family, and the consequences for individuals and the social order should the Vietnamese family disintegrate. (Some veterans of the Agency for International Development working in the camps believed this had already happened under the stress of the war and was the reason the South Vietnamese government fell. They were determined to reconstruct what they thought was the traditional Vietnamese family among the immigrants, believing this to be the only way for them to survive in America.) School teachers, curricular coordinators, and administrative and resettlement personnel time after time emphasized the role of education in reinforcing the Vietnamese family and the supremacy of the father, which they assumed was characteristic of both Vietnamese and American families. It was through the reinforcement and/or reestablishment of patriarchal relations that immigrants could "adjust" well to America. And, as the curriculum coordinator of the adult school pointed out to me in one of our lengthy interviews, the school's role was not just to teach English; its mission was to help its students "adjust" to America and live happily there.

The teaching materials were not the only elements in formal English instruction that attempted rob Vietnamese women of their social and economic roles and put Vietnamese men into lower-class and female work-force jobs. In-class instruction also worked in such a manner. An incident in an English class designed for illiterates illustrates this best This class had more women in it than any other class I observed at Fort Indian Town Gap. (The other classes appeared to be predominantly male; advanced English classes had almost no women in them.) Because the students were illiterate, written materials could not be used. The six-week course had but three units: (1) parts of the body and their names; (2) foods; (3) jobs. All this was constructed by the teachers with the assistance of the curriculum coordinator. Vocabulary was introduced by pointing to an object or a picture of it and learning the English name for it. When pictures or objects were not available, charade was used. In one class the teacher clucked and flapped his arms like a chicken to introduce the term "chicken." He then drilled the class on the phrase, "I want some chicken to eat."

The major emphasis in the classroom was on occupations--teaching Vietnamese refugees how to describe their work skills to prospective employers. In class the teacher began with the phrase, "What kind of work do you do?" He then drew stick figures showing different kinds of work--ditch digging, selling, and so on, naming them all. After introducing phrases like "I am a ditch digger; I am a mechanic," he asked each of his thirty-or-more students, "What kind of work do you do?" The first student to respond was a young man, obviously a former soldier. He responded by imitating a gun with his fingers and replied, "I rat-a-tat-tat." The teacher corrected him with, "I work with my hands." Next to recite was a middle-aged woman, who had lacquered teeth (indicating she came from a rural lower-class family). She made a motion that looked like casting nets (I found out later she came from coastal Vung-Tau and fished for a living). The teacher responded with, "I am a housewife." The woman looked puzzled. The teacher then drew a stick figure on the blackboard representing a woman with a broom in her hand, inside a house. He repeated "I am a housewife," pointing to the woman. She and the women sitting with her began a lively discussion in Vietnamese and started laughing. The teacher then drilled all the women as a group repeatedly with the phrase "I am a housewife."

English classes were the major formal education provided within the refugee camps. The adult school, however, did offer six vocational courses, on electricity, plumbing, carpentry, and home economics. All except the home economics class were simultaneously classes in English terminology appropriate to the skills immigrants already possessed. Perhaps this explains the poor attendance at the classes. Only five or ten students came regularly. The home economics class, conducted in English without a translator, was the only vocational class that taught skills rather than terminology. It was designed primarily for women to teach them how to use and maintain appliances found in American homes--electric stoves, refrigerators, mixers, and blenders--how to shop in supermarkets; how to tell the difference between non-prepackaged and prepackaged foods and their nutritional values; and how to cook American-style (make chili; pickled beets, gingerbread, jello molds, and so on). Attendance at class averaged seven persons, none of whom spoke English.

Formal education in schools is but one means by which immigrants were prepared for living in America. Within the refugee camps, outside the school, similar efforts occurred. The Pennsylvania Commission for Women, believing that the school and camp authorities were inadequately preparing women for life in America, set up a series of programs called "Women in America" to rectify these "deficiencies," much to the chagrin, I might add, of camp authorities and school personnel.

"Women in America": A Counter to English Classes?

"Women in America" represented to some extent an alternative to the kind of sex role socialization evident in the English language classes. Those who designed it firmly believed in women's rights and fluidity of sex roles, and that Vietnamese women were in a stage of bondage similar to that in nineteenth-century China. The program coordinator, an American woman in her late twenties, had lived several years in Taiwan, Hong Kong, and Japan and saw the Vietnamese family and women's roles within it in light of her limited observations abroad. To her, it was only recently that these women had stopped having their feet bound. According to her, their role was only to produce male heirs for the family and to accede to their mothers-in-law's and husbands' wishes within the household where they were confined. Camp authorities, she told me, through their educational programs and their practices (specifically the practice of not intervening in known cases of wife-beating at Indian Town Gap) reinforced Vietnamese women's traditional roles, which, she believed, were both oppressive and impractical in America. The "Women in America" programs, thus, were set up to explain to immigrant women their roles and rights in the U.S.

"Women in America" was initially designed as a series of meetings dealing topically with life in the American family, women's rights (the right to hold property, abortion, birth control and so on), women at work, and organizations that assist women in whatever they choose to do. What was planned as a series of meetings became six single evening presentations covering basically the same ground each time. This occurred because few of the same people came to more than one session, either because they had found sponsors and left the camps, or through lack of interest or difficulty in finding someone to care for their children.

The content of the classes varied in minor ways at each meeting, depending on responses to them. At several meetings discussion centered on snow or shopping as women, excluded from English-language classes, sought out information about America in general, and took the opportunity to meet Americans to ask questions that intrigued them the most. Generally, the class organizers tried to cover four topics each night before allowing refugees to change the topic: family life, women's rights, jobs for women, and women's organizations. Each of these was presented by the four women from the Pennsylvania Commission for Women, who spoke in English with simultaneous translation into Vietnamese. The first speaker covered the family. Her presentation stressed men's participation in housework and child care and was accompanied by pictures of men bathing children, doing dishes, shopping, and so on. There were almost no pictures of women engaged in these tasks. The second presentation told women they had a right to abortion on demand, could divorce their husbands, could vote, own property, and work if they chose to. It stressed women's right to plan family size, and said that two children was the desirable number for happy families. The third presentation was on jobs. It told Vietnamese women that some American women worked, some chose not to work. With the aid of photographs, the speaker surveyed the world of work for women, showing photos of women as bulldozer operators, nurses, teachers, librarians, salesladies, karate teachers, engineers, corporate presidents, and so on. The person giving the presentation paused when she showed the picture of a nurse at work, and told the class that it was an excellent occupation for women. At this point, a middle-aged immigrant asked if women could be butchers. The response given was that the presenter knew of no woman butchers in America. The final talk was on women's organizations. This was primarily a detailed enumeration of groups like the YWCA, Planned Parenthood, the National Welfare Rights Organization, and the League of Women Voters.

These classes did, indeed, present women's roles and work in quite a different light than did other formal education within the camps. Unlike the English-language classes, women were depicted outside the home, with the possibility of financial independence. The series, however, did not have as much an impact as did the English-language classes, for no more than thirty persons attended the meetings. Several of those who attended were men who, in the discussions following the presentations, made speeches claiming that men in America had no rights at all. The impact of the programs was all the more limited because there was no real incentive for refugees to attend them or take them seriously. Camp authorities and school teachers openly disapproved of the meetings, and ran movies and English classes during the times they were scheduled. Further, camp authorities made it clear to refugees that only by learning English would they adjust well to America. By September, when the Women in America series began, area commanders who were responsible for barrack sections of the camps pressured adults into going to English-language classes; they did not exert any such pressure for persons to attend the series. Most openly, they resented the classes apparently because they believed "Women in America" would disrupt the Vietnamese family, make Vietnamese men anxious about resettling in America and having to cope with aggressive women, and in the long run would make camp authorities' task more difficult.

The Written Word

A discussion of sex role socialization for Vietnamese refugees in the camps would be incomplete without considering other parts of camp life. Refugees learned about American life every day by shopping at the camp (usually done by men); going to the various recreation centers in the camps; watching nightly movies; hanging around resettlement agency offices, chatting with American soldiers and refugee workers about snow, Montana, dating, and hot dogs; and reading materials written in Vietnamese circulated within the camp. The most widely circulated and read material at Fort Indian Town Gap was *Dat Lanh* (Good Land), the daily bilingual camp newspaper published by the U.S. Army Psychological Operations Unit. *Dat Lanh* was not merely a news sheet summarizing national, international, and camp events, it was also a journal intended to supplement the work of schools in preparing Vietnamese to live in America. It was the only bilingual reading material at Indian Town Gap, other than camp notices and government documentary information.

Dat Lanh, which began publication on May 28, 1975, carried three types of articles: camp announcements (meeting and meal times, lists of incoming refugees, notices of sponsorships available to refugees, barrack rules, immigration laws); how-to articles (how to work a telephone, register for a sponsor, buy a car); and informational articles about the United States and its culture. The informational pieces about the U.S. will be the focus of this section, for in them the paper spelled out social behavior expected of persons living in the U.S. The informational articles were broadly of two types: American history and geography, designed to teach the basics of patriotic identification; and information on social behavior. The history and geography articles appeared almost daily. They consisted of atlas-type descriptions of each of the fifty states and the lives of American presidents. On holidays, *Dat Lanh* ran two-to-three-page stories explaining the significance of the day, particularly Memorial Day, Flag Day, the Fourth of July, Labor day, Armed Forces Day, Halloween and Thanksgiving.

The articles on social behavior were in keeping with sex role molding of the English-language classes. Most of these articles, called "The American Way of Life," were addressed to heads of households, presumably male, and explained tipping in restaurants (when the man takes his family out), getting insurance for *his* car and family, buying *his* family clothes, cars, and houses, and so on. Following these articles were short tips on pregnancy, child care, child health, toys, and so on, addressed to mothers. A front page article on July 31, for example, was entitled "Attention Mothers," and described mother's duties in getting health care for their children. Articles of this nature assumed sex role divisions along stereotypical lines for the Vietnamese family. Other articles openly promoted such sex roles as crucial for Vietnamese to follow if they wished to get along in this country. A *Dat Lanh* front page article on September 7, 1975, for example, entitled "Men and Women" advised men to take their wives on trips, to rise when a woman enters the room, open doors for women, help them push revolving doors since they are not strong enough to push them themselves, pay bills at restaurants, buy tickets, and so on. Further, it told them not to be "frightened" by American women who seem "noisy, aggressive, dominating," and reassured them that most women in America are "quiet, content and gentle" and enjoy being taken care of. The following two issues carried articles on single women's behavior. One of them counseled women on how to find single men. It advised them to join sports clubs, or photography or ballroom dancing classes. Girls should not ask men out, it continued. "In this county the man... does the inviting and the planning." The article then pointed out that girls could ask men to their homes for dinner, if they really wanted to impress them.

Education, Role Imposition and Role Reality

This article has described educational efforts directed at Vietnamese immigrants to the U.S. in one resettlement camp, Fort Indian Town Gap, Pennsylvania, particularly the sex role behavior taught through both formal and informal education designed for adults. The roles suggested for women had little correspondence with roles Vietnamese had historically assumed in their own country. Through circumstances of social class, war, and inflation, almost all Vietnamese women had worked to support their families, and through their economic contribution had gained a degree of power within the family, often serving as heads of families. They were not confined to cooking, cleaning, shopping, and child-rearing. The education in the camps proposed to take these women out of the workplace and put them back in the home. Access to English classes, initially restricted to adult males, meant that the women were deprived of an opportunity to enter the American workplace. It was men, not women, who were to be taught the language or how to fill out job applications. Women's education was initially confined to birth control, child care, and maternity classes, conducted in Vietnamese, and home economics classes, none of which involved preparation for life outside the house and the family.

When women entered English-language classes that were key to entering the American economy, they found class materials that relegated them to roles in their homes--for women could only shop and budget and marry. They did not work for a living, even though most Vietnamese women had; nor did they make decisions. "I am a housewife" was the only role model offered, and that role model was presented in such a manner as to imply that assuming such a role was required for living in America. This role socialization was deliberate. Americans, teachers and camp officials alike, believed in the primacy of the family and women's place as housekeeper. Despite their insistence on teaching these roles, they claimed that such relationships were intrinsically Vietnamese, and that retaining such "Vietnamese-ness" would facilitate immigrants' adjustment in the country.

Even the camps' definition of "the family" was somewhat of an anomaly, given the breakup of the Vietnamese family through resettlement. Americans defined the family as nuclear rather than extended, and resettled only nuclear families as units. Thus nuclear families within Vietnamese extended families were settled at different ends of the continent. Solidarity of the Vietnamese family, which depended far more on the trigenerational extended unit than it did upon male supremacy, was therefore not especially preserved.

The Pennsylvania Commission for Women and its representatives, while scarcely able to speak for refugees as a whole, or for Vietnamese women in particular, tried to offer a different view of American life for Vietnamese women and their possible role within it. To some extent, their view was more realistic about changes necessary to survive. Vietnamese were being resettled in an American society in an economic recession, where there were few jobs available to Americans, let alone to immigrants who barely speak English and possess few skills. Jobs for which most refugees were qualified were the lowest-paying in the society. Under American definitions of the nuclear family, the Vietnamese family averaged seven persons. Men working as day laborers, nurses' aides, and so on were not likely to earn enough to sustain an entire family, so that women would be forced to work, either to supplement family income or as the sole source of family income. A year after the camps closed, seventy-three percent of the immigrants who had once been professionals, technicians, managers, and businessmen found themselves blue-collar workers; another seventeen percent became clerical and sales personnel. Only ten percent went into jobs equivalent to those they had held in Vietnam. Most worked in jobs paying minimum wages; many of these jobs were temporary. Yearly incomes were so low that close to fifty percent of all Vietnamese families in the United States received some form of welfare.

While the camp educational programs were a point of entry of Vietnamese into the society and culture of Americans, they did not serve this purpose equally for men and women. Rather, they prepared only Vietnamese men for integration into the U.S. work force and society; Vietnamese women were not the focus of integrational efforts. "Women in America" alone tried to prepare the women for entry into the U.S. work force. However, like the other educational efforts, this program impinged upon Vietnamese culture and set U.S. terms for Vietnamese adjustment to the society. The educational programs also fostered the lowering of Vietnamese expectations, by preparing men for occupations usually reserved for women in U.S. society. While preparing men for women's roles, they also prepared Vietnamese men to usurp women's roles within the family. The schools taught Vietnamese men to take care of schooling, medical care, shopping, and the like.

English language programs, *Dat Lanh*, and even the "Women in America" programs, regardless of their points of disagreement, were all directed toward getting Vietnamese to enter the society and culture of Americans regardless of their desires. Most Vietnamese were ambivalent about becoming integrated into American society; they opposed the U.S. resettlement policy, openly expressing their desire to remain Vietnamese within the United States. Of this, Americans were well aware. Article after article in *Dat Lanh* derided Vietnamese unwillingness to leave the "Little Vietnams" of the camps and become Americans. After the camps closed, Vietnamese opposition to U.S. resocialization policies became overt, as they abandoned their original places of resettlement and left the diaspora designed for them, to form their own Vietnamese communities.

Reprinted by permission of David Kelly.

A slightly different version of this article was published by the author as "The Schooling of Vietnamese Immigrants: Internal Colonialism and its Impact on Women," in *Comparative Perspectives of Third World Women: The Impact of Race, Sex and Class*, ed. Berverly Lindsay (New York: Praeger Publishers, 1980), pp. 276-296. The editors have added a conclusion to this essay, drawn entirely from that version.

Page 179 from "To Become an American Woman:Education and Sex Role Socialization of the Vietnamese Immigrant Woman" by Gail Paradise Kelly. Originally published in *Comparative Perspectives of Third World Women: The Impact of Race, Sex, and Class*, ed. Beverly Lindsay (New York: Praeger Publishers, 1980), pp. 276-296. Reprinted with permission of David Kelly.

Women in American History

More of Herstory

Edited by

Dolores Delgado Campbell
American River College

The McGraw-Hill Companies, Inc.
Primis Custom Publishing

New York   St. Louis   San Francisco   Auckland   Bogotá
Caracas   Lisbon   London   Madrid   Mexico   Milan   Montreal
New Delhi   Paris   San Juan   Singapore   Sydney   Tokyo   Toronto

McGraw·Hill

A Division of The McGraw·Hill Companies

Women in American History
More of Herstory

See Pages 189-190 for permission disclaimers.

McGraw-Hill's Primis Custom Series consists of products that are produced from camera-ready copy. Peer review, class testing, and accuracy are primarily the responsibility of the author(s).

1 2 3 4 5 6 7 8 9 0 DEH DEH 9 0 9 8

ISBN 0-07-428888-1

Editor: Todd Bull
Cover Design: Maggie Lytle
Printer/Binder: DeHart's Printing Service